For Casey

"Suffer women once to arrive at equality with you, and they will from that moment on become your superiors."
—Cato the Elder, 195 B.C.

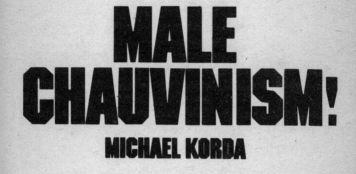

MALE CHAUVINISM!

MICHAEL KORDA

A BERKLEY MEDALLION BOOK
published by
BERKLEY PUBLISHING CORPORATION

BERKLEY MEDALLION BOOKS are published by
Berkley Publishing Corporation
200 Madison Avenue
New York, N.Y. 10016

BERKLEY MEDALLION BOOKS ® TM 757,375

Printed in the United States of America

Berkley Medallion Edition,

Second Printing, AUGUST, 1976

The author wishes to express his gratitude for permission to reprint from the following books:

Simone de Beauvoir, *The Second Sex,* translated by H. M. Parshley,
published by Alfred A. Knopf, Inc., New York, Copyright 1952 by
Alfred A. Knopf, Inc. Reprinted by permission of the publisher.

Erik H. Erikson, *Childhood and Society,* published by W. W. Norton, Inc., New York, Copyright 1950 by W. W. Norton & Co., Inc.

Virginia Frankel, *What Your House Tells About You,* published
by Trident Press, a division of Simon & Schuster, Inc., New York,
Copyright © 1972 by Virginia Frankel.

Jill Johnston, *The Lesbian Nation,* published by Simon & Schuster,
New York, Copyright © 1973 by Jill Johnston.

Norman Mailer, *The Prisoner of Sex,* published by Little, Brown
& Co., Boston, Copyright © 1971 by Norman Mailer.

Thomas Mann, *The Magic Mountain,* translated by H. T. Lowe-
Porter, published by Alfred A. Knopf, Inc., New York, Copyright
1927, and renewed 1955 by Alfred A. Knopf, Inc. Copyright 1952 by
Thomas Mann.

The author also wishes to express his particular gratitude to Ms. Phyllis Starr and Ms. Ruth Whitney of *Glamour* magazine, and to Condé-Nast Publications, Inc., for permission to reprint certain sections of "Women in the Office," an article which appeared in *Glamour* in February 1972.

Contents

For obvious reasons, I have changed the names of many people in this book, and I am thus not in a postition to thank all of them here for their patience and cooperation. I would like, however, to mention the names of some of those who have helped through interviews, enthusiasm, encouragement: Janet Bachant, Barbara Bannon, Helen Barrow, Louise Bernikow, Helen Gurley Brown, Elizabeth B. Dater, Jonathan Dolger, Phyllis Grann, Brooke Newman Hecht, Abby Hirsch, Julie D'Alton Houston, Phyllis S. Levy, Jeanette Mall, Mildred Marmur, Leona Nevler, Jane O'Reilly, Dorothea Scher, George T. Serban, M.D., Claire Smith, Phyllis Starr, Stephanie Waldman, Barbara Walters, Victoria Wilson.

In addition, I would like to thank particularly Judy Feiffer, who first suggested that I write this book, Lynn Nesbit, who took the idea of my being an author in stride and buoyed me up with her enthusiasm, and Nan Talese, for reasons she knows.

"It's a terrible problem. You run a $1.5-billion business, and it boils down to whether some chicks look good in their uniform. If you have fat stewardesses, people aren't going to fly with you." (1)
—*Airline executive, quoted in* The New York Times

This is a book about the ways in which women are discriminated against by men in the working world, about the reasons men feel, think and behave the way they do, and about the alternatives to a system that makes all sorts of special demands on women and rewards them, on the whole, with lower pay, fewer opportunities and thinly veiled contempt.

When most men look at a woman they do not see before them an equal human being. They see an enigma, a challenge, a mystery; the person is obscured by the sum total of their feelings and experiences about women, by a hundred thousand years of legend, myth, comedy and domestic uneasiness. Freud may have been wrong to say that a woman's destiny is her anatomy, but a woman's *legacy* is certainly the fantasies that men have created about her. She need not share these fantasies, and rarely does; she may even be unaware of them, and often is, but in the working world where men still hold the positions of power they affect her status, her salary, her chances of promotion, her future.

Women are becoming surer of themselves, more determined to be treated as equals, and less inclined to automatically accept inferior roles, but in offices across the country their status remains unchanged, and the impetus of their struggle for equality with men peters out into a bad-tempered and unproductive war of attrition for trivial and limited gains. For it is at work that men are making their last stand, and making it very effectively. Whatever women have achieved for themselves in obtaining an equal education, in redefining their sexual self-image, in coming to terms with the realities and legends of their biology, in the world of ambition, career and profit that is at the very heart of this country (pending its unlikely transformation into some green New Jerusalem) "she" is still mostly preparing things for "him" to sign, decide, *do*.

Much has been written about the anthropological interpretation of office life—each executive a killer-ape defending his desk in obedience to the territorial imperative. But the very popularity of such a view among men is probably the best proof that it's false. It may be comforting for a man faced with yet another tedious day in the office to imagine that his survival comes from applying the ancient masculine virtues of the prehistoric hunting band to the air-conditioned offices and corridors of a modern corporation. But this kind of dramatic fantasy is often nothing more than a further justification for discriminating against women, whose function in prehistory was to wait for the hunters to return home laden with bloody game and exciting stories of the chase.

There is no fantasy more enduring in office life: the miniskirted secretary (cave woman) waiting breathlessly to greet the conqueror (caveman-hunter-warrior-*Man!*) with a carton of hot coffee and to listen adoringly while he tells her of the wily traps that were sprung for him and how he fought back and won acceptance for his plan, his copy, his memo . . . But this kind of fantasy (even when it is put forward as a serious explanation of office psychology) is merely masculine self-indulgence, gratifying to a man's self-esteem, justifying the exclusion of women from "his" world, but very far from the truth. Office life is neither a modified test of doubtfully inherited prehistoric skills, nor the rationally conducted activity we like to pretend it is; rather it is a self-perpetuated masculine myth, the basic impulse of which is precisely *to escape from women*. The reason men behave the way they do toward the women who work with them lies not in their claim to possess special qualities of strength and cunning, but in their weaknesses and fears, in men's age-old fear of the demands of the woman, whose sexual demands must be met and sat-isfied—woman, who knows his strength and weakness as no other man can, and can judge his potency and thus, in his own eyes, his value.

The dynamics of business life are not therefore rooted in happy hunting groups, but rather in the legend of Samson and Delilah and in the terror of failing to live up to a woman's offer of herself—

> "Life, young man, is a female. A sprawling female, with swelling breasts close to each other, great soft belly between her haunches, slender arms, bulging thighs, half-closed eyes. She mocks us. She challenges us to expend our manhood to its uttermost span, to stand or fall before her. . . . The defeat of the feel-ings, their overthrow when confronted by life— that is impotence. For it there is no mercy, it is pitilessly, mockingly condemned. . . . Shame and ignominy are soft words for the ruin and bank-ruptcy, the horrible disgrace. It is the end of every-thing, the hellish despair, the Judgement Day. . . ."(2)

The quote is from Mynheer Peeperkorn in Thomas Mann's *The Magic Mountain*; his passionate declara-tion merely reflects what lies deep in the unconscious of every man. If Life is a demanding, challenging, mocking female, what are we to make of the all-too-real females with whom we must deal every day in our business life, and who are, so to speak, handmaidens of that very force we are trying to master and placate? Luck is a lady ("Luck, if you've ever been a lady to begin with, luck be a lady with me!"). (3) Fate is a lady, or at any rate, a fe-male. Success is the bitch-goddess, or a whore. Glory is a woman (in Napoleon's words, *"La gloire, c'est une femme"*). Even justice, blind as she is, is a woman, not to speak of Mother Nature. Women may complain that Father, Son and Holy Ghost form a masculine Trinity, and suggestions have been made that God should be re-ferred to as "She," but the fact remains that on any im-

portant matter of intercession and at all times of crisis
and fear, it is to Holy Mary Mother of God that all
Catholics pray, rather than to the fearsome Father, the
elusive Holy Ghost or the Son, Whose sufferings, on
reflection, always seem rather worse than ours.

Men do not live in fear of women on any conscious
level, but they recognize that women are *different*, that
behind their personae as executives, secretaries, stewardesses, teachers, bureaucrats, doctors, taxi drivers, lurk
other deeper, more mysterious roles. It is not just that
the *homme moyen sensuel* is aroused by a pretty
woman, though that is a familiar complication in the
working life of any attractive woman; men fear women
because women have the power to challenge them sexually, because they expose men to the possibility of failure and humiliation at a basic, biological level, and because as representatives of the maternal instinct, they
have the terrible power to withhold love, should we be
courageous enough to demand it.

Perhaps Germaine Greer is right in asserting that
women do not after all suffer from penis envy, that it is
merely a Freudian myth imposed upon women by men.
It has always seemed to me doubtful that small girls look
at the male genital organs and immediately decide that
they are lacking something; might they not just as easily
come to the conclusion that boys are malformed in possessing a protrusion where every girl sensibly has a cav-
ity? Blacks, after all, do not want to *be* white, they
merely want the same opportunities and rights as whites.
So it is, I suspect, with women. They do not envy the
penis, but rather the privileges and opportunities that it
has come to symbolize. It does not take women long to
learn that there is no particular magic attached to the
mere possession of the organ. Even in the Eleusinian
Mysteries of ancient Greece, the phallus symbolized the
regenerative power of the man when united to the
equally essential fecundity of the woman, rather than
any particular or preeminent masculine power in itself,
(4) but as long as the penis represented the power to
control a woman's life, to reach for self-fulfillment,

wealth, glory, to refuse such humble and distasteful tasks
as washing socks, sewing and cooking and cleaning for
others, women were doubtless inclined to envy it, since
it signified the right to a different kind of life.

If women have freed themselves from penis envy by
going out in the world, men are still involved in penis
worship, with all its attendant fears and uncertainties.
First of all, they are saddled with the responsibility of
potency, since there is no point to having a penis if it
does not function adequately when it is required to; and
this responsibility, which underlies most of the more
common masculine neuroses, leads in social life to an
easily assumed desire for omnipotency. Power and success
in the business and social world reinforce man's sexual
potency by symbolizing it where the real thing cannot
be demonstrated (a dinner party, an office, a convention), or frequently mask the lack of it.

This is not to say that women are powerless innocents
caught in the grip of a world dominated by fearful, neurotic men. This is no more true than the argument that
all men are "male-chauvinist pigs." The possibilities for
equality at work exist. What blights them is the fact that
every woman who goes to work brings to her desk, from
a man's point of view, all the unrelated, accumulated
problems, desires and feelings he has about women in
general, in much the same way that the first black
worker in an office comes to represen *all* blacks, is
treated as if he or she were an expert on ghetto life, on
Southern politics, on the Black Panthers, is either ignored because nobody knows how to begin a conversation, or patronized because everybody is trying to cover
up their prejudices by being nice. To men, a woman represents women, and like a black, she is in constant
danger of losing her identity, of becoming invisible,
sometimes clumsily courted as the possessor of some special knowledge that will explain why one's wife was in
tears at breakfast, sometimes appealed to for the rein-
forcement of one's masculine sense of self when it is en-
dangered, sometimes reviled and attacked in a simple
demonstration of male power and superiority.

Even when businessmen attempt to do something about what they call "Women's Liberation Problems," they unconsciously reinforce their own antifeminist attitudes by treating all women as if they were a defined group, with shared needs, ambitions and demands, instead of as individuals. This is a particularly convenient assumption in corporate life, since the only way to deal with a group is to use rhetoric and make small concessions, and it is much easier to justify the way things are by giving in to women on small points than to deal with the individual problems of, say, a secretary who is talented enough to be doing her boss's job, or a woman executive who is making $10,000 less than a man with a comparable title. Hence an airline may well give way to the pressures of the stewardesses by changing the weight regulations so that women who have put on five pounds aren't grounded or fired, but by surrendering to the group on this point, they can retain a whole host of other restrictions, and above all ignore the far more threatening possibility of a stewardess who applies for flight training and wants to be a pilot.

Similarly, business executives are happy to throw themselves into the problems of whether or not women should be allowed to wear pants in the office (a major struggle in office life that is now almost part of history) not only because it is comparatively easy to make concessions over such matters as these, but also because their comparative triviality confirms the basic masculine myth that women as a group are somehow less "serious" about business than men. Just as it is easier to discuss "the national problem of housing for minority groups" than to face the real black family that has moved in next door, so it is easier to talk about the company's policy toward women ("Harry, if you just *listen* to them instead of losing your temper, they'll shut up") than to face the fact that your assistant is smarter than you are and works twice as hard and can only be kept in her place by treating her as a woman—i.e., one of a subservient class unfit to hold power. After all, if they're not kept in their places, they may take ours.

By treating women as a group, with group characteristics, men effectively protect a masculine hierarchy, ensuring that *they* (women) are admitted into *our* world only on sufferance, assuming that we as men have some special kind of responsibility both to preserve the institutions we work in and to protect the women who work there. Men are accustomed to being members of a group and to the serious business of defending their position within that group. To begin with, they belong to the basic group—the male sex, and share in the benefits, demands, shibboleths and beliefs of that group. Their education, their participation in anything from sports to stealing hubcaps reinforces their sense of belonging to a group that demands a special kind of group loyalty feeling, which they find it difficult to extend to women. Masculine experiences tend to be collective *group* experiences: military service, boarding school, prison, sports teams, street gangs—the male is taught from the very beginning the importance of his membership in the male group and all its subgroups. At the same time, he is taught to seek, in any group, his own position of power, to compete within the group while still remaining loyal to its principles. Hence, in men, comradeship and rivalry are supposed to go hand in hand, and though they seldom do, men still suppose, in a yearning romantic way, that the formula works somewhere. Thus the legends about the French Foreign Legion, the rosy recollections of Army life, the attractions of clubs and dim "masculine" bars, all of which give men at one time or another of their lives an opportunity to feel the sense of membership in the group, of *belonging*, even when they may be, in fact, lonely and alienated. In dealing with women, they confront another group, one which seems to them less involved in the complexities of group loyalty and to have no clearly defined hierarchy of its own. It is difficult for men to fit women into their existing scheme of hierarchy, with all its masculine, collective assumptions, and inevitable that most men fall into the habit of treating them as members of a separate and rival group.

Until men have freed themselves from fixed attitudes

toward women, we are never going to be free as men. Seeing other people as stereotypes, whether from fear or habit, makes stereotypes of ourselves. In so many ways, men unconsciously treat women as an inferior species, then devise complex systems that prove themselves right and justify their own behavior.

It is often the small, casual phrase that best sums up an attitude that permeates our everyday life. The dynamics of male chauvinism may be varied and hard to define, but the spirit of them is instantly recognizable. *"The girls Kissinger takes to Chasen's,"* wrote Hugh Sidey in *Life* magazine, *"can't even imagine those endless, tedious hours of thinking, straining, groping for answers in a bewildering world."*(5) Repeat this phrase to yourself several times. If you are a man and it still seems to you a fair enough comment, one you might make yourself in a different context ("If only you girls were able to understand the kind of thought and responsibility that has to go into running a company like this, you'd understand why we've reached this decision"), then try substituting for the word "girls" the word "Negroes" or the word "Jews." Could you bring yourself to say "The Negroes Kissinger talks to can't even imagine those endless, tedious hours of thinking, straining, groping for answers in a bewildering world"? Would such a sentence be published in a national magazine? Obviously not. Would you, at a large dinner party or a business meeting, argue that "Jews are bad drivers" or that "Negroes are too emotional to make first-class business executives"? No. Both comments, however, are frequently made about women, though usually in a more elaborate, and in these days more self-defensive, form.

Nothing is stronger than a fortress of our own built against ourselves. It is my purpose in this book to examine the fortress that men have built to protect themselves from women—which is to say from acknowledging women's completeness and humanity—and the defenses they have erected to make insecurity appear in the guise of power.

"I came up in the elevator this morning with my boss and his boss, and John didn't even speak to me he was so busy talking to the Chairman of the Board. He saw me all right, but he looked right through me. I mean, what did he think? That if he said, 'Good morning,' the Chairman would think we were sleeping together? Or is it just that when men are talking business, women become invisible? When a man wants to be friendly, it's 'Let's have lunch, What about a drink after work?, Gee, that's a sexy dress you're wearing,' then suddenly, Wham!, you're a secretary, which is to say shit. *It's so inconsistent!"*

—*J*

A DAY IN THE OFFICE

Nine o'clock in the morning on a cold winter's day in the city, the steam writhing from the dirty asphalt through mysterious vents, the grit windborne directly into your tear ducts, the morning's traffic jam reaching its paranoid peak . . .

At this hour in New York, Park Avenue seems to belong to women. Stand in front of the Seagram Building's fountains, and everywhere you look women are striding briskly to work, bare-legged in zero weather, weaving in and out of the traffic on bicycles, jaywalking across the bows of furiously thwarted taxi drivers. If you are a man, you notice women; if you're curious you wonder who they are, where they're going. This endless procession of women of all ages and appearances, seemingly overwhelming the thinner, slower-moving stream of dark-coated businessmen, who look by comparison like a different, lesser species, surrounded, outpaced, outnumbered by an irresistible horde of women, Vinyl-booted, brightly-clothed, energetic, purposeful, apparently more likely to conquer the city than to be conquered by it . . .

"Every time I'm in New York I'm awestruck by the women in the streets," says a French businessman.

"They're so tall, so sure of themselves, so full of energy. They make me feel like a timid midget, *moi qui suis francais*. If a visitor were to arrive from Mars and land in New York, or Los Angeles, or Chicago, he would have no doubt which was the dominant species in this society —women!"

Alas, appearances are deceptive. Most of these women are striding toward their typewriters and yesterday's unfinished dictation, toward a banking job where they count money rather than make it, toward work with no future except more of the same. Married or unmarried, ambitious or not, they are making their daily rendezvous with a world in which women are largely *tolerated*, on the grounds that men can no more be expected to use a typewriter or answer the telephone than to wash socks or clean house.

For this, they have made excruciating arrangements with a sitter to care for their children, strange and sometimes humiliating compromises with their husbands, or simply left behind them family, friends, boys who think they love them, safety and comfort, to undergo the process of character-building (or destruction) that being a working woman in a man's world so often represents. Perhaps if they are young enough and from out of town they have exchanged clean air, the prospect of a "nice" marriage, a wall oven, two cars, for two bitchy roommates in a walk-up apartment on 89th Street, for the incredible, earsplitting Saturn-rocket shriek of the D train as it lurches through a subway station that isn't an express stop when you thought it was, the casual obscenities of passers-by ("Hey! Chica! Wanna fuck?") and hardhats ("Shake it, baby!"), the air that makes cigarette smoking seem like a healthy antidote to breathing, for the nights when you can hear the scratch of the lock-pick on your tightly bolted window as you lie there waiting for the burglar-murderer-rapist-junkie-psychopath-pervert to force his way past the dying philodendra on the window ledge, casually determined to commit unspeakable atrocities on your person before making off with the second-hand television set, and you clutch the hem of your nightdress you haven't paid Bloomingdale's for yet and say to yourself, "Mother, Mother, I'm coming home, I never meant it, I'll join the Junior League, Hadassah, the DAR, I'll marry my cousin in the insurance business, I never wanted a career. What am I *doing* here?"

Women are fast becoming America's true proletarian class. Life is squalid and dangerous in the ghetto, but the blacks have begun to learn how to use their numbers and their anger to make the system work for them, though the problems of black women remain worse than the problems of white women. Union workers, once proletarian, are now a privileged aristocracy, journeying into the inner city every day to raid its wealth, staunch protectors of man's prerogatives and the *status quo ante* in matters of jobs, pay and domestic life. It is women who find themselves doing the cooking after a hard day's work, who are shunted into "women's" jobs (by definition lower paid and static), who get harassed, patronized ("She's really good; I mean she doesn't think like a woman. . . ."), saddled as if by God's will with the everyday problems of children (teething, diapers, school grades, low-grade viruses—all the things men profess not to understand or be able to cope with). If they are married, they work mostly on sufferance; it they are unmarried, they bear the brunt of urban disintegration, praying their fillings will hold out because they can't afford dental bills and Blue Cross doesn't cover teeth, living in buildings that union workers have fled from, where security is a peephole, a police lock, a heavy chain and a steel bar to wedge against the door, or accepting the alternative: a dormitory life with three other girls in a "luxury" apartment where everyone sleeps on Castro convertible sofas, where someone else's wet panty-hose is always hanging in your face when you take a bath, where you can't bring a man home without worrying about whether your roommate is out as she agreed to be or has reneged and is home on the couch watching the *Tonight* show . . .

"I get to my office at nine and already I'm uptight. I've had a lousy ride on the B train, with the usual creep trying to feel me up, and a piece of grit in my eye and my mail is an IBM card from Con Ed threatening to cut off my service over $23.92 that I *paid* them months ago and their computer lost, and I spent last night reading a report that my boss should have been working on, one of those little jobs I don't get overtime for because I'm a secretary-assistant with a college education, not a transit worker or a garbageman, and here I am, twenty-four, pretty good looking, sitting at my desk in a fluorescent-lit cell, my purse locked in the filing cabinet with Mr. Smart's bottle of Jack Daniel's because there's more thievery here than there is outside on the streets (Last week someone even stole my carton of cottage cheese out of the office refrigerator, and it had my initials on it in Chinagraph pencil, for God's sake), waiting for the bell of the coffee wagon (Who can I borrow twenty-one cents from this morning?), and suddenly I don't feel like a human being at all because there must be a million women like me all over the city at this very moment, just little bits of some huge machine . . ."

9:45 a.m. The hallway of a large corporate office. Those who habitually arrive early are already at their desks, glowing with the satisfaction of people who have already caught up with the work they didn't finish yesterday (No sexual differentiation here; assuming the management is not anal-neurotic about punctuality, this kind of distinction is merely a question of metabolism and working habits). Those who habitually arrive late have sauntered in casually if they are executive of either sex, or have arrived short of breath and preparing their excuses if they are secretaries ("My cat was sick," "The babysitter was late," or perhaps if they're pretty and look "swinging," and can therefore get away with it in the eyes of most men, "I was out late last night and I have this terrific hangover").

Leaning against the water cooler, two men—both minor executives—are nursing their cardboard cartons of coffee, discussing last Sunday's Giant game, postponing for as long as possible the moment when work must finally be faced.

A vice-president walks by and hears them talking about sports. Does he stop and send them back to their desks? Does he frown? Probably not. Being a man, he is far more likely to pause on his way and join in the conversation, anxious to prove that he too is "one of the boys," feigning an interest in football that he may very well not share at all. His hobby may be stamp-collecting or lepidoptery, or simply making a profit, but all the power and money in this immediate world doesn't save him from the necessity of proving that he too is interested in the small change of masculine concerns. These men—*all* the men in the office—are his troops, his comrades-in-arms.

Now, let us assume that two women are standing by the water cooler at 9:45, discussing whatever you please: women's liberation, clothes, work, any subject except football, of course. The vice-president walks by, sees them, and moves off in a fury down the hall, cursing and wondering whether it is worth the trouble to complain— but to whom?—about all those goddamned bitches standing around gabbing when they should be working. "Don't they know," he will ask, in the words of a million other men, "this is an office?"

What he *cannot* do is to join in. Two women talking together, from a man's point of view, represent a closed circle. To enter it is to lose a portion of your power by entering a woman's world, to expose yourself to things that are unfamiliar, vaguely threatening, and frivolous at the very least. Note that there is another aspect to this curious social phenomenon: men are always given the benefit of the doubt, in that two men talking together in the hall will generally be presumed to be discussing business matters until it has been proved otherwise, whereas women are "wasting time." If the men are not in fact discussing business, they will be forgiven on the grounds that male shop talk contributes to office solidarity and good feeling—there is no onus on the comfortable dirty joke, a discussion of the stock market, sports news, politics, no feeling on the part of management that time is being wasted in this kind of exchange, so reminiscent of Arab gentlemen in the bazaar as described by Simone de Beauvoir:

> I recall seeing in a primitive village of Tunisia a subterranean cavern in which four women were squatting. . . . As I left this gloomy cave, in the corridor leading upward toward the light of day I passed the male, dressed in white, well groomed, smiling, sunny. He was returning from the marketplace, where he had discussed world affairs with other men . . . at the heart of the vast universe to which he belonged, from which he was not separated.(6)

An office is like a bazaar: it exists in part to reaffirm the bonds that exist between men. Their privileges of conversational freedom, shared experiences and the all-important sense of *member-ship*, that universe to which they belong, are not extended to women.

Thus women talking together in an office tend to do so furtively, guiltily pretending to be working if they are not, conscious that the mere fact of not being at their desks condemns them in the eyes of men, unable to adopt the relaxed attitude of men, and by their very nervousness drawing attention to themselves. It is hardly surprising that the women's liberation movement, when it finally reached offices, should have concentrated so much on getting women to *talk* to each other, to open up.

No man, I think, can really understand the ways in which women are made to feel *guilty* in the course of the working day. It is not just that they mostly have duller jobs than men, or make less money, or have fewer opportunities, all of which is true but can be explained or at any rate rationalized; it is that men find in women exactly those qualities they are afraid to admit to in themselves, or that lacking, they despise. A man who is sloppy will not only expect his secretary to compensate for his sloppiness, but will inevitably suggest that her neatness and capacity for organization are proof of a tidy, and therefore limited, mind, while his sloppiness is the sign of unfettered creativity, making her feel guilty for possessing exactly those abilities he lacks, so that the more successful she is at straightening the mess, the more she proves her inability to *really* succeed.

An executive whose desk looks as if it would take a couple of stable hands with pitchforks to clean it up: "I haven't time to mess with details. I need a girl who looks after things for me, a nice, uptight, compulsive, organized girl who needs the money, so she'll work, with no back-talk, because she can't afford to get fired. I don't want to know her opinions—I just want her to *handle* things for me, to hold my calls when I'm in a meeting, to keep tabs on things, to open my mail and deal with the stuff I don't have time to look at. . ." The ability to do this argues some skill and intelligence, and it is therefore necessary to pretend it is donkey work, it being a cardinal rule of male chauvinism to prevent women from feeling the challenge of a responsible job. A man who has just completed a difficult task is likely to ask for praise and to bask in it contentedly when it is received; most women, given the ambivalent attitudes that surround their work, are more likely to feel that praise merely confirms their subservient status, reinforces their guilt at doing exactly what has been asked of them, and doing it in just the way that satisfies men.

How many women are in a position to present their work as their *own* in American business, rather than handing it over to a man at some stage in its path up the decision-making process, at which point it tends to become "his," if only because without him it cannot move any further toward implementation? That this is true of women even in fairly high executive positions, has its effect on women in subordinate positions—one of the reasons that success is not as universal a goal among women as it is among men is that women can see just what the limits of success *are* for most women. A woman's success inevitably takes place within a man's world, on *his* terms: praise is praise for him, status, position, salary are granted by him.

It is hard for a woman who achieves some success to escape the slight suspicion that she is guilty of having sold out for any gains she has achieved.

10 a.m. The mail is being opened, the tempo of the day is picking up. The first part of the working day in many offices is social, the members of the tribe reaffirming their membership as if it might have vanished overnight, exchanging stories from that mysterious other life that begins at five-thirty and ends every weekday morning, the legendary home life where one is a different person, loved or lonely, possessor of a mortgaged house or inhabitant of a one-room apartment. It is similar to the moment of first light, when a herd of animals reassembles restlessly, each one anxious to see that nothing has changed during the night, that the leaders are still there, the small ones still alive, the familiar companions still close: it is a time for standing close together and exulting in the continuation of the herd's existence and one's membership in it. So, early in the working day men and women make the transition from one world to the other, retelling the events of the night before to their colleagues to reestablish contact, just as they relate the events of the working day to their wives, husbands, friends in the evening to clear them from their minds. On the whole, the men are more forthcoming about themselves but they make up for this by a probing and sometimes prurient interest in the outside life of the women they work with, trading unasked-for revelations of their domestic experiences for detailed information on the private lives of young women, eager to know what's going on in those mythical "swingle" bars, ever hoping for some confirmation of drug parties, orgies or some sign that other people's lives are more interesting than their own.

In many places the first sign of women's liberation could be discerned in this period of the day, traditionally reserved for coffee and mail. There isn't much to do about mail—you either open your own or open someone else's, and women executives are just as fond of having theirs opened for them as male executives are, perhaps because the sheer quantity of mail in the modern world has changed the task of slitting open the envelopes from a pleasurable, anticipatory experience to a chore. But coffee is a great source of conflict. Women's liberation has brought to an end the old-fashioned coffee pool, in which women more or less voluntarily grouped together to keep a percolator going, or even provided what amounted to a running buffet table. It is obvious that this system was organized entirely for the benefit of men, who were not expected to take their place in the roster for making coffee or cleaning the pot, and in any office its demise is the first warning signal that women are beginning to think about their roles. It is hard to define your identity as a working person when you begin each work day with a domestic act, providing a second breakfast for someone you're not even married to or living with, as if anything to do with food and drink were by nature a part of woman's functions. It is not just that men are inclined to ask their secretaries or even other men's to wait on them ("Ask your girl to get me a cup of coffee, would you, Sam? And some cigarettes—I'm out of them"); they unconsciously expect it of women executives too, accepting as if by right the cookies that a woman brings in occasionally until she soon finds herself obliged to bring them regularly, pressured into becoming a supplier of domestic comforts, a role which effectively takes her out of the competition by reducing her in everyone's eyes to a den-mother or a *cantiniere*.(7) So long as a woman is willing to bake cookies and make coffee, to wash glasses and get the ice, she can get away with a good deal with men, and even rise to a position of some power and influence without worrying the men around her.

10:30 a.m. The serious routine of the day has long since begun. For those women who are lucky enough to have jobs that are defined, that have a precise purpose and limits, their work is being done (or not being done) like anyone else's. But this, of course, is the great dividing line. Men tend to have jobs that are quite easily defined—they know what they can be expected to do and what they *aren't* expected to do. Most women in offices are not so lucky. They must simply take the work that is given to them, either in the form of routine or in sporadic bursts, often without any explanation of why the work has to be done in the first place. Few women realize how vital it is to have their job functions delineated precisely —hence the familiar open-ended working arrangements between men and women, in which ambiguity so often leads to unlimited slavery. By contrast, a male secretary was recently quoted in *The New York Times* as saying,

> I have never been used as a "go-fer," because I have taken the initiative to show that I am a secretary, and one who has a mind of his own and can offer constructive criticism about management problems.(8)

Leaving aside the question of whether "constructive criticism about management problems" would be accepted quite so easily if it were offered by a woman, which I doubt, it is obvious that most women have begun—out of fear, or guilt, or helplessness—by accepting the role of "go-fer" in the first stages of their working careers, partly because it's expected of them and partly because many of them have been brought up to feel that this kind of subservience is natural to them. Having failed to define their jobs at the beginning, they can only do so later on by an extreme effort of will and courage, which as likely as not will be misconstrued as "temperament."

11 a.m. A senior executive who is going on vacation drops in on his former assistant, a twenty-seven-year-old woman, recently promoted to an office and a job of her own. "Listen," he says, handing her a list after a few minutes of conversation, "I'm going away, and I'd like

you to look after a few things while I'm gone. My new girl is good, but she doesn't know as much as you do, and I don't want to pile too much on her right at the beginning. So be an angel and look after these things, OK? I can *trust* you!" Should she—can she—say no? Their relationship was built upon her willingness to say yes, she has been promoted as a reward for accepting unlimited amounts of work; now that she is an executive instead of a service, she is still unable to define the point at which work must be refused. Because she is unable to discuss this kind of thing with a man, and because he himself is embarrassed by any kind of pragmatic business conversation with a young woman, he is in a perfect position to take advantage of her.

"We talked, but I couldn't get through to him. I tried to tell him why I couldn't do what he wanted me to, and he just listened, but he didn't even *hear* me. So I said 'OK, I'll do it,' it isn't worth hassling about, but I feel as if I'd been blackmailed."

Because men and women communicate through screens of guilt, fear, ignorance, habit, social assumptions and repressions, it is particularly hard for men to discuss reasonably anything involving a woman's self-interest, and even harder for women to take a stand for their own interests without seeming obstinate or ill-tempered. Knowing this, all but a few women are inclined to pull back rather than run the risk of men losing their tempers and it is thus that women are frequently saddled with work they ought not to be doing. Not to discuss the limits of a job—what is expected and what is voluntary—makes it possible to ask someone to do anything and to resent it if they object. Many women are unable to say No because they don't know what they're entitled to say No to, and when they do finally say No, they do it out of exasperation, and often over the wrong thing.

Noon. An executive's secretary goes out to the receptionist's desk to bring in a young man—in fact some years younger than she is—to be interviewed for a job. As she shows him into the office, her boss says cheerily,

"Hey, June, you write that letter for me, OK? Tell him no, but make it nice, and I'll sign it after lunch. Oh, and make me a reservation for two at twelve-thirty, usual table."

. . . A reservation for a lunch with this bright young man just down from Harvard who isn't sure he wants to go into business, but is undeniably smart. So June, who came down from Radcliffe with a B.A. and had to take a typing test before being hired as a secretary-assistant, and still wonders why her interest in Erik Erikson, her unforgettable paper on Ezra Pound, Harvey Cox's lectures on "The Electronic Icon," have merely led her to an IBM Selectric typewriter and $120 a week, books a table for the young man from Harvard, who has compromised his integrity to the extent of wearing a suit and a tie reluctantly knotted on an old work shirt. June knows he will be told across the bread sticks:

"The thing is, we're looking for talent, for people who will stay, who will bring something special to us. You'd start as my assistant, but I'm easy to work *with*, and I want you to do your own thing, to find your feet as quickly as possible, to *contribute*. Dress the way you want, tell us what we're doing wrong. We'll learn some things from you, you'll learn from us. Can you start at $7,500 a year? I know it's low, but we'll make it up to you later if it works out. How about a dessert? They have a terrific Coupe Jacques here."

. . . Whereas she was told (no lunch, an office interview), "What I'm looking for is someone who can really work *for* me, someone I can rely on. It's very important that I get my messages, and there's a lot of routine work that has to be done and *matters*. Anyway, I like you, and if you want the job, it's yours, assuming your typing is OK. I can start you at $110, but we can get you $120 at the end of the year, if it works out. And of course you get Blue Cross and all that . . ."

June watches the two men go off to lunch, knowing that she will soon have to teach yet another young man the ropes, show him how to make out the expense account she doesn't have, watch him sit in on meetings that she can't go to, because men like to give a young man a chance to participate right from the beginning and will even listen to him respectfully, whereas a woman may have to nag and nudge for years to be allowed entry to the process of decision-making, and will be resented when she gets there. It's not that men are brighter or, these days, better trained. More success oriented maybe, but the main thing, June knows, as she unwraps her meatloaf and Swiss cheese sandwich, is that they get a head start. Recruited for a specific job, they begin their careers generally at exactly the point most young women spend years trying to reach. They don't have to begin as secretaries, to survive the long period of initiation in which a woman is valued not just for what she does, but for those negative qualities that her role so often requires: lack of independent judgment, absence of initiative, fear of displaying ambition. Do men realize that most young women are being asked to not compete by the very nature of their jobs, that it takes extraordinary strength and guile to break out of this trap?

"I couldn't give a damn," says Lee, now an executive in her own right at twenty-three. "I figured I'd get myself hired as a secretary, then *move*. OK, I was lucky. The guy I worked for was this real *schmuck*—smart, sure, but he always wanted to know what I thought, and I told him, and when I said what he was doing was terrible, he just *took* it, with this little-boy smile, and liked it. I mean, he *needed* me, he treated me as an equal (which was stupid, because I'm twice as smart as he is), and so I put it to him straight: no shit-work, no making lunch reservations for him, I mean, I have a *mind*. The girls around the office think I'm a spoiled brat, but who cares? I'm making twice as much as they are, and getting somewhere, and when it's a question of using my sex, I use it. I don't mean I sleep around—I don't. But if you have any kind of looks and you're not scared yourself, you can get what you want. You listen to them, flirt a little, cry when things go wrong, and say 'Gee, I wish you could show me how to do this, you know so much more about this than I do.' It's a snap."

Men should be aware, although they seldom are, that women can and do turn men's prejudices and chauvinism into a weapon against men. Lee, now a copywriter who has made it, has simply beaten men at their own game by playing the roles expected of her, using the license which men give women on the grounds that their behavior can't be expected to measure up to men's. Few men can handle tears, or the sight of a woman in a rage, but fewer women have the courage to use these ultimate deterrents, having been brainwashed into the belief that to do so is somehow "unfair," like the use of a switchblade knife in a barroom fistfight. This, of course, is nonsense. If women are to succeed in business it will not be by following the rules of behavior made by men, but by exploiting their own possibilities of action to the maximum. A woman who reacts to a working situation as if she were a man is simply playing man's game. Lee has gone from secretary at $115 a week to copywriter at $15,000 a year by acting out most men's fantasies about women to the maximum, and taking advantage of every conventional male reaction to women. Naturally, she is hated by her fellow women, who are busily working at the impossible task of being treated as equals by men. Lee doesn't believe any man is her equal; she is both a female chauvinist and a canny exploiter of her own sex and personality. As her former boss says of her:

"I never even knew what hit me. I hired this pretty girl with big eyes, and I have to confess I thought she's bright, and also a terrific looking girl, and she had this *soulful* look. She said she wanted to learn, and I guess she did. I'd have to admit that I'm not all that secure about women—I got married straight out of college—and suddenly I had this great looking girl in my office, telling me how wonderful I was, asking me to teach her everything I knew, building up my ego, flirting with me, or letting me flirt with her, I'm still not sure which. OK, I made a fool of myself, we went for lunchtime walks, had drinks together, all that, everybody was talking about us, and what I didn't know was that she was telling everybody else that she was really doing most of my

work, and doing it better than I could. I hadn't realized
that a smart, pretty girl, if she's ambitious, can make
more friends in management than any male executive
who's simply doing his job. When I couldn't handle the
whole thing any more—I mean, my wife was beginning
to ask me about what was happening, and the executive
vice-president spend half an hour talking to me in the
steam room at his country club about my 'problem'—I
tried to get her fired. I'd already lined up a good job for
her somewhere else, I mean, I owed her *that*, but by that
time she had enough contacts in the office to simply walk
into the copywriter's job, leaving me looking like an
idiot, and a vindictive one at that. All I can say is that I
hope I never live through anything like that again.
What are you going to do when somebody says, in effect,
'OK, you sexist pig, I'm going to turn it right back on
you'? Sometimes she'd appeal for protection, sometimes
she'd cry, sometimes she'd give me hell, and I couldn't
find any way to talk to her as if she was just another
human being, because she was a woman, so I was defeated before I'd even begun. My next assistant is going
to be fifty years old, with a blue rinse and no ambitions."

It is interesting to note that men who want to have "interesting" women working with or for them are frequently unwilling to accept the consequences, somehow
expecting that a strong, gifted woman will sublimate and
hide her qualities simply because she's a woman. Men
want women to be bright but subordinate, and are unwilling to accept that the two things seldom go hand in
hand. What is more, there are pitfalls for men who deliberately go out of their way to hire women who are
bright, ambitious and good-looking as props to the male
ego. One executive I know hired in succession as his assistant: an attractive young lady who tried to take away
his job while telling him that she couldn't understand
why he didn't have the courage to leave his wife, then a
woman who promptly married his most important client,
and finally the mistress of his boss. A three-time loser, he
now has a male secretary and is therefore thought by ev-

eryone to be a homosexual. Men who cannot talk to women as equals stand an excellent chance of being ripped off by the women they overtly or covertly despise.

It is past two o'clock. People are drifting back from lunch or throwing away the remnants of their sandwiches if they have "eaten in," executives are coming back with the leaden steps of people who wish they hadn't had that extra drink, more of them men, of course, than women, not only because men are more likely to have expense accounts than are women, but also because women are less expense-account oriented than men, even when they're entitled to have one. Women in business are thought, rightly or wrongly, to be more cautious about money than men, perhaps because for generations they have represented to men the domestic side of life, with its implicit demands for economy and stability, its opposition to the large gambles in favor of the certain and secure. Assuming that women were in fact cautious, one would think that this ought to be a respected character trait, particularly in business, but caution about money is equated with cowardice and lack of vision when it comes from a woman. Men are perfectly prepared to listen to cautious advice from other men, and every business above a certain size has a respected elder financial statesman whose job it is to give just such advice. But cautious advice from women is unacceptable to most men, conjuring up visions of Mother telling you to be sure to wear galoshes, centuries of domestic arguments in which men are thought to have argued for moving farther West while women pleaded the advantages of staying put. The truth is that women have come to business later than men, and have arrived there after the great period of capitalistic romanticism; they tend to be practical and pragmatic in their aims and their ambitions, while men are still haunted by the vision of the great entrepreneurs of business, and yearn on for infinite expansion.

Men seldom appreciate the extent to which women are governed by the fear of criticism, even when they are successful—in fact, the more successful they are, the more they feel exposed to it, with some justice. A woman who has made her way up the ladder to a fairly high rung knows full well just how difficult it was to get there, and how much more severely her performance will be scrutinized than a man's. Not that there aren't exceptions, but women are seldom as lavish or high-handed about money in business as men are.

In that early hour of the afternoon, when the day still seems long enough to encompass everything that has to be done, four men are meeting to discuss a promotion. A job is open—the head of special sales, a major responsibility, historically one that has been held by a man, and that has often led to a vice-presidency. The job requires an infinite capacity for detail, a gift for negotiation and a genuine enjoyment of making deals and profit. It would be possible to appoint a man who does not seem quite up to the job, to bring someone in from "outside" —or to promote a young woman who seems to be qualified in every way, the former assistant of the previous incumbent—knowledgeable, ambitious, bright, tough, a little assertive, determined to have the job. The four executives whose task it is to make the decision have put it off as long as possible, well aware of the issues involved, hoping that some miracle will make the choice for them. None has, so they now sit around a marble coffee table, faced with a problem they have discussed over dinner, lunch and drinks for so long that they have managed to make it a subject of office gossip, thus adding to their discomfiture to no small degree.

"My secretary says the whole office is talking about what we're going to do. She says if we don't give the job to Pat, we'll have insulted every woman in the office."

"Ed, I've been in this business for thirty years. I'm damned if I'm going to let myself be herded into a decision by a lot of women. We have to decide who can do the job best."

"Yes, but maybe she *can*. I mean, the man we interviewed wasn't all that good, and poor Alex isn't up to it, you know that."

"Alex has been with this company for twenty years. Anyway, how are all our customers going to react to doing business with a woman? I mean, Pat is a pushy broad, they're not going to like that. She's great on detail work, sure, but saving on stamps isn't the way to make a big deal, we all know that . . ."

"If we give the job to Pat, it's a saving, there's that to think of. I mean, we can bump her up to $17,500 and she'll be happy. We'd have to pay Alex at least $25,000."

Long pause. Clearly, Alex cannot do the job. Clearly, bringing in an outsider would lead to Pat's quitting, without doing anything for Alex. Unspoken is the fact that the head of special sales has always been a member of the executive committee, and will therefore join these four men in certain circumstances as an equal.

Ed, the oldest, speaks. "Look, there's no way I can see to keep Pat from having the job, but that doesn't mean we can't change things. Why not give Alex a title and put him on the executive committee, that will make him happy, and give Pat the department and have her report to us through Alex? We can invent a new title for her, something that will sound good, we'll give her a big party, that should keep the office quiet, right? And everybody will be happy."

And thus a job which was formerly independent is reshaped in order to give it to a woman, ensuring that she gets the work without the titles and prerogatives that would normally accompany the promotion. A common game-plan of men, when confronted by ambitious women: when a woman deserves to be the head of a department, and there is no alternative to promoting her, men tend to create a committee or alter an existing one, without making her a member of it, to control whatever it is she does. It is an index of this attitude that most of the decisions that are passed down to men can be broached to them quite simply, whether they are calculated to make for pleasure or pain, whereas a major question in any executive decision regarding women is to determine just how the news will be passed on, and by whom, nobody, as a rule, wanting to take on the un-enviable task. In part, this is because men always expect women to act "like women," and fear tears, rage or sexual blackmail, but it's also because women are subjected to a far greater number of compromise decisions, to promotions that are arranged in ways as likely to enrage as to please, to jobs that have been whittled down to make them "suitable" for a woman, to raises that are less than a man would have expected in the same circumstances. Male executives quickly learn to begin any such conversation by saying, "You have to understand our problems . . . ," but the real problem lies in the fact that in a hierarchical world women are already thought to be further down in the hierarchy by the mere fact of *being* women, and it is assumed that they will naturally respect the ego problems of men—even that they will be amused by them and tolerant of them. If men find it difficult to talk business with women, as they often do, it is surely because they seldom have anything very nice to say to them.

Or *about* them. "Have you seen the new girl in marketing?" a man will ask his secretary, "What a pig!" Insidiously, by small doses, men tend to undermine women's self-confidence by drawing them into a network of masculine attitudes, a task which is easy enough, since in most cases men have the power, and therefore form a ruling group. It is hardly surprising that women fall so easily into the habit of being Quislings, currying favor with those who have power by joining in the denigration of their fellow women. It's not that women are more bitchy than men—this would scarcely be possible—but rather that most of them have few alternatives to accepting the general bitchiness of men and pretending to enjoy it, that women seldom have a power base from which to operate. Women know that the power to change things usually lies with men, that appealing to their fellow women is simply linking the weak with the powerless. So long as the person who gives you a raise, authorizes your promotion, determines your place in the corporation, is a man, then it is clearly more pragmatic to humor him than to offend him, more important to be liked by men than respected by women. Few men can understand that they have imposed upon women a kind of guilty, searching anxiety about their own relationships with other women, created problems of loyalty that would be unfamiliar to men.

3 p.m. An unlucky executive is explaining to Pat the conditions of her promotion, effectively destroying her pleasure in it by making clear just how the executive committee has hedged its bets, and probably further offending her by any number of injudicious remarks while his secretary, hastily commandeered to play a domestic role, organizes an office party.

"You have to understand our problems. I mean, this is an important job to give to a woman, and you're going to have to take a lot of responsibility. Well, you understand, Alex has to be taken care of, and anyway it would be sort of tough to have a woman on the executive committee. Some of the older members would find it hard to accept, but we all think you'll do a terrific job. A lot of guys were worried about giving this job to a woman anyway, but I said, Hell, Pat doesn't think like a woman, she's got a practical mind, she's a realist, she's somebody we can work with. Anyway, it's yours, and we're going to treat you the way we'd treat a man: you'll have a year to put it all together, and if it doesn't work, you're out."

Men are experts at suggesting that while they believe personally in complete equality, their older colleagues would find whatever is being discussed unthinkable. Most men are eager to be *liked* by women, *respected* by other men, and so will cheerfully fire a man, with a minimum of fuss and guilt, while in conveying bad news of any kind to a woman they will invariably assign the responsibility to someone else, trying desperately to retain the woman's sympathy. A natural consequence of this is that women frequently feel they are the victims of some nebulous conspiracy, since they can seldom find any male executive who will admit to having shared in whatever decision concerns them, or who will profess to agree with it. Not surprisingly, a woman finds it hard to understand why she has been, say, turned down for a raise or a promotion when every man she talks to says she'd doing a wonderful job and lavishes sympathy and understanding on her. A good part of women's irritation with the world they live and work in comes from the Kafkaesque consequences of men's inability to talk to them frankly. Lucky the woman who works in a place where there is a confirmed misogynist who is capable of telling her just why something has been decided in a certain way!

Promotions are given to men with all the obligatory courtesies of trust and confidence; they are given to women with elaborate warnings and cautions, with expressions of mistrust and doubt, as if men were saying (and they frequently do, in so many words), "We don't think you can do this, and we didn't want to give it to you, but we haven't got any choice, so take it, but don't think we wouldn't rather have a man if we could find one, and remember that we'll be watching you all the way." Watching, of course, for signs of "feminity," for the tears, loss of temper, "pushiness," overcaution that men suppose to be characteristic of women.

If Pat objects to being short-changed on her promotion, she will be accused of "acting like a woman." When a man criticizes, he is being constructive or obstructive, as the case may be; when a woman criticizes, she is being a bitch, or nagging, the worst of sins in the lexicon of male/female relationships. If a man asks another whether or not he has done something he was supposed to do, he is likely to take it in stride; the worst that can happen is that he will resent an authority figure. A woman who reminds a man about something is a *nudge*, a Jewish mother. It is hardly surprising that many women retreat from the burden, quickly learning to keep their mouths shut, thus making themselves invisible and impotent.

Throughout the business world, in every decision, at every turn, the social attitudes we have grown up with affect women in their relationships with the men who

are at once their rivals and their masters. Women are
not supposed to be ambitious, therefore ambition in
women is generally regarded as a negative trait, even
though it is highly prized in men. Attention to detail is a
necessary adjunct to a man's other talents (if any), but
in a woman—because she is *supposed* to be good at it—
it tends to prove she is unsuited for anything else but detail work. Arguments from men are stimulating, or at
least men are generally obliged to pretend they are; arguments from women are tendentious, and if prosecuted
with any vigor, ego-destroying.

The echoes of our domestic differences underlie every
encounter between a man and a woman, obscuring the
issues under discussion, transforming the most innocent
remark into a pointed shaft. Men are generally able to
deal with one another on the basis of the business at
hand. They may lose their tempers, but when they do, it
is because of some substantive disagreement or difference. A woman's opposition touches a deeper level of
feeling. A businessman suffering from a temporary bout
of impotence may react with unexpected violence to a
pretty young woman's reasonable request for a raise, a
man who has just quarreled bitterly with his wife is not
likely to hold his temper in a heated discussion with a
woman executive, a vice-president who has spent a lifetime persuading himself that his wife cannot add up her
checkbook is not going to be reasonable about the possibility that a woman might be promoted to run the accounting department. Pat need only disagree with the solution that has been found to make her promotion
acceptable to the male hierarchy in order to ignite the
fires of overt sexism.

"Look," says Pat, "I'm not sure I agree with the way
this is being done . . ." Instant reaction, the microsec-
ond connection of irrelevant impulses that makes discussions between men and women *different*. She's behaving
like my wife (who wants to take a beach house for the
summer instead of going camping in the Grand Tetons),
like my girl friend (who made an ambiguous remark last
night that might mean that all things considered she's

known better lovers than me), like my mother (who still
thinks I should listen to my father's advice about business), like my daughter (who told me it was none of my
business that she spent her Easter vacation sitting in the
Autopub drinking whiskey sours with a bunch of boys, at
sixteen, for God's sake, what the hell next?). Flushed
cheeks, a sudden reddening at the back of the neck, a
troubling pounding at the temples (My God, I've got to
watch my temper, cut down on cigarettes, lower the old
cholesterol rate), "Listen, Pat, don't make waves, OK? I
was on your side, but now you're behaving like—*a
woman.* You have to learn to accept things the way they
are, I mean, you're getting a terrific break for a woman in
this business, and you're already complaining. You don't
understand how things work, you want everything your
own way. *Can't you see that I'm on your side?*" ("On
your side so long as you recognize my prerogatives, on
your side so long as you keep your mouth shut, on your
side so long as you accept benefits gratefully without
reaching too hard for them. I respect your ambition.
God knows I wish my wife would get out and work instead of sitting around the house doing nothing all day.
There are a lot of things women could do if they'd get
up and try, but running this department isn't one of
them"). *

Pat is left alone to relish her ambiguous promotion
(Men generally prefer to deal with women executives in
the woman's office rather than in their own, since it
leaves the man free to make an exit, rather than exposing

---

* Of course women do much the same thing in talking to men,
easily equating one individual man with some real or imaginary
concept about men in general. There is no greater misfit in
working life than the woman who takes every remark from a
man as a sign of male chauvinism, even when it's a perfectly
reasonable comment or request. One of the dangers of women's
consciousness-raising lies in the ease with which it becomes
possible to regard every transaction of the working day as a
proof of tyranny. It is important to distinguish between the
normal unpleasantnesses and difficulties of work and those that
are abnormal, unnecessary and possibly "sexist" in nature. But
on the whole, women have fewer illusions about men than men
have about women, and therefore have less at stake.

him to the risk of a scene that he can't bring to an end
and giving the woman the possibility of having the last
word).

3:30 p.m. The point at which the day's work actually
has to be accomplished, or left over to pile up until the
next day. In most businesses, it is the time when a certain hysteria begins to build, an anxiety to finally make
all those telephone calls, answer the morning's mail,
deal with the problems that seemed easy to postpone before lunch. As every woman in a subordinate position
knows, this is the bad time, when male executives tend
to move everything off their desks and onto those of
their secretaries and assistants. "Take a letter, Phone
him back, Tell them to order more stock, Find out the
name of his lawyer and make an appointment with him
for next week, Say yes, Say no, Say that I'm out of the
office, Say that it's on my desk, Make up a list of all our
suppliers by geographical area, it's all nonsense but they
want to see it, This has to go out today, before five, *now*
. . ." If real work in all its petty detail were not done,
there would, of course, be no business and none of us
would be employed, but women, cut off as they so often
are from any connection to the meaning of their work,
can be forgiven for taking little pleasure in it.

" . . . *Do* this, do that." "God," a woman told me,
"I'm so tired of being told to do things, or told what to
do, as if I just existed so people could give me orders. I
read about the army, and I think, Right, that's what I
am, a private first class in a world where every man is at
least a corporal." But of course you can't be a corporal
if there aren't any privates, and men have become used
to giving orders to women even when they are relatively
powerless to give them to other men, rather like the poor
Southern whites who needed the Negroes to give them a
sense of power and identity. Working women know better than anybody just how much of the work they are
asked to do is in fact *make*-work, manufactured to create
a sense of busyness and self-importance, an extension of
someone else's anxiety and stress, the proof that some-

one else is harassed and overworked and therefore a member of the team. Women have their problems, God knows, but men suffer to an extraordinary degree from the fear of being thought idle by their superiors, and it is a part of American legend that successful men are *driven*. And if one doesn't have enough to do to make this kind of intensity possible or plausible, one can always create it by imposing on female subordinates this vision of constant *Blitzarbeit*. (9) The Board of Directors may not notice, but one can make damned sure one's secretary or assistant notices. Most of us need only look around to see examples of men proving their own worth by demonstrating it to women, in the absence of the possibility of doing so to any superior in the hierarchy.

An executive rushes down the hall, struggling into his topcoat while firing orders at his secretary, who follows him down the hall. "Phone him back and tell him I'll deal with it this afternoon, My God I'm already late for lunch, Remind me to go through those folders when I come back, Fit him into my calendar for Wednesday . . ." The fact that he may have spent the morning reading *The New York Times* and doing his taxes, and that he may well be on his way to spend an hour and a half in the fishing tackle section of Abercrombie & Fitch, changes nothing. It may be true, as Helen Gurley Brown says, that "fifty per-cent of women aren't doing their best," but given their vantage point, they can be forgiven for opting out of what often seems to be nothing more than a hysterical charade played out at their expense for other people's benefit.

Very few men in any business are likely to be respected by women who have spent years observing them from behind a secretary's desk, even when they have risen since then to become major executives themselves. Men have an instinctive fear that women at work can see through the poses, games and rituals by which they preserve positions in the hierarchy, that women's experience places them in a position to judge just how effective men's work really is, how much of what they claim to be doing is really necessary and how much is faked.

"God, I have to go to the convention," says a male executive to a senior woman executive, in the compulsory world-weary tone that signifies exhaustion, sacrifice and a willingness to perform yet another odious chore. Another man may well sympathize, but many a woman will object. "Listen," says one, "don't give me any of that. I spent years arranging for conventions, I know what goes on there, and I know you'd be screaming with rage if you couldn't go. Sure—it took years before I was allowed to go, and do you know why? Because the men didn't want anyone to see them cruising the bars, and sitting in the hospitality suites drinking and playing poker, and making passes at the girls. But there isn't one of them who *wants* go, oh no! It's all work, and it's tough being away from home, and if only you *knew!* I know. When I was a kid, I used to fill in those expense sheets—that was before Diner's Club and American Express—and try to find a way to justify why some guy who was supposed to be sharing a room with some other guy took a separate room in another hotel one night. When you're a secretary, you know everything that goes on, they even *tell* you, like you were some kind of mother-confessor. Now that I'm an executive myself, I don't have to believe any of that, or pretend to. I work harder than most men do, and I know when a man is really working, and when he's just faking it. After all, I've worked for some of the world's great fakers, and even made it possible for them to fake it—I mean, that was my job, right? 'For God's sake, Greta, fix that report we did last year so it looks like something new; Anybody calls, tell them I have a big meeting out of the office; My expense account has to come out at about $500, look at my diary and fix it so it comes out that way, but make it an odd number, right?; Tell them I'm in conference and get me a black coffee and three aspirin; Cover for me.' Now that I've made it, I can see through them."

It is going on five, the time when an office shakes itself down into three basic groups: those who go home on the dot, most of them either young women or very senior male executives; the men who stay on because they don't want to go home, who have gotten into the easy habit of pretending that this is the time when they work best; and the senior women executives who are committed to stay later than anyone, to demonstrate even to an empty office that they can do more work and carry more responsibility than all those men who left for Westport two hours ago.

Today, however, is Pat's promotion party, hastily organized to compensate for the somewhat humiliating compromise she has been presented with. In a large office the usual signs of festivities have been laid out on a desk: Great Western Champagne, paper cups, trays of sandwiches from the nearest delicatessen, mixed nuts in ashtrays, a couple of bottles of Scotch for those executives who are known to need their stiff shot in the late afternoon, Tab for the nondrinkers. A scattering of early comers surround the desk, either members of Pat's own department who have helped set things up, or secretaries who feel they ought to make an appearance but want to cut out for home just as soon as they decently can. Already the air is slightly ionized by a crisis, so typical of male/female relations at work. The executive in whose office the party is being given has instructed several of the "girls" to be sure to clean up afterward. Some of them would possibly have stayed on their own—or he himself might have stayed to help and made the task a kind of easy, shared obligation—but having been given their marching orders, there are already half a dozen sullen and mutinous faces at the festive board, polarizing the occasion into the usual confrontation between pig-man and chained-woman. Slowly, the staff of this particular happy working family assembles, the more important men gathering together to continue the business discussions of the day; then, as the room fills, separating to flirt with the prettier women, sowing the seeds of new dissensions and resentments for tomorrow. There is a period in all such office festivities when, momentarily, all things seem possible, when the undercurrents of sexuality that run through office life are briefly released, when men take that extra drink, miss the next train, begin to wonder if they could find a plausible excuse for staying overnight in town. There is even a social pressure against men who *do* go home early, for in a world that has absorbed half of Freud's teachings without paying any attention to the rest, the worst sin is to fail in the Darwinian struggle for sexual survival. It used to be that making a pass was essentially a private act, whatever its wisdom or chances of success. These days, as men of a certain age find themselves forced to deal with a tougher and more realistic generation of women, a pass seems hardly worth making unless it's one in public, its real importance being the demonstration that one is still in there fighting, game for yet another maladroit approach to a young woman who more than likely is eager to be on her way home where a younger and more attractive boyfriend impatiently waits for her.

Pat's arrival brings conversation to a stop. The senior executive of the corporation takes advantage of the hush to make a short speech: "When I first met Pat she was a secretary, as a matter of fact, *my* secretary, and she really took my life over and learned more about what I was doing than I knew myself. So I promoted her. And she's never looked back . . ." Applause. Pat thinks, Yes, but it took you five years to do it, and then it only happened because I nagged and pushed you into it, and you fought every inch of the way, and now I work harder than you do and still know more about the business, but you're a director and a *macher*. Thanks for nothing.

And then, gradually, the party subsides, the women slipping out to avoid the late-stayers' propositions or absenting themselves before the cleanup call, the more realistic men making their way homeward before that magic hour of temptation when it is just late enough to make an evening of it, until only the hard-core romantics and the now openly rebellious cleanup brigade are left. One by one, the lights go off, until the office is empty except for one lone executive at the Xerox machine, making copies of a report himself because he knows that if he leaves too much shit-work for his "girl" to do in the morning, she will make his life not worth living over the shit-work that he will have to give her anyway in the course of the day. A melancholy victim of women's liberation, he stands hunched over the machine, intending to slip the copies into the files without her noticing, which would only prove that he doesn't have the guts to ask her to do the job. Where is a man to turn, he wonders, How did it come to this? If I leave it all on her desk with a note saying "Rush! Please Xerox," she'll start the morning in a vile mood and accuse me of giving her nothing but drudge work. If I do it myself, she'll say, "For God's sake, I would have done it if you'd *asked* me! What kind of a person do you think I am anyway?"

But that's the way it is, communications have broken down, men have become aware of women's protests and even sensitive to them without really coming to grips with the substance of women's *demands* or making an honest effort to change the way things are. It is now fashionable to "understand," even to "sympathize"; it is not yet fashionable to think about a solution to the problems of inequality or to admit that men will have to give up some things once women are to make real progress toward their goals. It is even less fashionable to examine the reasons behind the continuing inequality of women, to ask just why so much of a woman's working life should be irritating and unsatisfying, or why women who work at full-time jobs should still earn, on the average, only three dollars for every five dollars earned by a similarly employed man, why women professional workers should earn on the average $7,878 a year while men in the same jobs earn on the average $11,806 a year, why since 1955 women's earnings as a percentage of men's have *gone down* by 4.5 percent(10) despite the ever-increasing number of women who are working full-time and despite their growing militancy and self-assurance.

Behind the practical, financial facts of discrimination lie the attitudes that make them possible, even inevitable. In the language of sexual chauvinism, women have been screwed.

TWO

> *"Could you ask one of your girls to help me? I'll send a slip of paper, with a personal inscription to the recipient of the book, paper-clipped onto a description of that person's address; your girl—or some intelligent mailroom boy—would then paste the slip into the blank front page of the book and mail it off . . ."*
>
> *—Author to editor*

> *Twenty-year-old Dourniese Hawkins will don a hardhat, overalls and boots and work in the trenches of Consolidated Edison's Manhattan gas operations . . . A former cab driver and letter writer, Miss Hawkins will continue her studies at Staten Island Community College at night after wielding a jackhammer, a pick or a shovel during the day—'side by side with big, brawny men,' a company spokesman added. The only problem may be the signs that say, "Men at Work."*
>
> —The New York Times (11)

THE DYNAMICS OF MALE CHAUVINISM

Some time ago I was on a television talk show with a group of fellow publishers, discussing books and how they get published, aiming our rather incoherent explanations to a formidably cheerful woman interviewer. Staring open-mouthed at the red light on the television camera, I was astonished to hear one of my fellow guests, a portly citizen in his Mod-forties, decked out in the casual, expensive tweeds of his profession, reply in answer to the lady interviewer's question about the way in which the manuscripts of unknown writers find their way into his particular cell of the cultural conspiracy: "Well, we try to give everything a fair reading. If a manuscript comes in to us by mail, a junior editor gives it a first reading. If it's any good, the junior editor passes it on to a senior editor to look at it. She prepares a report for him, and if he likes it—and that doesn't often happen— he gets in touch with the author . . ."

46

There was a brief angry flutter from behind us, where a group of women writers and agents were waiting their turn to talk about women's liberation in book publishing, but our interviewer went blithely on, and my colleague sat back, smiling with the satisfaction of a man who has explained the obvious. Of *course*—"she" gives it to "him" for a decision. If you are a man, try reversing the proposition. "The junior editor passes it on to a senior editor to look at. He prepares a report for her, and if she likes it she gets in touch with the author . . ." Does not the tongue find it difficult to wrap itself around those reversed pronouns, to verbalize the idea of "him" doing menial work for "her"?

"Have your girl phone my girl, and fix a lunch date." The opposite of "girls" is not "boys," of course, but "men," as if women were automatically classed with children, rather than with adults. It is easy to pick up these slights when listening to other men, it only requires a modest amount of sensitivity, but just the other day I found myself saying that someone was remarkably smart for such a pretty girl, the "girl" in this case being a thirty-five-year-old businesswoman, who probably makes twice what I do. Not long ago, I sat in on a meeting at which two famous lawyers were present, a man in his fifties and a young woman in her thirties, who had not met each other before. When the man came in, he smiled, turned to me and said, "Listen, you should have told me she was a great-looking chick, kid." Leaving to one side the fact that our discussion was doomed from the start by this ill-placed compliment, the point is that I could see quite clearly why it was offensive. Would *she* have said to me, "You didn't tell me that he was really well-hung for an old man"?

OK, I was brought up in a family where women were expected to keep their mouths shut (My father's answer to any comment from a woman was "What do you know about it?). Women were a mystery, and there seemed to be nothing very much men wanted to talk to them about, except sex, which was the one thing we *couldn't* talk to them about.

My first experience with women at work was on a
newspaper, where I swiftly reached the conclusion that
most of them knew a great deal more about the inner
workings of the business than the men did, that in fact
the whole enterprise depended on them on a day-to-day
basis. The men went out and wrote the stories, made the
connections, did the interviews, but all this activity
would have been impossible without the staff of women
who filed, kept records, checked, corrected spelling,
watched deadlines, pointed out to young reporters like
myself that we weren't allowed to used the word "however" more than once in any story and in general
assured that the chaos of editorial activity was channeled
into the daily appearance of a newspaper. For all that
these women were cordially despised, and all the more so
since they had clearly come to terms with their situation,
accepted their roles, in effect *surrendered.* Yet their surrender was never complete enough—What human surrender is?—to convince the men that they had nothing
to fear. The women had found a weapon to use even in
defeat, by attaching themselves to larger powers, by
becoming the mysterious reflections of the Chairman of
the Board (in the case of his personal assistant, a wid-
owed lady of awesome precision); the Treasurer (his secretary forever saying, "I don't think they will approve
this, you know, they'll want to know if all these items
were really necessary as expenses"); the managing editor (his amanuensis warning any supplicant, "I
wouldn't advise you to bring it up with him, frankly;
he'll be very angry") . . .
The men could interview the Prime Minister and
come back with a story, they made more money than the
women, worked in the limelight—to the extent that
journalists ever get into the limelight—but in the office
they faced an impenetrable barrier of women who had
managed over long years to transform themselves into
the guardians of power, formidable vestal virgins whose
authority was all the greater for being ill-defined and
unofficial. You might curse them, placate them, charm
them, but ill-paid and unheralded as they were, their

pride lay in a fierce loyalty to principle. Like so many many women in business, they were *"plus royaliste que le roi"*; men might think of leaving, going over to the competition, cheating on their expense accounts, fudging a story, "taking advantage," as the phrase went, of the company; women were the Praetorian Guard of management, the frowning representatives of morality, truth, justice and a good day's work for a day's pay. As such, they were naturally unpopular—the currents of tension, stress and anxiety that characterized the relationships between the sexes were so strong as to be overpowering, at any rate to a young man like myself who had never observed an office in action before. Here were experienced, middle-aged men whom I admired, spending their office time in bitter and protracted disputes with women who earned a tenth of their salaries. Here were respected figures in journalism trembling with rage at their desks over some insignificant dispute with someone's secretary, lashing out in furious diatribes against women in general, reading into an office quarrel all the rejections and difficulties of their married lives.

A newspaperman's bar, a newspaperman's standard litany after the third drink and putting the paper to bed (that phrase, with all its implications of wife, home, domesticity): "I could have been anything once, boy. I used to be able to write, I had ideas. Well, even if I couldn't have been a novelist, I could have been a foreign correspondent, but I got married, had kids—don't ever marry, you get tied down and you end up like me. Well, you saw it today, you saw how that bitch treated me when I wanted to see the chairman about that feature. You'd have thought I was a dog, and believe me, it's a dog's life. I could have had Vienna, Paris, and here I am living in the suburbs, and paying off the mortage, and saying please and thank you to some bloody woman, and coming home to have some other bloody woman ask why the hell I'm late. Stay single, boy, fuck 'em and leave 'em, they'll drain the blood and the guts out of you. They even live longer, for God's sake! Here, let's have another!"

How easy it was (and is) for men to blame women for their troubles, to accuse their wives of having enslaved them, so that their days had to be spent doing this work, earning the money to pay for home and children, and how easy to extend this blame to the women in the office, so that the whole world became a prison created by women, in which men worked for their benefit. Yet the women were not happy—the wives were unsatisfied, the women in the office clearly resented their lower pay, their inferior positions; they were serfs for unhappy and defeated rulers, a never-ending circle of misery and regrets. The men thought that "freedom" could only be found away from women; the women knew that "freedom" was merely a synonym for rejection of women. Male chauvinism did not, for all practical purposes, exist as a theory then, but the *practice* of it flourished; it was clearly not a result of ruthless strength and selfishness on the part of men, but the sign of inner weakness, fear, frustration—the ultimate rationalization of self-hatred and self-contempt. It struck me then, as it does today, that the male chauvinist is not the proud (if obtuse) figure that men take him to be, insisting on his legitimate superiority over women, but rather a man who cannot accept the responsibility for the failures in his own life and therefore assigns them to women, in much the same way that the Germans, unable to accept the defeat of World War I, transferred all blame magically to the Jews.

Male Chauvinism! A phrase that men usually use with pride, or at any rate with bravado. But what is it? What do we mean? Why is it necessary for men to assume, as so many of them do, that the difference between men and women involves a question of superiority?

The simple truth is that male chauvinism consists above all of classifying people by biological function, as if this were a determining factor in entirely nonbiological activities and situations. Millions of words have been written by men, and not a few by women, illuminating these biological differences, seeking to understand them, yet it explains nothing to dwell on woman's biology while refusing to promote her to a job she's entitled to, or when giving her a smaller salary increase than a man in the same position would expect.

Biology is a trap. It neither explains nor justifies any assumption of masculine superiority, yet it remains the traditional weapon to use against women. Norman Mailer's *The Prisoner of Sex* provides a good example of this tendency to assume that biological differences determine woman's place in the world, much of it reading like one of the more tenebrous medieval tracts on woman.

Mailer expatiates at length on the biology of women, giving them the dubious benefit of his sympathy for possessing a genito-urinary system more complex than man's:

> The womb was a damnable disadvantage in the struggle with the men, a cranky fouled-up bag of horrors for any woman who would stand equal to man on modern jobs, for technology was the domain of number, of machines and electronic circuits, of plastic surfaces, static, vibrations, and contemporary noise. Yet through all such disturbance, technology was still built on conformity of practice. If it could adjust to rhythm, tide, the ebb of mood, and the phasing in and out of energy in the men and women who worked its machines, nonetheless such adjustments were dear to technology, for each departure from a uniform beat demanded a new expensive control. The best operator was the uniform operator, and women had that unmentionable womb, that spongy pool, that time machine with a curse, dam for an ongoing river of blood whose rhythm seemed to obey some private compact with the moon . . .(12)

If I understand his meaning, it is that a woman's monthly period may in some way disqualify her from running a computer, controlling a subway train, flying a Boeing 747, piloting a 100,000-ton tanker into harbor

("I can't con the ship today, First Mate, you'll have to take her into the slip for me, it's my time for the curse and I can't tell port from starboard I'm so on edge"). Even if we leave to one side the fact that women have long since proved they can do anything—after all there is a woman astronaut, women ferried fighter planes across the Atlantic in World War II, one of the stars of the NASCAR stock-car racing circuit is a lady who drives a pink car and wears a pink helmet—Mailer's suggestion is still absurd, ignoring as it does the nature of the work ordinary women do, and overlooking man's biological weaknesses as if they didn't exist.

"A private compact with the moon . . ." It is the old cry that women are somehow different, connected to some larger and more mysterious force of Nature, spiritual descendants of the unfortunate witches of Salem. Underlying Mailer's concern about the womb is the unspoken assumption that the penis is somehow a cleaner and simpler organ, as well as the larger and more tenebrous assumption that man stands alone while woman moves with the tides, driven by cosmic forces that no man can understand. Nobody disputes that women's sexual organs differ from men's, but what does it matter? Of course the vagina is not a penis, of course women menstruate, of course their internal organs require more upkeep and expose them to greater dangers than do those of men, but to dwell upon these differences is to ignore the fact that they are both obvious and unimportant.

Yet the false concepts men have about women are not as damaging to the relationship between the sexes as the more subtle misunderstanding that men have about themselves. Just as the old idea about woman's biology being a kind of compact with the Devil or some other dark force lingers on the edge of the unconscious, perfectly expressed in the Gypsy belief that women are unclean, or *marhime*, from the waist down, and that her skirts must not touch anything a man uses, so there persists the ideal of man the tamer of things, a Promethean force acting on the physical world, as woman supposedly responds to the spiritual one. For men worship strength, associate their assumption of superiority with physical prowess, justify their position in the present by their reading of the past.

At the heart of male chauvinism is a false concept about modern man. When men had to till, plow, fight with a sword and spear, tame horses, lift the stones with which civilization was laboriously built, there was some justification for their feeling that a man's physical strength was a special gift, a counterbalance to the more mysterious ability of woman to reproduce the race. Woman's power was secret, miraculous, associated with magic (there are still tribes that have not connected sexual intercourse with the act of reproduction, and they will probably learn to do so at just the moment when we have succeeded in separating the two). Man's power was simple and obvious, the ability to lift a heavier stone, plow a straighter furrow, wield a quicker broad-sword. In our culture it is, for most of us, some fifty years since this division of powers has ceased to exist and among the middle and upper classes it was declining rapidly a full century before that, even then cutting men off from the source of their pride and their superiority over women. Most men in business are not very much stronger than the average woman, if at all, and a lifetime of sitting behind a desk and picking up the telephone is hardly likely to give any man a physical edge over a woman who has spent twenty years lifting children, carrying groceries and cleaning house.

Masculine ideals are formed around the image of physical strength and work, but the modern male chauvinist does not possess or require this strength. What is more, male chauvinists tend to be aggressive in their relationship to women, at least in the verbal sense. They want to impress, seize, capture, subdue women; they dream of obscure sexual triumphs, they confuse sexuality with strength. The men who lived by their bodies seldom did. If they were indifferent to women or embarassed by them, it was because their energies were turned toward work and physical skills; they lived in the heroic present, and women seemed to them peripheral rather than threatening. As Larry McMurtry wrote of the old cowboys in his collection of essays *In a Narrow Grave*:

> Cowboys could perform terrible labors and endure bone-grinding hardships and yet consider themselves the chosen of the earth; and the grace that redeemed it all in their own estimation was the fact that they had gone a-horseback . . . To be a cowboy meant, first of all, to be a horseman. Mr. Dobie was quite right when he pointed out that the seat of the cowboy's manhood is the saddle . . . I do find it possible to doubt that I have ever known a cowboy who liked women as well as he liked horses . . .

Men who work together in professions that require strength and skill form powerful bonds: they are simply more comfortable with each other, *dependent* on each other; they do not trust strangers and outsiders—and women, except as mothers, are outsiders by definition. Anyone who has served with a group of regular soldiers soon learns that they have their own world, that they have excluded women from their lives *except* as sexual objects, and those mostly prostitutes.

To a cowboy, a sailor, a cavalry trooper, marriage was simply a luxury, not only because a woman was a burden in a hard career ("Down to Gehenna or up to the throne/He travels the fastest who travels alone," as Kipling wrote), but because until recently these professions made marriage economically impossible or imposed intolerable hardships on a man's family. The modern male chauvinist, by contrast, wants to live with women and still retain the image of those men who had to live apart from them. *They* left the world of women and family to live in a private world of their own; he lives in the middle of the domestic world, surrounded by women, dependent upon them, anxious for their approval, but unwilling to accept their presence, bolstering his doubts and weaknesses with the myths and legends of a masculine ethos that would, in most cases, have rejected *him.* What is so special about being a man, if you're sitting in an office using your mind, or pretending to? Where is "the seat of one's strength" in an air-conditioned cubicle? There do not in fact seem to me to be *any* important physical differences between twentieth-century urban man and twentieth-century urban woman *except* the sexual ones, and it is difficult to imagine any convincing reasons why one should be more capable of filling a role in our technological society than the other. The only reasons, in fact, that can be found are just those philosophical abstractions that Mailer is concerned with, and which prove nothing except the obvious fact a woman isn't a man.

Biological arguments seldom prove anything. Women have pointed out to me that it is the lioness that does the hunting, not the lion, that female spiders are not only larger than the male but devour him after copulation, that in many species of fish the female is larger and more aggressive than the male, but I cannot see what this proves unless it's that Nature is marvelous in the diversity of its life forms. We are not lions, nor spiders, nor fish. Our cousins among the higher primates seem to live in a society organized rather like ours, in which the males are larger and display abundant evidence of male chauvinist attitudes, which would suggest that the problem of male chauvinism lies rather deeper in our genes than is generally admitted, that it is part of the mixed blessing of heritage, along with the opposing thumb and the upright back. It is not that man's physical superiority is a myth invented by men; it is that we have created a society in which strength no longer makes men superior. Nothing is proved by searching the Table of Species for examples in which the female is dominant, since Nature seems to have tried both systems of dominance on land, at sea and in the sky without coming to any general biological conclusion for life on this planet.

No purpose is served by simply reversing male chauvinist arguments and inventing a feminine universe in which man is an aberration, an idea which has already been passed down into the popular culture, as cogently expressed in the words of Valerie Solanis, the founder of

SCUM (Society for Cutting Up Men): "(We can) reproduce without the aid of males and to produce only females. We must begin immediately to do so. The male is
a biological accident: The Y (male) gene is an incomplete X (female) gene, that is, has an incomplete set of
chromosomes. In other words, the male is an incomplete
female, a walking abortion, aborted at the gene state . . .
Being an incomplete female, the male spends his life attempting to complete himself, to become female. He
attempts to do this by constantly seeking out, fraternizing
with and trying to live through and fuse with the female,
and by claiming as his own all female characteristics—
emotional strength and independence, forcefulness, dyna-
mism, decisiveness, coolness, objectivity, assertiveness,
courage, integrity, vitality, intensity, depth of character,
grooviness, etc.—and projecting onto women all male
traits—vanity, frivolity, triviality, weakness, etc."

What is this but the language of male chauvinism reversed? What is more, it presumes once again that one of
the sexes must necessarily dominate the other, that there
exists some transcendental "feminine" quality, the "female characteristics" that man is supposed to have
claimed and stolen for his own.

Mailer's lunar preoccupations are even more strangely
echoed in Elaine Morgan's *The Descent of Women*,
which argues that the evolution of the human race
began when female apes led their mates to take refuge
from the hostile land in the ocean, where they lived for
10,000,000 acquatic years, shedding superfluous body hair
and acquiring the characteristic human form. Noting
that the female prehominoid ape not only had to put up
with the rigors of a scorched and dying land, but also
had to deal with the attentions of her "greedy and hec-
toring mate," Ms. Morgan shows how the female, bereft
of the male's "fighting canines," was forced to use peb-
bles to crack open shells, and thus became a tool user,
while "The male watched her and imitated her." Well
maybe. Quite apart from the fact that no evidence exists
to show that male prehominoids possessed large canine
teeth and females didn't, it seems unlikely that our an-

cestors could have spent so many million years in the water while remaining so badly adapted to their environment. It is certainly pretty to imagine that female apes shed their body hair to swim better, and developed subcutaneous fat to protect their body heat, while their children clung to the long hair of the head, evolved especially for this purpose—one can't fail to imagine with pleasure the spectacle of our ancestral mothers frisking through the African surf, as sleek as dolphins, children floating beside them clutching to strands of flowing hair with their tiny hands, each woman a water-nymph Eve or Rima the Fish Girl. But if this is where we sprang from, why didn't we develop webbed feet, why are our mouths and noses so ill-suited to breathing in the water (acquatic mammals usually have nostrils they can close), why do we lose body heat so rapidly in water? And by what magic did women grow longer hair on their heads than men? We need only look around us today to see that men can grow a head of hair that equals in length that of any woman.

No, it seems unlikely that Mailer's unease or the current conflict between the sexes can be alleviated by inventing an Atlantan evolution for the human race. More serious attempts to provide a theory for feminine superiority like that of Mary Jane Sherfey's *The Nature and Evolution of Female Sexuality*, are hardly more enlightening. In it, Dr. Sherfey argues that "All mammalian embryos, male and female, are anatomically female during the early stages of fetal life," and goes on to suggest that not only does man develop from a woman (a kind of reversal of the Biblical legend of Eve's creation from Adam's rib) but that the rise of modern civilization and society derives from man's suppression of woman's enormous sexual energy. But the replacement of phallic worship with vagina worship seems to me to merely substitute one form of superstition for another, this time in the name of science. Besides, men have always given tacit recognition to the notion of the Earth Mother, the symbolic womb of fertility and procreation, and even managed to integrate this pagan notion into Christianity in the person of the Virgin Mary. It does not disarm the arguments of male chauvinists to argue that woman is the Great Matrix; chauvinists are perfectly willing to concede this role to her and go on to run the world as they please.

As the genuine necessity for physical strength has waned, men have turned to sports to symbolize the ancient values of strength and courage. Here, at any rate, was an activity in which men could effectively reassert their membership in the male group, and from which women were as a rule generally excluded. It is hardly surprising that sport should have taken on, in Western society, such an importance that its rules, its language, its legends, have passed into the male consciousness, making themselves felt as much in business as anywhere else. Men talked of sports, thereby excluding women from their conversation, they admired sportsmen, and identified with them, which women were in no position to do, they used the terminology of sports, as many older businessmen still do. As a general rule, when an executive speaks of "our team," he is unlikely to be including the women in the organization in his thoughts.

But here too, modern reality has sapped the sports ethic of its original vitality and meaning. Some men play sports, some don't, but those who do find themselves playing games that a woman can excel at—tennis, golf, sports that don't embody the heroic team ethic or demand a weight-lifter's strength. It is not in the actual arena of active sports that the male chauvinist is most at home, but in that nostalgia for the locker room and the trials of physical strength that the major team sports vicariously provide, the old romanticism of muscle and physical daring in a world which increasingly needs neither. The male chauvinist attitude toward sport is a kind of surrogate pride—most men are more concerned with knowing and reading about sport than doing it, and it is a woman's ignorance of sport that attracts their ridicule, rather than her inability to play. The male identification with sport has its effects in the *confining* of women, their sense of being limited. As Jill Johnston points out, "What's in it for a woman to go out and play with the men and feel like a dope for being no good. Or to go out and play with women and receive no cultural feedback, mirror action. In all the media across the land the men can see themselves playing all their sports while the women can see only a fragment of themselves occasionally occupying a small space as a strange exception . . ."(13)

Yet this is changing, and Ms. Johnston's comment is probably applicable only to the more specialized and commercialized sports, which constitute mass entertainment, rather than to physical activity in the traditional sense. The notion of sports as a male preserve is gradually being undermined as women athletes begin to pursue sports which were hitherto almost entirely masculine. Even here, the roots of male chauvinism are being sapped, destroying some of the basic assumptions about what a woman could or couldn't do, making the artificial distinctions in other areas seem just that much more offensive and arbitrary. So long as women merely became doctors, or business executives on the level of middle management, or lawyers, the myth of masculine superiority could still somehow be preserved in the physical area. But that territory becomes smaller and smaller. Few worlds were more exclusively "masculine" than the track, yet there are women jockeys now. The only reason anybody could think of for arguing that women shouldn't be jockeys was that they might find it easier to meet the weight requirements than men, opening up the possibility that the majority of jockeys in races might soon be women. Happily, it seems they find it no easier to keep their weight down than men do, and as for the other requirements of being a jockey—riding ability and courage—the exercising and training of Thoroughbreds, an arduous and dangerous business, has long since been taken over by young women, to such an extent that they have become familiar fixtures at every track, demonstrating, if any proof was necessary, that they can get up just as early, ride as hard and take as many risks as any man, and providing a natural pool of talent from which many more women jockeys are likely to emerge.

Robyn Smith, for example, rode 309 horses during the 243-day New York Racing Association season. Twenty-seven years old, she "is quite sure" she will have a Kentucky Derby mount soon, and says of her career, "It has nothing to do with femininity." She attributes her success to hard work—harder work than most male jockeys are willing to do. She arrives at Aqueduct at six to work the horses, exercising them to keep fit herself. "I make the rounds every morning to find horses to gallop or breeze, four or five. It makes no difference to me whether or not I get to ride them in the afternoon, just so long as I can work them in the morning . . . Some of the boys usually don't get to the track until it's time to report for riding races."

As for the traditional male chauvinist sport of football, there already exists a women's football team, in fact a whole league of them: the New York Fillies play against Midwest Cowgirls, the Pittsburgh Powderkegs and the Detroit Fillies, wearing NFL kits with the addition of foam-padded plastic breastplates. Though one New York team member is said to have quit after breaking a fingernail in a practice session, the teams seem to play with the same toughness as male players.

Women golfers, it seems, are already in revolt, complaining that they can't play against the top-ranking men, but have to play against each other in what amounts to an inferior tournament, and that they make less in prize money and endorsements than men do. "If women got as much national publicity as men, we'd be making just as much money . . . It's only March and Jack Nicklaus has already made $100,000. Once you say you're a woman athlete you have two strikes against you."(14) Mrs. Marlene Bauer Hagge is of course protesting against a very obvious injustice. Why should women play golf separately from men? It is all very well to argue that "women will never be strong enough to match drives with men," but is it true? And if it is, need it always be so? I doubt it, and there is no reason not to have a handicap system anyway.

Golf is not the only sport that produces discontent. Mrs. Patty Martinez Cash, a champion table-tennis player, says: "Women are discriminated against in tournaments all the time. Prize money for the men is much greater. I've played in tournaments where the men won $3,500 for first place, the women only $500. That's not fair . . ."(15)

If it isn't biology that makes men superior, or physical power, real or expressed in the surrogate of sports, what exactly is the male chauvinist's justification for his supposed superiority? Can it be sex itself?

As a final argument, there is always that: the pride of the erect penis. God knows, you have to be man to understand the depth of feeling behind this particular male concern, and the way in which the slightest uncertainty about it (and what man is ever completely certain?) can lead so quickly to the fear and distrust of women. But potency, however desirable in the relationship between the sexes, is not a convincing argument for male superiority, and the assumption that virility is an index of ability in other areas is very doubtful. Men, of course, tend to regard virility as the basic standard of judgment within their group, thus automatically excluding women from membership in the various subgroups, since they cannot compete in that particular game. Women sometimes make the same dubious correlation; Gloria Steinem, for instance, was guilty of *reverse* male chauvinism in saying that she thought President Nixon was the most "sexually insecure" President to hold power in recent years. Perhaps he is, but so what? A virile and aggressive sexuality is not a prerequisite for a successful Presidency. There is abundant evidence that Napoleon suffered from premature ejaculation, and a careful reading of his love letters to and from Josephine seem to indicate a certain anxiety about the size of his penis. These sexual concerns did not prevent him from winning the battle of Austerlitz or writing the *Code Napoleon*. Suggestions have been made that Frederick the Great was a repressed homosexual, and even if it is true, it does not seem to have had any very great influence on his success as a general. Even Winston Churchill was accused of being a homosexual as a young man, and fought a libel action to prove that he wasn't, with rather inconclusive results. Yet men are so convinced that an erect heterosexual penis is the proof of competence in other areas that they have even persuaded women—radical women like Gloria Steinem, at that—of its influence. Mailer, for example, tends to equate male heterosexual aggressiveness and competence with the ability to create, which leads him to complicated rationalizations about D. H. Lawrence's obvious sexual insecurity:

. . . He had lifted himself out of his natural destiny which was probably to have the sexual life of a woman, had diverted the virility of his brain down into some indispensable minimum of phallic force— no wonder he worshipped the phallus, he above all men knew what an achievement was its rise from the roots, its assertion to stand proud on a delicate base.(16)

This is, of course, the gonad view of life, the root, so to speak, of male chauvinism. Note the statement that Lawrence's physical weakness would probably have led him to have "the sexual life of a woman," with the implication that a woman's sexual life is somehow less vital, less creative than a man's. And how could Lawrence have had "the sexual life of a woman," being a man? What Mailer means, I think, is that Lawrence was lucky not to have become a homosexual, given his problems, neurotic and physical—but is a male homosexual's eroticism equivalent to a woman's? One wouldn't have thought so. The suggestion that Lawrence diverted some part of his genius downward, where it was mysteriously transformed into "phallic force" is fascinating, though difficult to take seriously, but far more interesting is the use of the phrase "the virility of the brain." Why was Lawrence's literary genius a function of this putative "virility" whose site is the skull rather than the groin? Does Mailer mean that great writers have some kind of erection of the mind?

A man's sexuality has very little to do with his ability as a writer or anything else, and a woman's sexuality does not have any great bearing on her capacity to work. Modern writers, particularly Mailer and Hemingway, have been inclined to equate the act of writing with virility, yet we can just as easily put the act of creation in feminine terms, sometimes even applying the female function to a man, as in "he nursed this great idea for many years before giving birth to the first volume of his *oeuvre*." Alas, if virility were a determining factor in writing, we should have to award literary prizes in quite a different fashion!

Virility guarantees nothing, and phallic power has no innate claim to superiority over "vagina power." Our grandparents, whatever their pruderies, did not make the mistake of assuming that a man who was sexually secure was naturally more trustworthy or capable than one who was not, but this proposition now enjoys wide currency in post-Freudian America, without anyone's apparently having noticed that it more or less excludes women. If a man's sexual self-confidence is a value test (say, for the Presidency), it is at least theoretically possible to gauge it; either a man has an erection or he doesn't, and he can maintain it for seven seconds or seven minutes. Judgment can be made. But how is one to test the sexual self-confidence of women? There are no visible signs that cannot be faked, it is perfectly possible for a willingness to engage in sexual activity to conceal an inner passivity. In this way the idea that sexual performance somehow qualifies one for other activities works against women.

Love, sex, are mysteries, and it is perhaps just as well that in a certain measure they should remain so. Henry James, who was hardly Mailer's idea of an aggressive sexual man, could still write very great novels, a woman in her period can still operate a complex computer, the most sexually potent man in a business organization might be the mailroom boy rather than the president. It doesn't matter. What matters is that men have unconsciously convinced themselves that virility is a factor in their careers, and since they cannot compete with each other in terms of their comparative virility (not because they don't want to, but because there's no practical way to do so), they use their assumption of virility against women. Your business rival may be more virile than you are—who can tell?—but both of you are by definition more virile than any woman, and therefore better. In a game where men have made all the rules, every man can win.

But the rules are changing, men are left high and dry with an attitude that they cannot support with facts or reason, left with nothing but the vague feeling that surely men must be different from women in some way beyond the physically obvious one, that perhaps the very fact that women covet the privileges of men may be a proof of man's superiority, a position to which Mailer ultimately withdraws in *The Prisoner of Sex,* and which is a popular Maginot Line of male chauvinist thinking:

So let woman be what she would, and what she could . . . Let her cohabit on elephants if she had to, and fuck with Borzoi hounds, let her bed with eight pricks and a whistle, yes, give her freedom and let her burn it, or blow it, or build it to triumph or collapse . . . So women could have the right to die of men's diseases, yes, and might try to live with men's egos in their own skull case and he would cheer them on their way—would he? Yes, he thought that perhaps they may as well do what they desired if the anger of the centuries was having its say. Finally, he would agree with everything they asked but to quit the womb, for finally a day had to come when women shattered the pearl of their love for pristine and feminine will and found the man, yes that man in the million who could become the point of the seed which would give an egg back to nature, and let the woman return with a babe who came from the roots of God's desire to go all the way, wherever was that way.[17]

In Norman Mailer's acceptance of women's liberation are contained all the cliches of male chauvinism: the concentration on biological factors, the ego that implies that her spirit craves, needs the one man (guess who) who will implant in her the perfect seed, the notion that man carries the burden of a special ego that women will have to learn to cultivate and carry for themselves, the whining undertone of the implication that men suffer from special more lofty diseases which women are somehow spared, the basic belief that women's liberation is a question of fucking, that women are essentially motivated by the Masters and Johnson discovery that they can sustain limitless orgasms,(19) rather than by any simple desire to be treated like intelligent human beings and given the training and opportunity that an intelligent human being has the right to expect. The male chauvinist in effect says, when he tries to be reasonable, "All right, you may join us," without seeing that there is no "us" to join. Men have designed society and the structure of work around their own impulses and their sense of belonging together, as if they were in some mysterious way guardians of the sacred flame of progress, wealth, energy, achievement—all those ambitions which are primarily meaningful because they separate men from women, give men added value. This baroque structure of myths, constructed over the centuries, is the means by which men cling to their masculine pride while sitting at their desks doing a job that a woman could, in all truth, do just as well or better if she had the training and the motivation. But if she could, then who the hell are we, and why are we sitting there, shuffling papers and answering the telephone, heirs in fantasy to the power and authority of Frederick the Great, Barbarossa, the Plains Indians, a hundred, a thousand million men who believed that it was a man's function to deal with the physical

world, to conquer it, to tame it, to mold it in his image;
who left to women that magic, inward mystery of childbirth, of continuity, the impulses that silently, instinctively connect one generation to another and provide the
rationale for expansion and adventure and work. To ask
men to allow women into this dream castle, this vast
Neuschwanstein of dreams and ambitions, is to ask them
to dismantle it, to admit that man has finally been
domesticated, that the dreams and illusions are over and
done with, that nothing is taking place in this office, at
this desk, behind this typewriter or computer but work
without glory, without special significance: Man's world
is no longer infinite, but limited, no longer special, but
ordinary, no longer a heavy burden with earned privileges, but merely the same world as every other human
being's, in which he is free to make just those choices
that everyone else is free to make, and no more, and in
which his goal is simply survival, to be bought by work,
as woman's has been survival, to be purchased until now
by attaching herself to him. As women push into man's
world, making their way through the loopholes of the
crumbling structure of men's dreams about themselves,
demolishing the ancient prerogatives, they are destroying
man as God, reducing him to human proportions. When
men fight back they are defending far more than the
right to earn more money, not to have to begin as a secretary, to achieve a place in the hierarchy of a corporation; they are fighting to maintain the last bastion of
their identity in a world that no longer offers them an
easy path to glory or even imposes on them the burden
of carrying women on their shoulders—a burden that
men have complained about through the ages, but in
which they have always taken a perverse pride, since it
proved them the stronger sex.

It is ironic that Mailer's book, which ends with a
kind of blessing to woman (But do they want our
blessing? Do they *need* it?), begins with his secretary
warning him that he may be about to win the Nobel
Prize, and looking up at him, as she transmits this message, "with eyes so rich in admiration that she could

have been confronting the Honorable Ex-Supreme Court Justice Arthur J. Goldberg."(18) For this is what we want from women, expect from them, demand from them.

Events seem to indicate that we will soon have to learn to do without it.

THREE

"You can't put women in tough combat jobs. There are so many things they can't do physically. Tell one to take a mortar casing over the hill and, by thunder, she can't even get it over a log."
—Curtis Tarr, director of the Selective Service System,
            on the women's equal rights amendment

"So few women care any more. They're not interested enough in people or in men. A woman's real purpose lies in trying to give pleasure to those around her—to be courteous, attractive and amusing . . ."
—Princess Beris Kandaoureff

THE PSYCHOLOGY OF SERFDOM

I once had a friend who worked in a largish business corporation in New York City. About four years ago we had lunch together and he was, I thought, in a state of exasperation unlike his normally placid self. "I can't get any useful work done," he complained, "the whole office is like a madhouse, half my colleagues are behaving like madmen. And remind me, I have to buy copies of *Vogue*, *Glamour* and *Harper's Bazaar* on my way back." This unusual request intrigued me, and I asked the cause of this sudden interest in fashion.

"It's like this," he said. "We're concerned about pants suits. Some of the girls have been coming to work in pants suits, and when the management noticed they passed the word down: No pants suits. Well, my secretary turned up with a certificate from her doctor saying that she had suffered from rheumatoid arthritis as a child and that her condition required her to keep her legs warm in the winter. So they made an exception for her; she could hardly be asked to change into a dress at the office, so we had one girl wearing a pants suit. Up until then it had been a fad, something the young women, the secretaries, were pushing for the hell of it—

you know, just to annoy the old arteriosclerotic brigade, and they succeeded. I mean, my God, we even had memos from the chairman of the board, who hasn't been seen or heard from in ten years! Then all the senior women executives turned up in pants suits, it was like solidarity, and that really scared the pants off the men, if you see what I mean, so we had a meeting in the board room to discuss the problem, and everyone said pants would destroy our image, that some women don't look good in pants, that it was the thin edge of the wedge. Still, when our assistant treasurer, a pretty formidable woman in her fifties, had turned up in pants, there didn't seem much that anyone could do about it. So we decided pants *suits* were OK, provided they were really suits. No slacks, jeans or separate pants. I said, Who the hell knows the difference, but I should have kept my mouth shut, because now we have a committee, the three senior male executives, and we're supposed to decide whether it's a pants suit or just pants. So I have to buy fashion magazines."

The spectacle of three middle-aged men sitting in judgment on the women in their office—like the judgment of Paris by committee—was undeniably comic, and even my friend could see the humor of it. A few months later, I visited his office to find that half the younger women were in pants or blue jeans, a clear failure of policy. "Well," he said, "it's because it's a rainy day, for Christ's sake. On a rainy, slushy day, it makes sense." By the end of the year, his office looked like a women's college on a weekday morning, and the rapid progression toward total freedom—hot pants, granny dresses, boots, paisleyed gear and braless T-shirts had begun—obliterating all standards, and leaving the men to stagger after it, discarding their ties for turtlenecks and exchanging their Brooks Brothers shoes for a fantastic variety of varnished footwear hitherto seen only on the feet of pimps.

And the battle still goes on. In June of 1972, *The New York Times* reported that the women workers at

Revlon's head office in New York, from typists to senior executives, were in a state of simmering but unsuccessful revolt over a company regulation that prohibits their wearing pants in any form—including pants suits—to the office. Jay Bennett, the corporate vice-president of personnel and industrial relations, seems to have faced the same problem as the men described above, and to have dealt with it in the same manner, but with rather more firmness. "Questions began to arise when pants suits became fashionable," he explained, "so I held a meeting in 1970." The result was the prohibition of pants suits in any form. One secretary was quoted in the *Times* as saying, "It's like being supervised at school." Another reported that women who are suspected of not wearing bras are summoned to the personnel office for inspection, a facet of management/employee relationships that must set some kind of new high for male chauvinism. The *Times* did not mention whether the alleged inspection is carried out by a male executive or a female— one assumes the latter—but those who fail were apparently sent home to change and have their pay docked.

One woman executive rightly pointed out that clothing regulations impose severe financial strains on young women who have to buy two wardrobes, one for social life, the other for work. Another made the touching comment that when women leave the company "for other reasons" they always wear pants on their last day, a gesture of defiance which seems rather restrained under the circumstances.

It is interesting to speculate whether Mr. Bennett, of Mr. Revson, for that matter, exert the same control over their wives. One doubts it. But there you are: men have an urge to control women at work, in any way possible, perhaps to compensate for the increasing difficulty of controlling them on the home front.

In business men still rely on the collective impotence of women, as if they were conscious of John Stuart Mill's words, written over a century ago, in defense of women's rights:

All causes, social and natural, combine to make it unlikely that women should be collectively rebellious to the power of men . . . All women are brought up from the earliest years in the belief that their ideal of character is the very opposite to that of men; not self-will and government by self-control, but submission and yielding to the control of others.

The social attitudes of women—or rather the social attitudes that are forced on them—prevent their exploiting the value of their own work in the ways that are instinctive to men. Men find it difficult to react to success signals from women, and convenient to ignore them. Women have been taught at an early age to be compliant and polite. And if they put their work forward politely and compliantly, it is easy for men to give them the ritual smiles of approbation and approval that govern so much of traditional male/female discussion—and then ignore them. (If, on the other hand, a woman attempts to push her work forward, to seize credit, then she is being "pushy.")

Nothing contributes more to the psychology of serfdom of women in business than the subtle notion that the corporation is not "it" but "him." Women know that beyond each man is a door leading to a more powerful man, each step up the ladder moving nearer to the magic inner core that is essentially masculine. The process of rewards and promotions in business, above a certain level, remains in the hands of men, and most men not only expect "submission" but are unable to see the mechanism of success except in masculine terms.

A woman's decision to break out of the ranks and into the race for success is not as easy as simply making up her mind to do so. Women complain that they have been "programmed for failure." As one young woman in business told me, "Success frightens women, I think, frightened me any way. It means giving up the comforts of irresponsibility, of being a little girl, of asking for admiration and approval. That's hard to do when your idea of success has always been to be praised by other people, mostly men. I realize now that I've spent years asking to be treated like a dog, or a bitch, I guess, looking to men to give me a pat on the head and say, 'Well done.' Men don't seek approval for its own sake, the way women do. They sometimes please other men to go after what they want, but not just for the sake of pleasing, which women *do*. When I first began work, I didn't understand this at all, the whole thing scared me. I'd always thought of men as equals, and here they were in charge of this whole system, determining just what was going to happen to me. I couldn't find a way to break into the system, and the more I tried, the more I made a mess of it. The men who came in when I did were simply more at ease with the whole thing, they *fitted in* . . . I thought that I was afraid of failure, that was my big worry, then one day I realized that what really scared me was succeeding, attracting notice, having to come out into the open as a person in a world full of men who simply wanted me to be quiet and productive and not make trouble. It's tough to be an outsider."

Even today, the advice that women are given on going to work seems somehow to miss the point. A recent publication for married women going to work advises:

Professionalism means being objective and willing, cheerful, presentable, and polite, no matter how strange, lonely, unhappy, or irritated, you feel . . . This might not be easy at the outset while you are trying to adjust in so many ways; however your primary satisfaction in the work world comes not from emotional gratification but from a sense of accomplishment, and if you look to your accomplishment first, the rest will follow . . . Your appearance and demeanor should show good taste, but forget about creating a big impression. Striking clothes or a pronounced "way" with men won't get the job done, and if you get noticed, it'll be the wrong kind of notice.(22)

As advice, this is not very much better than the old dictum of convent schools that girls should never wear patent leather shoes because men can see their underwear reflected on the shiny toes. The only realistic note is that advancement is dependent on men (". . . a pronounced 'way' with men won't get the job done, and if you get noticed, it'll be the wrong kind of notice"). The implication is obvious and largely true: if you want to get ahead you are going to have to be noticed by men, and the question is merely what kind of notice you will manage to attract, i.e., what role in the battle of sexes you will agree to play. But we all know that many a career has been launched by attracting "the wrong kind of notice," and that given the choice between two equally qualified women, one pretty and the other not, most men will prefer the former. Given the nature of the working world, there are few things more valuable to a woman than "a pronounced 'way' with men." To be sure, it is also necessary to be qualified for the job, to work, to have ideas. Quite apart from the evident unreality of this admonition in terms of relationships between the sexes, it seems odd to tell women that "the primary satisfaction in the work world comes . . . from a sense of accomplishment." Generally speaking, the purpose of work is to exploit one's potential to the maximum, to earn the maximum amount of money, to reach for success. Men may or may not have a sense of accomplishment (none would deny that it's a nice thing to have), but if they're going to get anywhere, they also have to fulfill their potential, to move actively as far as their talent and opportunities will take them. There is no reason for women to have lesser goals. Finally, would any advice to young men going out to work include the necessity of being "cheerful, presentable and polite"? These qualities may very well be desirable, but as an approach to business success it resembles kindergarten instruction. You may be as cheerful and presentable and polite as you like, but there is no substitute for shrewdness, judgment, a realistic appraisal of one's possibilities and a

weather eye for the moment of opportunity. Even the editors of a work deisgned to *help* women find it impossible
to talk frankly about the reality of the work world.

In one sense only women do have a small advantage
over men. They can get *into* a corporation more easily
than a man, since they come in as secretaries as a rule,
whereas men usually are hired for a specific job, and are
therefore subject to a much more demanding and strin-
gent hiring process. But because women do begin, so to
speak, in the ranks, they remain at least one step behind
the men who began on a more exalted plane. There is a
sense that men were picked out, chosen because they
were likely to succeed, whereas women have somehow
emerged from an altogether less prestigious apprentice-
ship. Even to have been a salesman, for example, is a
badge of knowledge and courage in business, proof that
one has been out on the road, known the harsh realities
of selling a product, been exposed to the tough world of
moving merchandise. Like battle scars, sales experience,
however lowly, is regarded with esteem. It is hard to
imagine male business trainees being asked to put in a
year as secretaries, learning to type, take dictation and
put up with the demands of an executive. Being a secretary earns a woman no *kudos* in the business world; it is
not the kind of humble work that pays dividends or en-
forces respect—rather the contrary: it tends to make men
feel that a woman forever preserves the characteristics of
a secretary, that her experience and years of preparation
are not only negligible, but negative, the mark of servi-
tude overcome, but never quite forgotten.

From the very beginning, women tend to be pushed
into jobs where they are *relied* on to do what is necessary
without complaining, or at any rate to restrict themselves
to the kind of frivolous complaints that are fairly easy to
field. From a man's point of view a woman who works is
always in some mysterious way less "womanly" than one
who doesn't—For were not women supposed to be at
home, in the kitchen, looking after children, as God and
Nature intended them to?—and this attitude eroded any
respect she might hope to win from men by her success.

The more successful she is, the more unnatural. A man's success is by definition good, a woman's merely evidence of some deep flaw in her life, the consequence of hidden neuroses, of inability to fulfill her traditional role. A businessman remarked to me recently about some dispute with a woman executive, "You have to expect it, you know: a woman in her forties who isn't married, whose whole life is in her work, you've got trouble. I don't say she isn't good at her job, she *is*, but it's not a natural life, living alone in an apartment, putting into her job all the psychic energy that most women put into marriage, children. I'm *for* women's liberation, I think it's great for the kids, but I don't think most women want to be liberated—I think they resent it instead. They're hoping someone will come along and unliberate them, and when nobody does, they become impossible."

The pressure to keep women in traditional roles, to think of them in the traditional ways, is not restricted to businessmen. The counterculture and even the juvenile-crime culture operates with the same disregard for women, the same tendency to revert to the old stereotypes. A recent story in *The New York Times* about teen-age street gangs contained some perfect gems of male chauvinism and female submissiveness. Noting that officers of the special police surveillance units do not consider the girls to be a menace and that the boys themselves keep the girls "submerged," the reporter went on to describe life in the gangs in a way which makes it sound remarkably familiar:

The girls reciprocate for the protection they receive by acting as housekeepers for the boys. Savage Nomad girls are charged with keeping the clubhouse decorated and clean. The Savage Skull girls wash and iron the boys' laundry. "They're like our wives, they do everything a wife does," Blacky, a club president said. In the Savage Nomad headquarters, Janet concurred. "The guys take care of us. It's their job to protect us, so whatever they do has to be right." A spokesman for the Gang Intelligence Unit explained, "We don't consider the girls a particular problem. They are primarily passive . . . The boys risk getting killed, the girls risk getting pregnant.

Even in the subculture of street violence and crime, the girls are only allowed to fight against each other, never to join in the larger, more organized warfare of the gangs themselves—they are, therefore, excluded from the central activity of the organizations they belong to, and restricted to the minor, supportive roles that men everywhere traditionally reserve for women. "Sure we hang out with the girls," said the president of the Young Sinners, "but we don't talk to them much."

The counterculture is no different. Communes break down because life reverts sooner or later to the same domestic patterns that exist everywhere. As one ex-communer told me, "It started out to be OK, but it just turned to the same old shit, I mean, OK, you were living in total freedom, but the women were still ironing the shirts, and the men were doing all the big talk about farming and preparing for the winter and stuff. Preparing for the winter meant the women had to learn how to can, right? And sexual freedom turned out to mean that the guys play around, but the chicks still get stuck with the same old jealousy bag. So I walked out."

In a recent discussion of men's reactions to women's liberation, I was even more astonished to find that many young radical men blamed women for destroying the radical movement in the United States. One participant in the discussion remarked in detail on this phenomenon:

"In early 1970, there was born a forum called the Seattle Liberation Front, which was touted as the successor to SDS, as a format which might provide new energies to the radical movement in this country . . . That was in February, 1970. By September of 1970, the women in that particular movement had decided that the leadership was male chauvinistic, and they realized that women occupied a secondary position in that movement, in that community, and so at a meeting of the Seattle Liberation Front the women stood up and denounced the leadership of the SLF, then walked out of the meeting, which depleted the SLF by one half. Soon thereafter, the women went to the home of one of the leaders of the SLF and "trashed it up," in the sense that they painted slogans all over it saying, "Sexists are not revolutionaries." This was disconcerting because the slogans they painted on this man's house were so obscene that his neighbors complained, and the city came to his house while he was out of town and painted the slogans over with orange paint, and so there was this garish building in the middle of this working-class community. The women issued a statement through the underground press detailing their reservations about the SLF leadership, and some of the points were very well taken, but the fact was that the women's revolt had effectively destroyed the SLF, in the sense that half the people had suddenly walked out . . . Suddenly half the movement had departed to form its own clique in the women's liberation front, so much of the energy of this nascent revolutionary movement was brunted, set aside, shut off, depleted, and I think that unsettled everyone so much— I know that it unsettled me enough so that I simply couldn't feel active in broader terms than my relationship with a specific woman. I mean, all of a sudden the revolution had become *personal*. It stopped being some external phenomenon which we could confront. But when I saw this deterioration in my travels around the country, I began to have my suspicions that women were being selfish, right? Then when I saw the deterioration of relationships and marriages among my own friends, I began to think: there is something wrong with these demands women are making upon us . . ."(22)

The underlying theme is clear: *We counted on women and they failed us.* In the radical movement, as in business, men expect women to follow the leadership. A young radical woman told me, "Sure we walked out, and why not? I mean, there was a lot of talk from the leadership, but the leadership was all male, a bunch of guys organizing nothing demonstrations and pretending that they were Trotsky or Che, and like the chicks served up the food, and got to paint signs, and run the mimeograph machine, and do the typing, for Christ's sake, and of course fuck. Big deal! I believe in revolution, man, but being in the movement was just like being in an office, with the guys doing all the talking and the chicks doing all the shit-work."

The issue of women and "shit-work" is not only central, but in a certain sense transcendental. In Victorian times, "women's work" was supposed to be genteel, and the tradition lingers on, but this was never more than a convention of the upper classes. Woman's work has always been shit-work, connected as if by natural law to the monotonous and degrading task of cleaning up, of dealing with the feces, sweat and grime of a race that cannot groom itself. In all cultures, human feces is considered an abomination, yet women have always been laundresses, have always cleaned diapers and babies, accepting as inevitable what men have shunned. Arabs, for example, use one hand for eating, the other for performing their ablutions—it is a deadly affront to eat food with the wrong hand. But Arab women, who must use both hands to wash clothes, clean up babies, deal with their menstruation, do not partake of this dexterous separation of functions, and are assigned to a lower order of humanity. Throughout our cultures this common assumption that women are somehow formed to cope with filth and dirt runs unchecked, forming a sociological background that permits men to assign women to menial tasks without guilt. Washing up is women's work, nursing is women's work, looking after babies is women's work, cleaning is women's work. Something of women's mystery for men even lies in the dichotomy between the lacquered, elegant image of the ideal woman and the functions that men have unconsciously assigned to women in general, as if, in the words of a medieval writer, women were "a flower rooted in dung." Shit-work is therefore more than a phrase: it represents an attitude, one of the basic myths of male chauvinism, connected to, stemming from, every man's relationship with his own mother, his deeply ingrained knowledge that she is the person who will deal with the small, messy wounds of childhood, with illness, with dirt, with the regulation and management of the bodily functions that take up so much of a child's time—Brush your teeth, wipe your nose, use your handkerchief, wipe your bottom, wash your hands afterward, clean your fingernails.

What must, of course, be particularly irritating for a woman is that men are inclined to argue that shit-work is rewarding in itself. By and large, women still have to do *duller* work than men, and theirs is the boredom of waste, rather than the boredom of overextension. "We all have to do shit-work," says a business executive earning $30,000 a year. "I have to attend meetings I don't want to go to, settle problems I don't want to think about, make decisions; my secretary has to type letters. Everybody has to do things they'd rather not do." True enough, but the difference lies in the fact that men's shit-work is supposed to lead somewhere, it is done for purposes of self-expansion. Most of the shit-work that women are called upon to do leads nowhere.

A further example of this attitude is the kind of reverse sensibility that makes it necessary for men to *apologize to* women for work, or worse, to pretend that whatever has to be done is *fun*, as if they were dealing with children. This tendency to sugarcoat work in presenting it to women has of course been intensified by the growing sensitivity of men to the demands of the women's movement. An example:

M: "I wonder if you'd mind just going through all these clippings, marking off the most interesting passages and Xeroxing them. Actually, it's not such a boring job as it looks. I think you'll find some of them very interesting."

W: (who already has ten other things to do and knows perfectly well that she is being asked to do a secretarial chore when she's already been promoted to an executive job): "Well, I'm awfully busy now. Couldn't someone else do it?"

M: "Just because you've been promoted doesn't mean that you don't have to help out with the shit-work everyone else has to do. Now just *do* it and stop complaining!"

Oddly enough, in this kind of situation, the woman will usually win, if she is persistent enough, for, having left his desk and come to her with the papers he has, by the rules of male chauvinism, signaled the weakness of his position—if he had called her into his office and handed her the clippings, he would have established his authority. All the same, in most offices, when a woman wins a battle like this, as she often will, women are still the losers. The man will simply give the work to a woman lower down the pecking scale who won't complain—once he has categorized it as work for a woman by offering it to a woman, it becomes impossible for him to do it without losing face. In many offices, men will offer a difficult clerical task to a number of women in succession, even suggesting that it can be treated as overtime work, and frequently by-passing their own secretaries or assistants for fear of annoying them.

Some younger women in offices have pretty much given up on work as an area in which anything can be changed, putting their psychic energy into larger issues of self-definition while going on with their daily tasks unquestioningly. They assume from the start that business is unfair and opportunities are few, thus confirming men in their original prejudices.

And men have learned that there are two kinds of women's liberation in business. One derives from the struggle on the part of young women, particularly the better-educated ones, to define themselves as individuals; the other, involving as a rule older and more senior women workers, is concerned with salaries, titles, promotions and respect for work done. The former is irritating, the latter threatening, but it is the former that absorbs more attention, if only because it has the less practical relationship to the work at hand. The women who are concerned with promotions and salaries and titles are already deeply involved in the system; they are operating from within, and at a certain level can only make progress by showing that they are at least as interested in profit as the men, and possibly more so. The younger women who see in each demand a new demonstration of male chauvinism are open to attack precisely because they have very little to offer in the way of profit, because they are talking about their personal relationship to the work situation, rather than the *aim* of the work itself, which is simply money.

Even a distinguished sociologist can argue, in this day and age, that equality already exists, when it is visible to almost anyone that it doesn't. Joseph Adelson, for example, writes:

> . . . We should first distinguish between the banal and the extravagant aims of the recent outcry for a change in the status of women . . . I call certain aims banal simply because everyone seems to agree with them, men and women alike; they are now non-issues. Everyone believes in equal pay for equal work; most everyone believes that women should not be sharply limited in the economic roles available to them.(23)

But where is the proof that these are generally accepted, "banal" aims, with which "everyone seems to agree"? Very few women are getting equal pay for equal work, and most men, whatever they say, are very anxious to keep women "sharply limited in the economic roles available to them." It is a professorial conceit to suppose that the practical aims of women's liberation are generally accepted, in an age which still condemns women to the typing test and shorthand classes as the reward for a four-year liberal arts education. On the whole, a woman's possibilities still remain very limited as compared to a man's.

One bright young woman trying to get ahead, and

deeply involved in women's consciousness-raising, is battling openly on both fronts—personal and professional—and has managed to galvanize her office by fighting every sign of male chauvinism, while working hard to show her competence and intelligence. The result is that even the most impassioned pleading of her immediate superior has proved insufficient to win her a significant raise, let alone a change in status. The fact that she refused to make a cup of coffee for a visiting executive is remembered when her reports, analyses and suggestions (all of them very intelligent) are forgotten. The very mention of her name guarantees a bitter and protracted discussion among the senior executives. Her immediate supervisor, an otherwise reasonable and very pleasant man, says, "I've given up. I like her, and she's a bright person, and I *need* her, but she set out to fight on too many fronts at once. She might have beaten men at their own game, she's smart and hard-working, but you can't show them up by being bright *and* put them down as men at the same time. They have too many weapons, and hell, I'm no hero. When I mention her name at a salary meeting, everybody whistles and says, 'What's the matter, are you afraid of that little bitch?' OK, she's difficult and sharp-tongued, but the trouble is that she's really involved in all this women's liberation business, it *matters* to her on principle—not just a twenty-dollar raise or an office of her own instead of a desk in the hallway—the men just aren't ready to deal with the whole thing as a serious *life* issue. So they punish her. They say, in effect, 'You do it our way if you want to get ahead,' then they tell her, 'But you're not going to get ahead anyway, so don't think we'll be impressed if you do do it our way.' Sometimes we talk about it, you know, and I try to tell her about the whole shit-eating side of work, and she says, 'You made it one way. Why do I have to do it that way?' But there isn't any way to make it without giving up some part of our ego, and like a lot of young women, she's just in the process of finding hers. Half the trouble is a question of chronology. Women are learning to develop their egos and doing it out there in public, at work, where men have had centuries to learn to restrain theirs . . ."

In the same office, a woman co-worker complains, "I've always kept a low profile, it's not that I don't believe in women's liberation, but I guess I don't want to make a spectacle of myself, maybe I'm frightened to, maybe I just think that women's liberation is mostly about side issues, not about work. But doing what I'm supposed to do and working hard at it haven't got me very far, and I'm beginning to wonder just what the hell it's all about. A lot of the women's liberation people in the office, the first ones, seemed to be a bunch of cliquey, ugly, super-serious *dykes,* girls who wanted a lot without having put in their time, you know? They left, I guess because they were pushed out, but also because they moved on to other things, and now the women's liberationists around here are mostly young, pretty girls, who don't do a goddamned bit of work and use 'male chauvinism' as an excuse for not doing their share, the way Southern girls always used to have migraine headaches, or a bad period, or needed to leave early for football weekends. I work hard, but what do I have to do for someone to notice me? I've seen women here get noticed because of their looks—that really hurts!—or because they made a lot of trouble to *get* noticed, then 're-formed,' for which they got all sorts of Brownie points, but a woman who is simply doing her job get's treated like a faithful dog."

Her supervisor, a man, says, "She's terrific, sure. That's what this office needs, a lot more quiet, hard-working, rational women, who put in a good day's work and don't forget that we're all here to get things done— not to use the office as a place to work out problems."

Neither attitude works against entrenched habits— fight and you're a troublemaker, comply and you're beaten. Confronted by women's liberation sweeping through their own corridors and offices, men rely on the time-honored methods of corporate politics to solve the

problem, playing the games which are instinctive to successful men, and which women are only just beginning
to learn.

A case in point: three years ago, a strong-minded
young woman managed to bring the management of a
big advertising agency to its chauvinistic knees by sheer
dogged will-power. Using the methods that had made it
possible, for one brief moment, to organize the peace
movement within corporations, she managed to forge a
group of about a dozen active feminists, most of them either secretaries or assistants or junior copywriters, all of
them young, ill-paid and resentful of the fact that
women were not given a chance to rise to better-paying
and more important jobs. Jane wanted to bring in clients, but didn't have an expense account. She took them
out to lunch and signed the check, forcing the company
either to pay the restaurant or fire her. The company
paid. When the management refused to sit down and discuss the issues of women's liberation in the office, she
leaked her complaints to a variety of trade magazines
and even to *The New York Times*. The company listened. It was clear there was no hope of charming her
into surrender, and senior executives found themselves
on the defensive whenever they tried to reason with her,
for she was obviously talented and knew her facts. What
is more, she knew her job, which made it difficult to fire
her. "Jesus," one man said, "suddenly I'm the enemy in
my own office! Don't these women know we're all supposed to be on the same side?" But as Jane pointed out,
they *weren't* on the same side; he was the enemy.

At this point in time, Jane and her supporters seemed
on the verge of winning substantial gains. Even the
women who weren't radical feminists or who were afraid
to show any sympathy for her in public or who simply
weren't ambitious enough to see any practical advantages for them in joining her, began to take on a harder
attitude toward men and work, to force frank discussions
about their roles, their pay and their future, if only on
an individual level. Change was in the air, and the corporation sensed it, indeed little else was being discussed.

Hastily, Jane was promoted to the rank of senior copy-writer and given a raise, thus separating her from the other women, then given so much work that it kept her fairly quiet. Without her active participation, the movement lost impetus, and her very promotion served as an answer to additional demands, since the management had obviously responded to women. When business declined, about a year later, Jane was quietly fired along with a lot of other people, some of them men, her dismissal concealed in the larger issue of retrenchment and justified by the old adage of "last in, first out." It was even possible for the management to express great regret at the necessity of firing her. Now women's liberation has become a dead issue on an active level; everybody is willing to discuss it, everyone is involved, but no woman is attempting to confront the management about unequal pay, job opportunities, special training programs for women, new hiring procedures, etc. Instead, with Jane's departure, the agency has become women's-lib oriented in every way except the ones that count on the job.. "Sure," Jane says, "they're all trying to define their life roles, to work out their head problems, to think out the whole big subject of sexual exploitation. Well, there's a place for that, I don't deny it, I'm even into it myself, increasingly so since I left the company. I've gotten involved in a lot of things, including the whole lesbian thing, and I guess I'm a radical feminist in every sense of the word. But when I was there I knew none of that mattered from nine to five, that working out your private life is different from making damned sure that you get a decent chance at a promotion you deserve, instead of having it go to a man automatically. All those women are kidding themselves; they're just playing into the hands of men. At work, women's lib is *power*. Nothing else will get women what they want and deserve. Talking to men about male chauvinist *attitudes* is playing their game. It's male chauvinist *acts* that count, not what they think of you, but what they *do* in relation to you."

But to most men, working women are still cheap

labor. Male chauvinism is among other things a shrewd
method of extracting the maximum of work for the minimum of compensation. And like all prejudices, the prejudices of male chauvinism are self-fulfilling; by not given
women the incentives to develop their potential, men—
so long as they retain power—can ensure that the majority of women workers in fact justify the inferior position
of women. Because women are thought of as replaceable,
they are seldom given the training that would make
them more valuable, that would, in fact, make it difficult
to replace them. Men have arrogated to themselves the
enormous advantages of continuity, they have a sense,
however illusory, of permanency. Women rarely do, except in the sad sense of having stayed too long, of having
abandoned all their other options, being left at the age
of fifty the untrained and unwelcome ward of some corporation.

In most offices, men control, administer, decide upon
the security and futures of countless women. The reverse
is very seldom true. Women's liberation is not an ab-
straction: it is a struggle for equality of power. Its impetus comes from the realization of ordinary women, perhaps shocked at the psychological space exploration of
the feminist radicals, that their own modest journeys so
greatly resemble a third-class passage on the *Titanic*.
"Women's liberation isn't so damned difficult to
define," one young woman said, "it amounts to saying:
'OK, you've got yours, *now when do I get mine?*'" Or,
as one woman wrote forcefully: "There's a time when
you stop being a nice girl. You say, I'm going to be dis-
liked for the first time. I remember the day I said: All
right, no more everybody's darling. I know I can do this
better than this man, and I'll do *anything* to get this
job. At some point, it's no longer man/woman, it's I
want and I can do. And no one's going to stop
me."(24)

And over the short haul, who knows, nobody may; but
the long haul is a different story. A young woman, if
she's talented and ambitious, may jump the hurdles, but
as the years go by, men's attitudes toward her will tend

to change. Because to men, the fact that a woman *can* marry and stop working condemns her when she doesn't. Men feel that women have an alternative, while they do not; that men work from necessity, women from choice. Intruding domestic issues into the business world is one of the more effective means by which men encourage in women the psychology of serfdom, and find a support for their own lofty place in the power structure.

"You're ambitious, I understand that," an executive of my acquaintance recently told a young woman, "but you have something I don't have, *can't* have. I have to work a lifetime for financial security, and there's no short cut, no miracle that will change things for me. But you could get married tomorrow and wake up rich. I'm not saying you would do it deliberately, but still it could happen. Women don't realize that they're lucky, they can drop out, sell out, hope for a miracle . . ."

Men *expect* women to marry, and this is an excellent excuse for not giving them responsibility ("What if she marries and has kids, for God's sake?"), and not allowing them on the fast track that leads to promotions and financial security. True, a woman who doesn't get married and stays on in any reasonable corporation can derive considerable benefits from this attitude. By not marrying, she makes the company take on a certain responsibility for her future, as if the corporation were determined to be a surrogate husband. But this is not so much equality as a terminal dose of paternalism. She can sometimes arrange to be pensioned off quite generously simply because she hasn't managed to find a man, earning by what seems to be a failure in her private life a privileged position that success in her public life would never have won for her. But for this it is necessary to be a confirmed "spinster," to have dedicated one's life to the company, and if possible to be ugly. The least sign that a woman has the possibility of an alternative, even had at one time the possibility, and the men's generosity begins to evaporate. "A woman like that, why the hell didn't she get married? I mean, she's still pretty good-looking, she must have had a lot of chances, I don't see why we should have to pay for the fact that she missed out on life."

At heart, the question is whether women are "domestic" creatures or not. Men have rigidly divided the world into work and domesticity, and more or less abandoned the latter to women. When women emerge and join them at work, they undermine the structure men have created. Men's first line of defense is to treat these women as if they were still in some way "domestic," assigning to them the surrogate roles of wife, mother, daughter, refusing to take their ambitions and contributions seriously. They may be *in* the office, but they are not *of* it in the sense that men are.

Men tend to think of their careers as an obligation that requires putting in endless hours at the office, pouring their energy and concern into their work, sometimes for money but often because it is the easiest thing to do with their lives in our present culture. This attitude toward work implies a kind of aristocracy of function, against which everyone else must be measured. Knowing what they have given up, men are not only reluctant to admit that women can do the same, but doubtful that women *ought* to. A woman who works hard is not just a threat, the way any competitor is, but proof that the attitude most men have toward work is destructive to themselves and others. We find it difficult to see the ways in which we so often sacrifice our humanity as payment for our success, but the unfamiliar spectacle of a woman ignoring her children to make business trips, focusing her life on success, is an uncomfortable demonstration of just what we, as men, have done in the service of our careers. We have assigned to women a role of domestic happiness and then given up our own in order to make hers possible, without asking if it was what she wanted, what *we* wanted. Men work and some justify it by the domestic results—a house, money, a suburban garden, charge accounts. Someone, they argue, must be getting a benefit out of the work in terms of pleasure and gratification, and if it isn't them, then it must be their wives. We have created a dangerous myth, in which men sacrifice their pleasure—and often their health, energy and substance as well—in order to make other people, mostly women, "happy." The notion that the recipients of all this unwanted sacrifice are in fact not happy at all, that they too would like to go out and work, is an unwelcome and disturbing one.

In *The Pursuit of Loneliness,* Philip Slater argues that the American man's concept of "career" is "undesirable . . . a pernicious activity for *any* human being to engage in, and should be eschewed by both men *and* women."(25) It may well be that men have "Calvinist" attitudes toward work, but the disenchantment with which many American men speak of their careers and businesses is often a smoke screen to disguise the fact that they enjoy what they're doing, partly a means of extracting certain domestic comforts and privileges, partly an attempt to discourage women from wanting to pursue a career with any serious intent. For many men are aware, especially if they are married, of a slightly guilty feeling that they like their work more than being at home. A whole generation of American businessmen have been schooled to portray attitudes of fatigue, strain and nervous tension to mask the fact that they are deriving a good deal of satisfaction from their work. A group of men can be sitting comfortably in an office, discussing business in a relaxed fashion. Let a woman enter the room, and their feet will swiftly come off the desk, their relaxed manner will evaporate instantly. As if by reflex, they will hunch over in postures of suffering thought, clench their fists in tension, take up all those minor poses of men under strain—remove the glasses and massage the bridge of the nose between thumb and forefinger to indicate eyestrain and mental exhaustion, close the eyes as if in deep thought, raise the pitch of the voice to show that what is taking place is important. I have known one senior executive who smashed ashtrays and coffee mugs to indicate that his patience and nerves had been strained to the breaking point, another who affected a trembling of the fingers and a stutter to project fatigue; others who use such simple, but effective, devices as asking any importunate woman to bring them three aspirin *before* she has a chance to say whatever it is that is on her mind. Men are never so tired and harassed as when they have to deal with a woman who wants a raise. In these circumstances, they play the victim-game to its logical conclusion, using their own sufferings to justify the refusal of any request, however minor. "I'd love to talk about it, Sue, but not this week; if you could see my calendar, you wouldn't believe it." "I know, I know, I think you should have more money too, but hell, things are tough for everyone. I'm going to be here till eight going over these reports. I haven't had time to answer yesterday's phone calls yet." "Look, this just isn't the time, I have troubles already with the Board, if I try to get you money now, it won't work anyway."

Men even carry this tactic to the lengths of making it a preventive deterrent, complaining about their lot bitterly in order to shame women into not making embarrassing and difficult demands. This subtle mode of operation requires the man to sigh a great deal, to hold his head in his hands in a posture of extreme weariness, or slump his shoulders resignedly to convey to the women around him a suffering that discourages any woman from adding to it by bringing up her small problems (like the fact that she hasn't had a raise in two years). I would go so far as to say that this pose (oddly so "feminine" in terms of the traditional definitions of male/female behavior) is one of the central weapons in the arsenal of male chauvinism. Applied in advance, this attitude of *Angst* is usually sufficient to disarm women; it acts as an invisible screen against requests, demands and complaints—for how can you add to the troubles of a man overwhelmed by troubles (even though his salary is $50,000 a year, with an unlimited expense account and a yearly bonus of stock). The beauty of it is that the greater a man's success and the larger his income, the easier it is for him to assume the Position of Woe necessary to repel intruders. The variations are endless—

—To a woman who he thinks is going to ask for a few days' extra vacation time in order to go to Europe: "I don't know if I'm going to be able to get away this summer, it's a tough year for all of us, more work, less staff." (Ignoring the fact that he spent three days in Bermuda at the company sales conference, is on his way to a convention in Puerto Rico, and will take Fridays off from Memorial Day through Labor Day to spend three-day weekends at Easthampton, permitting him to argue that he "doesn't take vacations.")

—To a woman whom he suspects will bring up the subject of promotion: "God, I don't know, I can't go on like this, there's no future in my job, there's just no fair system here for rewarding merit, you know?" (Passing tactfully over the fact that he is already a senior vice-president, and could only advance further by hiring the dissidents from the Gallo family to wipe out the rest of the management.)

In so many ways, some unconscious, others not, men even attempt to reduce women to servility when they are honoring them. In April of 1972, the United States Navy appointed its first woman admiral. In announcing this appointment, Vice Admiral Davis, the Navy Surgeon General, praised Captain, now Admiral, Alene Bertha Duerk for having beaten out "the competition of several qualified girls." He added: "Pressures were indeed upon the Navy. Since the Air Force and Army have recently appointed several women as general officers, people were thinking, 'Why haven't you given your girls a break in this regard?' "(26)

This is a perfect illustration of male chauvinist thinking revealing itself. In the first place, there is the admission that the Navy has acted out of "pressure," rather than making Captain Duerk an admiral on her own merits. The implication is that the Navy was forced to have a woman admiral and that it might as well be Captain Duerk as anyone else. Then too, there's the word "girls," applied here to senior officers of the United States Navy. Admiral Duerk is fifty-three years old, served in the Pacific in World War II and in Korea, and commanded 2,300 Navy nurses at the time of her promotion. From the point of view of a man, however, it is still possible to refer to her as a *girl*, with all the word's implications of prepubertal dependence.*

At what point do "girls" become "women"? A recent book about women at work is called *The Girls In The Office*,(27) but several of the "girls" it deals with are thirty or forty years old, and all of them, after all, are self-supporting, working adults. Just as it used to be possible to refer to black men as "boys," in order to emphasize the fact that no black could ever achieve the status of a white adult, so the male chauvinist still refers to women as "girls" for the same reason. A great deal can be read into the male habit of switching back and forth between "girl" and "woman" in speech and writing. A recent article by a man on living alone in the big city notes:

> For every girl who lives alone . . . there are far more who have moved in with room-mates. Some girls need the continuation of college dormitory life,

* The problems of the armed services are by no means limited to male chauvinism toward senior women officers. *The New York Times* recently reported that a woman lieutenant of the U. S. Air Force was discharged after being accused of practicing witchcraft, or, as the *Times* put it, being "a professed worshiper of Satan." Her commanding officer was quoted as saying that Lt. Erika Uehlinger, of Detachment Eight of the 14th Aerospace Surveillance Force, Laredo, Texas, "was generally known to profess witchcraft." Her supervisor made the interesting comment that "she should be processed out of the Air Force for her own good and the benefit of the Air Force before she does something dangerous to the Air Force or herself." The implication that Lt. Uehlinger might be capable of doing "something dangerous" to the Air Force would seem to suggest that the Air Force believes in witchcraft. Would she throw a spell on the Early Warning System? Put a curse on SAC? It is reassuring to know that the strategic deterrent is being protected against witchcraft from within, though a less male chauvinist and more inventive group of officers might have seen the opportunity to use Lt. Uehlinger's alleged contacts with Satan to throw a curse on the Soviet missile system. The U. S. Air Force's witch-hunt does not seem to extend to warlocks; it would seem to be another case of women having a bad reputation.

Southern girls as a group tend to stick together anyway, four girls from Sweet Briar still sharing the
same hair dryer and dating from a common pool of
expatriate good ol' boys named Bobby Lee and
Billy Bo, whose idea of a good time is still six steins
of beer at the Red Onion and an occasional college
football weekend . . . In every apartment there is
one girl who thinks of the place as hers, usually because she was unlucky enough to have been the one
who signed the lease in the first place (landlords
frown on leases signed by four young women) . . .
What makes the business of finding a place to live
exacerbating is that sex cannot happen without a
place to do it in, and young women who come to the
big city to live aspire to some kind of sex
life . . . (28)

Here there is a very subtle counterpoint. Note that the
final sentence, which deals with sex, uses the phrase
"young women," implying that females who have sex
are "women," while females who live together are
"girls." It is possible to call Southern college graduates
of the male sex male children only by using a stock
phrase, "good ol' boys," to disguise and soften the use
of what would otherwise be an unacceptable description
of an adult male. The woman who is possessive about
the apartment is a "girl," whereas the cosignatories to
the lease whom the landlord frowns upon are "young
women," perhaps because possessiveness is one of those
male fears that automatically makes a man search for a
pejorative word to describe the possessive woman.

Language fraught as it is with male chauvinist under-
tones even constitutes a major weapon in men's struggle
to keep women in an inferior position. There is the common male habit of using profanity to put down women,
a game in which they cannot lose. Most profanity de-
fames women to begin with, and when used against a
woman it automatically reduces her to a sexual object on
the lowest level. Hence, a "cocksucker," though it has
homosexual implications as a pejorative, when used in

the presence of women implies disgust for an act which most men expect women to do and which is, in this age of sexual permissiveness, merely one of the many ways in which men and women communicate sexually. A woman can justifiably wonder why something she does in bed, is perhaps even asked to do, is a symbolic term for a person who is treacherous and untrustworthy. Terms like "ball-breaker" are too obviously chauvinistic to comment on; more interesting are such stock phrases as "they screwed us out of the deal," or "they fucked us," which are pretty much in current usage, and which imply very obviously that a woman's sexual role is automatically inferior and humiliating, that of a loser. To "screw" someone is to triumph over them (masculine), to "get screwed" is to be defeated (feminine). The use of the word "cunt" is less subtle: it simply means, in general usage, a person who is idiotic, obstructive, hostile. In its sub-form—"He's a poor cunt"—it has overtones of pity, which are even more humiliating to a woman.

Until a few years ago, men used obscenity to silence women, a simple tactic because women were more frightened and shocked by obscenity than they are now, but most women still don't like it, and have no reason to, and few can be unaware of the extent to which obscenities, when used by men, serve as a means for putting women in a lower place, asserting male superiority, for reducing all women to a lower caste, for insisting that the penis is the symbol of authority and power, the vagina the symbol of weakness, subservience. "Cunt" is a pejorative because men feel, at heart, that the sexual desires of women can only be satisfied by an act of surrender and self-abasement on their part, that in accepting penetration women are in fact giving up something, sacrificing themselves to the overwhelming power of their sexual needs, being robbed of some indefinable quality, the theft of which adds to the man's stature and diminishes hers.

Harder to catch are the polite euphemisms by which certain attitudes are emphatically registered or implicitly discarded. If a group of men are in a meeting and want some piece of information from an executive who is not present, one man may say to another, "Get his secretary on the phone and ask if he's got those figures." If a woman is present at the meeting, he is more likely to say, "Phone his office and see if they have the figures." Men frequently say "office" as a euphemism for "secretary," as in, "I'll be away next week, but phone my office about those tickets and we'll get them over to you"—this when the man is in fact one of twenty executives in a large office. When men say "my office" while talking to a woman they are signaling that they "understand," that they are too tactful to mention to a woman that they even *have* a secretary, particularly when discussing some tedious chore which will have to be done by the secretary in question.

There is also a system of meaningless upgrading that operates when men refer to the women who work for them; thus a man will refer to "my secretary" when she's not present ("Look, phone my secretary, Linda Bathurst, next week, and she'll give you the information"), and to "my assistant" when she is present ("I'd like you meet my, ah, assistant, Miss, ah, Bathurst, who'll show you round the office, right Linda?"). This is exceptionally humiliating, not only to the woman herself, who knows perfect well that she isn't an assistant except for parade purposes, but also to those women in the office who have in fact *become* assistants, with real job functions, only to find that their title is meaningless.

When a survey was taken of the effects of women's liberation on the nation's largest corporations, nearly every questionnaire was answered by a man, which makes one wonder by what logic a large company assigns a male senior executive to study and remedy the concerns of women. To quote from one reply: "Thank you very much for your recent letter to our president requesting information concerning our corporation's policy for the advancement of women in our business. As this subject comes under my administration, your letter has been referred for my attention." The letter comes from a male vice-president.

Why, one must ask, is a large corporation's "policy for the advancement of women" run by a man? How serious can they be about "affirmative action to assure the advancement of qualified women," in which they feel they have been "eminently successful"?

Well, and why not? What do women know? How much clout do they really have? Wherever we look they are humiliated and belittled, separate but not equal. In every magazine and newspaper we see them shown as objects of sexual fantasy, used to promote products they don't really profit from which are sold by companies in which they have no power. The whole motion picture industry, which formed so much or our culture in the absence of anything stronger or more interesting, has presented women as mothers/wives/girlfriends or sex objects for generations, providing a decisive and formative influence on men's idea of women. Nor have things changed that much for the better—we are simply shown more of the sex object, breasts where we used to see shoulders, pubic hair where we used to see thighs. Even when we turn to so distinguished an analytic figure as Erik H. Erikson, we get a highly ambiguous portrait of the relationship between the sexes at the basic level. In giving children of both sexes between the ages of ten and twelve a set of building blocks with which to construct "an exciting scene out of an imaginary moving picture," Dr. Erikson learned "to expect different configurations" in boys and girls. "Girls much more often than boys would arrange a room in the form of a circle of furniture, without walls . . . Only one boy built such a configuration. He was of obese and effeminate build." Dr. Erikson found that "the most significant sex difference was the tendency of boys to erect structures, buildings, towers," while girls "tended to use the play table as the interior of a house, with simple, little, or no use of blocks." He noted that "girls rarely built towers," and concluded:

If "high" and "low" are masculine variables, "open" and "closed" are feminine modalities . . . It is clear that the spatial tendencies governing these constructions are reminiscent of the *genital modes* . . . and that they, in fact, closely parallel the morphology of the sex organs: in the male, *external* organs, *erectable* and *intrusive* in character, *conducting* high *mobile* sperm cells; *internal* organs in the female, with a vestibular *access* leading to *statically expectant* ova . . . The girls' representation of house interiors (which has a clear antecedent in their infantile play with dolls) would then mean that they are concentrating on the anticipated task of taking care of a home and children.(29) (All italics in this passage are Dr. Erikson's.)

Well, there it is, from the couch's mouth. At an early age, girls build things that are open or circles, representing the vagina; boys, of course, build towers, except for the unfortunate lad who was "of obese and effeminate build" (Note how these two qualities are linked, as if obesity and femininity were somehow identical). Note also that sperm cells are "mobile," while the ova are merely static and expectant, waiting, as it were, for a man to build his tower in the vagina. And remark upon the final, somewhat sweeping conclusion: that girls are concentrating upon the "anticipated task of taking care of a home and children."

Nowhere does Dr. Erikson point out that if his ten- to twelve-year-olds are familiar with movies—as they must be in terms of his experiment, since they have been asked to construct scenes "out of an imaginary moving picture"—then they have already been exposed to the roles they are supposed to play, that comics, children's books, the example of their own families, television, all show them a world in which women are static homemakers, men dynamic adventurers. By ten, the girl may already feel a sense of loss, a premonition that she is in for less exciting prospects than a boy; by the time she is twelve, our culture has done its formidable best to fix these attitudes in her mind. Yet the implication is that Dr. Erikson is dealing here with some basic genetic difference, a proposition in which the ignorant and unsophisticated male chauvinist believes completely without the necessity for experimentation and "scientific proof." Clearly, even when a man of Erikson's sensitivity and intelligence approaches the problem of woman, he is unable to do so without remembering that he's a man. If he cannot be impartial, how can we expect the average businessman to be?

So pervasive is this kind of thinking, this assigning to women of sexual characteristics in their way of thinking and working—as if a man's mind were an extension of his penis, thrusting, mobile, erect; a woman's mind an extension of her vagina, open, circular, internal, receiving rather than intruding—that women themselves have come to accept the idea, and even take pride in it. At the first National Conference on the Visual Arts, held to discuss discrimination against women in the "male-dominated" art world, one of the principal subjects of discussion was whether "feminine" art existed. Several women argued that an imagery of "repeated circular forms" and "a preoccupation with inner space" could be seen in works by women, and advocated a movement of Feminine Art. It is surely an ironic triumph for men when women themselves proclaim the male chauvinist arguments as if they were a triumphant step forward for feminism.

Happily, one artist, Agnes Denes, responded to the idea of Feminine Art by saying that she denied any particular "vaginal sensibility." She went on to say, "The only inner space I recognize is where my brain is—and my soul."(30)

FOUR

"I don't do any fancy fucking at home. My wife would just wonder where I learned to do tricks like that, and pretty soon she'd start asking what the hell I'm doing when I work late at the office."
—Conversation overheard in a corporate men's room

*"OK, around here the conversation gets a bit—raunchy?
—you know, and I pretend not to mind it as much as I really do, but what makes me mad is that it's always so god-damned one-sided, it's always men putting down women, no woman ever answers back. The other day, I was out with a cold, I mean, I really felt lousy, and when I came back to the office the next day this guy who's a senior executive, twenty-five or thirty years older than I am, said to me, "We missed you yesterday, how was the abortion?" Well, who asked for that? It was a mean, ugly, nasty thing to say, but what am I going to tell him, and what's the point anyway? But for just one moment I really felt cheap and dirty, and he'll never understand why what he said hurt . . ."*

—B

SEX AND SEXISM

We do not as yet live in an Androgynous Zone, and our relationships with each other are inevitably colored by sexual reactions, often giving a dramatic meaning to what would otherwise be the most commonplace of business encounters. "Sex in the office," says one man, "is the same as sex out of the office, except that you have to spend eight hours together the next day, instead of just break-fast." Yes and no. Sex is always sex, but sex in the office is peculiarly complicated, for here as nowhere else, social distinctions, ambition, money and exploitation combine to make the sexual relationship between man and woman nerve-wracking to the highest degree. Every office has its famous affairs, past and present, and each is usually a legend of triumphant masochism, the sullen scenes at the office Christmas party, the endless, hard-drinking, weep-ish sessions of man-to-man confessional when things are going badly ("I mean, I really *love* her, but I haven't got the guts to tell my wife. I'm a coward, what would *you* do?"), the embarrassing moments of tenderness, displayed in highly inappropriate circumstances, when things are going well ("Wasn't that Mr. Sills and Nancy from Accounting kissing downstairs in front of the bank last night after work?"). Offices hold many dangers for men of a certain kind and age, especially those who have married early and spent a decade working hard, building a career, incarcerating their wives and families in Westport or Larchmont, and who now find themselves, at exactly the moment when they have money and some time on their hands, surrounded by attractive and intelligent young women. People like this are unprepared for the sudden complexity of an office love affair, and nearly always handle it as badly as possible, paying the maximum amount in exposure and marital stress for the minimum amount of pleasure. My favorite story of office love is that of a very senior executive who spent his spare time writing long love letters to his secretary, then, for reasons best known to himself, Xeroxed them, frequently leaving a trial-run copy in the machine, from whence it naturally made its way around the office, to the delight of his colleagues and subordinates—a delight all the greater because the letter-writer's hints of sexual conquest were very explicitly contradicted in his letters to the object of his affections.

In office affairs, as in the politics of the Seraglio, women are always in the wrong. When a man makes a fool of himself over a girl twenty years his junior, the odds are that *she* will be fired in the final reckoning, unless the management of the company was looking for an excuse to fire the man anyway. The "double standard" lives on, indeed flourishes. The aftermath of most office affairs is the departure of the woman, sometimes forced out by a hierarchy of men whose protective instincts are aroused by the sight of a fellow man in trouble, sometimes (cruel-est of all blows) fired by her lover "for her own good."

"Love," says a friend of mine, "requires equals as lovers";
but there is a conspicuous lack of equality between men
and women at work, and this inequality—of status, pay,
opportunity, position, responsibility—affects any personal
relationship that grows out of work, changes the balance
of friendship, affection, love, distorts what might be, in
other circumstances, perfectly legitimate feelings.

It is difficult enough for a woman to work in a world
run by men, without having to reflect back to men their
own fantasies about her; yet women are constantly
placed in the uncomfortable position of providing a passive audience before which men can project their chosen
roles in the sexual drama of their lives. Men impose
upon women the demands of their imaginations, making
them, in their minds, as captive as was poor "O," who,
in that dubiously authentic modern classic of pornog-
raphy,* was told,

"You are here to serve your masters. During the day,
you will perform whatever domestic duties are assigned to you . . . Nothing more difficult than that.
But at the first sign from anyone you will drop whatever you are doing and ready yourself for what is
really your one and only duty: to lend yourself.
Your hands are not your own, nor are your breasts,
nor, most especially, any of your bodily orifices,
which we may explore or penetrate at will." [81]

Of course, the office is not "O" 's house of torture in
any physical sense (though a young lady of my acquaintance claims to have been raped on the mahogany table
of the empty board-room of a major corporation by a
senior executive of the company who had invited her in
to talk about her future), but men often behave as if
they thought it *were*. Perhaps they share the feelings of
Ambrose Bierce, when he wrote: "To men a man is a
mind. Who cares what face he carries or what he wears?
But woman's body *is* the woman." Don't we tradition-

* The rumor still exists that it was written by a man.

ally believe that the more valuable the body, the less valuable the mind? An insurance salesman says, "When I'm talking to women about policies, if they're attractive, I'm always thinking, 'Jesus, I'd like to lay you,' and it gets in the way between us, but they *expect* it, they want you to feel that way, I beam that at them—subtly, you know?—and I can get them eating out of my hand, they'll sign anything. The whole sex thing is always there, it's *basic*, right?" And so it is, but mostly in the form of fantasy, of verbal sexuality, of the kind of sexual muscle-flexing that is intended to impress one's fellow men, in case they should have any doubts about one's intrinsic masculinity. There is no surer way to establish male-bonding than a quick leer at a passing woman, the shared reaction that can range from a furtive wink to a full-fledged sexual pantomime, that can even be expressed, particularly in elevators, by a completely blank expression of men's faces that in fact signifies *awareness*, the communication to each other, by immobility and unnatural silence, of sexual presence. "I notice the way men look at me," says a young woman who works in Rockefeller Center in New York. "You can't not notice when you step into an elevator full of men and they stop talking to each other as soon as you get in, and there are all these arteriosclerotic businessmen looking right through you with their washed-out suburban eyes and pretending that they're meditating or something, and I know when I get off at my floor, they're going to be digging each other in their fat ribs and saying, 'How you'd like to have that one licking your popsicle, Harry? Play any golf this weekend?' Everwhere I go, men are sticking their gluey little fantasies on my body, without even seeing *me*. Why can't I just be a person? What *right* do men have to use me to play with themselves? I work, I'm a human being, and yet I sit there eating lunch and all these guys are eating their Primeburgers and looking at me out of the corners of their eyes, with ketchup all over their chins, and even the counterman is doing a whole number, and for what? I'm not even that attractive, for God's sake, I know what my body looks like, and it belongs to me. What kind of lives do they *lead?*"

To which another woman adds, "I don't see a man on the street and think, 'I'd like to sleep with him,' let alone follow him or make obscene remarks. Right, there is a big difference between men and women. A woman looks at one man at a time, you know, given a certain situation and feeling. She looks at a *person*. A man looks at every woman, women just aren't people to him at all."

Not quite: Men have evolved two ways of looking at a woman: in certain circumstances, they do see her as a *person*—Mother, Lover, Colleague, Wife, whatever; in other circumstances, they see her as a *sexual object.* When they manage to see her in both contexts simultaneously we can say that they are experiencing what we commonly call "love." But most of the time men look at women with a curious kind of double vision: women are supposed to be looked at, to be visual objects, inanimate and passive, as well as functional, active human beings with roles, ambitions, personalities, lives.

Women are placed on the marketplace with fixed physical values—so much for good legs, so much for good breasts, so much for long blond hair, whatever points seem desirable. Men can have little idea of what it is like to be judged constantly on one's exterior, the endless small humiliations, the fear of old age, the jealousies engendered between women ("I'll never forget that dish-faced blonde in high school who was always so perfect and walked off with all the boys. I'm thirty-eight now, but if I saw her today I'd slap her silly"). The construction workers who hoot and whistle at a passing woman are not really seeing *her*; they are looking at their own image of what a woman is, at the projection of their own fantasies, playing out a game of sexual competition that exists only between men and has little or nothing to so with women. Men often compensate for their insecurity with women by proving their sexual prowess to other men. Thus, a group of construction workers calling out to a woman are in fact merely demonstrating to each other that they are sexually aggressive. If they met the same girl in different circumstances, say in her office, they would probably remove their hard hats politely.

The reason women can so easily become invisible as people is that men find it difficult to deal with the threat of a real woman—to admit that women are real people means facing up to the fact that they have demands, rights, minds, sexual fantasies and standards of their own, that—God forbid!—they may be judging us. Most men, in fact, don't much like women, precisely because of their individuality, and the less they like women, the more necessary it becomes to depersonalize them. Hence the fact that men so often make *confidantes* of the women they work with. Women are supposed to have no solidarity. Their relationship to men is assumed to be like that of a conquered race, happy to turn on their sisters, willing to listen calmly to the horror story of some other woman's marriage, hearing all the obscene little secrets of home in those bars that, in New York at any rate, sometimes seem to exist for no other purpose than for men to tell the women they work with about their failures with the women they have married. There exists in every man's imagination an ideal woman against which all women are compared, but at the same time—like someone shopping for a piece of furniture—he compares each woman to another, pondering the advantages offered by this pair of thighs as against those offered by this pair of breasts, comparing the excitements of an extramarital relationship in this walk-up floor-through in the West Eighties with the comforts of a solid domestic establishment in Connecticut—the perpetual comparison shopper of fantasies. As one young woman, twenty-eight years old, college-educated and successful, told me, "Where I work there's always this kind of *current* of sex talk, you know, and I don't really mind it—I mean, I know where I am, and I also know that most of the men around here don't. Like, the other day, I was leaning over to pick up something, and I was wearing leather jeans, and this guy I work for said, 'Hey, there's a split in the seam of your jeans. I can see your pants!' I said, 'Gee, that's funny, I never wear any.' Well, it isn't true,

I *do*, I mean it's not all that comfortable to wear leather jeans without pants, and who cares anyway. But I could see it was like a big sex revelation for him. No pants! *Wow!* All of a sudden he was thinking about me in a completely different way, as if not wearing pants were some kind of big deal—you don't wear pants, it must mean you're an easy lay, my wife wears them all the time and she's uptight, right? What a jerk!"

Already involved in the difficult struggle to acquire respect and opportunity at work, women are, at the same time, constantly exposed to the old familiar demands and difficulties of sexual role playing. Unlike men in business, they are often judged, classified, tested on two levels, sometimes simultaneously, a process which can always be relied upon to throw even the most career-minded young woman off-balance. A man sitting down to discuss a difficult business problem with another executive, perhaps over a drink at six o'clock, can be fairly sure that the conversation will remain within certain limits. In similar circumstances, a woman cannot be certain, for she is always aware that she is present in another capacity—that of Woman. Nor is it just that she will be looked at, appraised, in a way that no man would be ("They didn't tell me you were a very pretty lady, Miss Newman. What's a girl like you doing worrying about the language in this contract?"), it's that her presence puts the man in the position of playing whatever his particular role may be in the sexual theater: embarrassment, timidity, compensatory brutality, the refusal to make concessions to a woman, avuncular advice-giving . . . Obviously, a clever and attractive woman can more easily persuade most men to agree to things that they might refuse another man, but she also has to cope with more complex business situations than a man does. She has to be aware of subtle pressures, intimations, shades of meaning that derive from men's feelings about women—about *her*—rather than from any concern with the business at hand. When a man has finished whatever business he has to do, he can refuse the next drink and go home. A woman in similar circumstances may have to accept the onus of turning down a social invitation. If she refuses another drink and goes home, she may be making an enemy; if she accepts, she may be letting herself in for a torrent of autobiographical information or a pass.

A good friend of mine, an attractive businesswoman in her mid-thirties, told me a story which illustrates the curious way in which work and sex become entangled, turning a prosaic discussion into high comedy or drama. Once, when she was staying at home with a bad cold, her boss, a divorced man in his forties who lived nearby, offered to bring some papers from the office to her apartment on his way home. They discussed business matters over a drink, a perfectly ordinary discussion with an emotional content of zero. After they were finished, he had another drink and began talking about himself and his divorce, then made a pass at her. Failing, he had another drink, proposed staying the night (having by now convinced himself that she wouldn't have asked him to stop by if she hadn't expected him to make a pass), then passed out and spent the night on her sofa, occasionally waking to bang on her locked bedroom door. "I guess I might have finally let him in," she said, "except that I really did have a cold, and looked like the Wicked Witch of Endore, and felt worse. Of course, the next morning he had all the early morning sex guilt feelings, without any of the satisfaction. I wasn't too surprised when I got fired at the next cutback."

At least one major corporation, which, as it happens, is making a serious attempt to promote women and open up more opportunities to them, reported:

A year ago . . . we encountered problems with our annual golf tournament which had been restricted to males. One woman objected violently to the exclusion of females and we have agreed this year to run either a joint affair, or more likely, something which is "separate and equal." Joint company field trips have, from time to time over the years, produced some unfortunate by-products.

The "unfortunate by-products" can be easily imagined by anyone who has attended a convention or sales conference at a hotel or resort; indeed, such corporate gatherings are often treasured as spectator events, advance bets being placed on whether X will once again make a fool of himself with someone's secretary, or Y will finally make it with the woman executive he has been eying for the past six months. Corporate attitudes toward sex in the office differ. Some companies look with indulgence upon these more or less sanctioned Dionysian revels, on the grounds that they clear the air; others react against them vigorously, perhaps on the grounds that the spectacle of senior male executives mixing on intimate terms with women (mostly, by the nature of things, subordinates) savors not so much of sexual license as of revolution. And maybe with reason. The amount of sexual energy circulating in any office is awe-inspiring, and given the slightest sanction and opportunity it bursts out—from which one can only conclude that a great many ambiguous feelings are being held in check most of the time, their hidden presence doubtless altering, however slightly or subtly, the nature of our working relationships with the women around us.

The very idea of men and women working together in the same place is a comparatively recent one, hardly a hundred years old. Until then, men and women worked together only in circumstances of such degradation and slavery that sex cannot have represented a major problem—after all, in Victorian England, women, even children, hauled coal in the mines, stripped naked and harnessed to wagons, and worked sixteen or more hours a day in the "dark satanic mills" of the Industrial Revolution. If the Victorians segregated their women, kept them at home, it was in part because every man was conscious of the conditions under which life was lived among those who worked—the impetus to isolate women was not by any means a completely ungenerous one. Our immediate ancestors were strongly motivated by the desire to seal themselves off from the reality around them, to build small islands of domestic bliss in a sea of squalor, poverty and starvation. Among the evils they fled was the systematic exploitation of women as manual laborers, and it is scarcely surprising that the idea of women working should have taken on in their minds a peculiar horror, associated as it was with that hell into which every middle-class Victorian could fall by bankruptcy, sickness or bad luck. When women of the middle classes reemerged at the turn of the century, it was into a very different working world, one of offices and shops, rather than mills and mines, one where the problem soon became too little work, rather than too much. For the first time, men and women found themselves working together in relatively civilized circumstances, not quite as equals, to be sure, but under conditions which allowed the *idea* of equality to emerge, and that made it possible for men and women to talk and think more openly about sex than was ever dreamed of before the First World War. Freed from the sexual myths and reticence of the nineteenth century, women can hardly fail to be aware of the contrast between the modern ideal of woman as a sexual partner and the reality of a world in which men have come to accept, even admire, equality in bed but expect it to end at the bedroom door.

The modern office is still an *experiment*, a test of whether men and women can in fact work together. Historically women have been seen as drudges or players of domestic and sexual roles, the exception being in those intellectual and aristocratic circles where women have a kind of equality because of extraordinary intelligence (Mme. de Stael), longevity (the familiar figure of the Victorian matriarch), talent (Mme. Curie) or eccentricity (Florence Nightingale). Men have not yet acquired the cultural habit of talking to women as equals, and it is going to take some time before they do. Even on communes, where one can suppose that most members are less inhibited and trapped by past habits than in, say, a modern insurance office, the problem of dealing with the opposite sex as if they were simply fellow human beings poses difficulties. One reporter described the efforts certain communes are making to eliminate the barrier of received ideas and automatic stimuli that keep men and women in polarized roles:

> While most communes aren't into sex orgies, there does seem to be a lot of sensuality and nudity, especially on rural communes. People are more apt to touch each other casually, affectionately, and at Laura's, group showers were the rule because of the shortage of water and the difficulty of heating it up. Yet this didn't seem to arouse much sexual interest. Gordon Yaswen, writing of his communal experience at Sun-Rise Hill, explained nudity this way: "(Group nudity) . . . was a symbolic act of communion with and trust in each other, and helped to cement us. It seemed . . . to alleviate some of the natural curiosity the males and females had in each other, and . . . let us all breathe a little easier, not having to undress one another mentally."(32)

". . . Not having to undress one another mentally." People who work together closely in an office are involved with each other at a level of intensity often much higher than anything likely on a commune, but the standards of our culture prevent them from touching each other "casually, affectionately" or even admitting that they feel a need to do so.

Unlike the communers of Sun-Rise Hill, most men are still stuck with what Gordon Yaswen called "natural curiosity," they simply have had no opportunity to free themselves from the wandering sexual awareness, a kind of low-level satyromania, that either produces constant frustration of a series of bungled affairs, and that makes any attempt to deal with women on an open, equal and human level totally hopeless. Men are simply deprived of *feeling*, of emotional outlets, in just that area of life

which is often most important and exciting to them,
their work. The conventions of business life establish a
kind of artificial coldness and sterility that is unnatural
to both men and women, without providing any real
means of alleviating those sexual feelings which those of
us who do not shower together on communes, generally
speaking, seldom succeed in getting altogether under
control. Nothing has programmed us for life on terms of
some personal intimacy, within a rigid and formalized
hierarchy for eight or more hours a day in an age of sexual freedom and blatant sexual appeal. Modern office
life is a radical experiment in relations between the sexes
which is at least as revolutionary as any commune, and
far wider in scope.

In principle, there is something very attractive about
the idea of sex in the office, a sense in which sexuality
heightens one's pleasure in one's work, a complicity of
shared concerns that in itself contains a certain excitement. Indeed, so exciting is the idea of sex at work that
one of the major office games is pretending that it's taking place when in fact it isn't. On a basic male chauvinist level an office affair is a badge of status, always provided that it's handled well; that is, with the minimal
amount of emotional disturbance and with its course and
direction firmly controlled (or thought to be firmly controlled) by the male partner. Any display of emotion on
the part of the man, or the suggestion that the woman either initiated the affair or decides when and how it will
end, loses the man his status in his peer group. One of
the most enduring traditions of business is the summer
affair when the wife and the children have been safely
set up in some beach house, to be visited, like expensive
prisoners, on the weekends. The summer months are
open season, the time for putting into practice the fantasies of the winter, and nobody who controls expense accounts can fail to notice a certain unexpected rise in ex-
penditures in July and August, along with the repetitive
mention of those small, dark bars and restaurants on the
Upper West Side and around York Avenue, where the

nightly attempt to find a domestic substitute for the dog days of summer takes place, sometimes successfully, more often not. Lust is very often less a factor than the understanding unwillingness to be alone four nights a week in the big city, not to speak of the sensual quality of those airless, hot evenings that otherwise offer only eating alone with a copy of the evening newspaper propped up before them. Sex, of course, does take place, but even when it does not, most men are obliged to pretend that it has. An executive invites a woman to have dinner with him, drops her home and goes back to feed the cat. The next day, if questioned, he is likely to answer with a smile of complicity, unwilling to admit that there was never the slightest suggestion of sex on either side, but thus changing the status of his dinner companion in everyone's eyes, and making her relationship with other men in the office (including those who decide her salary and her chances of promotion) that much more difficult and complex. Many men cultivate meaningful reticence, broadly hinting that they have "something going" outside the office. While early-morning conferences in the summer months produce a kind of obligatory sexual recitation, the equivalent of campfire fishing stories:

"I don't know, last year was terrific, but it's already July and I haven't got anything going yet . . ."

"You're lucky. I'm exhausted. There's this magazine researcher I met at a party, and she's only twenty, and I'm using muscles I never even knew I had, it's like the Kama Sutra."

"Hey, Steve, didn't I see you leaving last night with Nancy? That girl has a great-looking ass on her."

"Mmmm. What's on the agenda this morning?"

Clearly, the last man is ahead on points, on the grounds that he who says least means most, though he may very well have bought Nancy a drink then gone home to read *Playboy.*

The status quality of office sex is such that women even collaborate to give the appearance of serious sexuality to what is often no more than a friendship or a banal flirtation. Each side gains something from such an encounter: the man gains the status of being a seducer, of having, if he's married, an extramarital affair; the woman gains the status of an individual, no longer "one of the girls," somebody to be reckoned with seriously. It remains, when all is said and done, one of the quickest and most effective ways for a woman to make herself noticed in any corporation; and at the lowest level of salaries and jobs, being noticed is half the battle. Being thought to have a sexual involvement with a man, particularly an older man of some consequence, gives a woman some prestige in her own peer group as well.

Thus play-acting plays a large part in office sexuality, and indeed the more obvious an office "affair" is, the less likely it is to have been consummated. I have seen respectable men in their late forties allow themselves to be interrupted in the middle of a meeting by young women to be told that it was time to go home, or that they were tired of waiting, and the only response was the sly smile of a man caught out in domestic *contretemps*. A friend of mine used to take his rather glamorous secretary to conventions, giving rise to rumors that he did nothing to discourage. He was thought of by his colleagues as a very real *mensch* indeed, except that during an evening of heavy drinking, his companion revealed that they had separate rooms and kept to them. "Of course I'm not sleeping with him," she said. "I mean he's never even suggested it, if he *did* I might, who knows? But we just traveled down together, you know, and he talks a lot about himself and about his wife, and I think if I turned up in his room and took off my clothes, he'd *panic*."

Needless to say, his loss of status was irremediable, and shortly after he fired her, he himself left to take another job. There was simply no way his colleagues could take him seriously any more. It is better by far to be caught out *in flagrente delicto* on your office couch than to have your sexual *machismo* revealed as a fraud. Some men, in fact, are partisans of the public sexual encounter, building up their reputation by a series of open (and often drunken) seductions which have the advantage of establishing their sexual aggressiveness once and for all in their minds of their colleagues, leaving them free to get on with their work for several months or years afterward, secure in status.

In the age of sexual freedom, sex *is* status, and it is for this reason that men are reluctant to let it be known that they have dropped out of the sexual competition. This alone makes it difficult for them to deal with women on a business level. At the back of their minds is the fear that a woman may think less of a man if he doesn't at least put up a formalized show of sexual interest, a kind of gesture to the gallery. Most men do not expect a response, and one woman I know, more courageous than most, has managed to stop this kind of chauvinism in her office by simply taking men at their word. "I just say, 'OK, let's stop talking,'" she told me, "and it works like a charm. Sometimes I just walk over and lock the door, then sit down on the guy's sofa and ask him what he's waiting for. So far I've had no takers, and now they've stopped hassling me, and they even *respect* me. They think I'm a very tough chick indeed."

Women who are less direct have more problems, for once a man has established a flirtatious and insinuating relationship with a woman, he acquires in his own mind certain rights over her. He has given her the offer of affection; she is expected to respond with an offer of submission. One young woman told me that she turned down a promotion twice because her immediate superior felt that a nice, pretty girl like her shouldn't take a job that meant working late at night, and going home unprotected on the subway. "The third time," she said, "I finally realized what he was doing. It was my coming out in terms of women's lib. I thought, 'You keep taking me out for drinks, and asking about my private life, and giving me the old daughter-incest routine, and the real thing is that you're just too lazy to find a new person for this job and train her, so you're trying to persuade me not to accept the promotion.' So I took it, and I haven't had any trouble on the subway, and I wish I'd had the guts to do it two years ago!"

Establishing false relationship is a perfect means of

keeping women, particularly young women, in check. For example, a distinguished broker has a brilliant and attractive young woman assistant, twenty years younger than he is. She is ambitious, hard-working, capable, and believes that her work will eventually be rewarded by promotion, more money, a better title, a bigger office. But the broker has fallen in love with her, idolizes her, has even told his colleagues that she's the only reason he goes on working. Unable to face the sexual nature of his feelings about her, he has begun to think of her as if she were his daughter. Having established an inappropriate relationship between himself and the young woman, he has effectively trapped her, placed on her the responsibility for his remaining in the office. Instead of rewarding her work with a better job, which would mean moving her away from him (the equivalent of a daughter's leaving home), he gives her warm advice, a paternal if slightly incestuous affection, flowers on her birthday, pleasant little luncheons. Her work is now reduced to the level of a beloved daughter's school grades. If she attempts to get out, to promote a better job for herself within the company, he will react with the fury of a lover spurned, a father offended, for he has given her the gift of his affection and invested his sexual fantasies in her person. By the rules of male chauvinism she belongs to him, far more surely than if they had merely slept together. "I couldn't go on without her," he says, thus ensuring that his colleagues will do everything they can to keep her right where she is . . .

Not, of course, that office sex doesn't take place from time to time, some offices being in fact notorious for it. Banks and IBM are said to be bad places for office sex, partly because they're so tightly organized, perhaps also because the kind of people who work for a bank or IBM are unlikely to let themselves go. Retail stores are reputed to be very sexy, insurance offices not sexy at all, advertising moderately sexy (perhaps the amount of drinking and the general tension reduces sex), book publishing mildly so, magazine publishing very high, networks fairly high, especially on the creative side. Well, who knows? No statistics exist, althoug the weekly news magazines are famous as hotbeds of sexual intrigue, and with some justification. In the first place, they employ a large number of intelligent and educated young women (and go out of their way to hire attractive ones); in the second, they work to strict deadlines, which means that a man and a woman (*he*, of course, a writer, *she* a researcher) may be together for days, working late into the night on something they're both deeply involved in, and with at least a degree of mutual respect. As one *Time* staff member told me, "It's a question of opportunity partly. Most men in ordinary businesses have to go home, and that limits their possibilities. If you're a banker, it's pretty hard to phone home and say, 'Gee, honey, we had such a lot of money come in today that I don't know when I'll be finished counting it. I may stay over.' And you couldn't do it twice. But a man who works for a magazine has deadlines, last-minute world-shaking events that mean the whole magazine has to be rewritten. He has a series of permanently valid excuses."

Now that most motels no longer require couples to have luggage, life is a good deal easier for those who manage to have sex at lunchtime, an important point because it is only the romantics or the neophytes who waste time or stay late to pursue their affairs. The sensible executive fits office sex into *his* schedule, at his convenience, rather than allowing it to disrupt the orderly routine of life. I know a man who always asks his secretary to sleep with him. Some do, some do not. When he finds one who will sleep with him, he takes her there and then on the surface of his desk, arguing that a certain brutality and swiftness of approach establishes him from the very beginning as the person who is in control of the situation. After that, they make love on his sofa, from six to six-thirty, when everyone else in the office has gone home, which not only frees him to go home at a reasonable hour but also gives him the valuable reputation of working late. At the first sign of "involvement," the suggestion from the woman that it might be nice to go

out for a drink or to have dinner together, he finds her a
new job and fires her.

Men do not find it easy, as a rule, to treat a woman simultaneously as a lover and a working colleague. A
young woman who had an affair with the man she
worked for commented, "At the beginning it was OK, I
mean he tried to give me interesting work and all that,
and I was ambitious. But then this whole personal thing
just built up between us, and he stopped thinking of me
as a working person. He couldn't handle both. I was either someone who worked with him, or someone he was
sleeping with, but he couldn't take on my being someone
who worked with him *and* slept with him. We had a period when things were OK between us, but then things
got heavy. I told him, 'I still *work* here, right? I came
here to work, and I even like what I'm doing, and it
doesn't have anything to do with what we do outside, or
whether you're going to get a divorce, or whether I want
you to, which I don't think I do. I'll handle my job, just
don't take it out from under me.' But he *did*, he
couldn't help himself, and I had to go. I suddenly realized that he was boxing me in, taking away my work so
that our relationship would be the only thing I had to
concentrate on, and I said to myself, 'Let his wife handle
that.' "

It would be impossible to discuss sex at the office without adding that the office serves many married men (and
perhaps not a few women) as a perfect place to work out
neurotic problems that would be difficult to solve at
home, if only because they would end in divorce. Many a
man who takes a liberated and sensible attitude toward
his wife (if only because he has no choice), compensates
by becoming a tyrant toward the women who work with
and for him. And there are domestic chauvinists who
compensate by a liberal and understanding attitude toward the women they work with, exacting obedience at
home and behaving like amateur psychoanalysts at work.

A very successful businessman, for example, was notorious for screaming at his secretary in the vilest and most

abusive way, flying into uncontrolled rages in public and belittling her, to the point where nobody could understand why she stayed on. In fact he was sleeping with her, and his rages were merely a kind of elaborate joke, a sort of precoital sadomasochism. Afterward, they would make love in his office, joking about the effect his rage at her had had on their colleagues, excited by the perverse contrast between their public images and their private relationship. Obviously an affair of this kind has its bizarre side for the two people involved, but the effect on other people is more important than the exact nature of the sexual relationship between the man and the woman. In this particular company, women are after all working for a man who flies into terrifying rages at his secretary, and they may be intimidated themselves, not knowing that the rages are merely a sexual contrivance, an in-joke between the two people involved.

Not every businesswoman is confronted by a superior who masturbates at his desk while talking to her, as one woman executive reported in a recent book on office life, but her story serves as a perfect example of extreme male chauvinist behavior in business life:

Jock had a brownish-yellow overstuffed chair at his desk, and I began to notice a darkening stain in the front of it. At first I thought he had dirty hands and was rubbing them on this one spot, but that didn't make sense. Then one day a young girl assistant came running out of Jock's office with this horrified look and said to me, "Stacey, that chair's wet. I can see it!" I said, "Bettye, it must be the light," and I shooed her out of there. When she was gone, I took a close look. Something white and frothy, like spit, was drying in that same spot I had noticed before. I bent over and sniffed, and the stuff had a sharp, acrid smell. I thought I knew what it was, but I couldn't belive it . . . I remembered that Jock usually sat up tight to his desk, and *anything* could have been going on underneath while he was talking to people in his office. Apparently, his kick was to call a girl in, have a conversation with her, and play with himself all the time.

Most interesting is what happens when Stacey finally reports this disagreeable habit to a senior executive. He refuses to listen, in fact treats *her* as if she were guilty. In her own words:

The feeling he gave me was that Jock could keep on drinking, keep on masturbating, keep on killing himself, and keep on his verbal assaults against all the rest of us underlings, and simply for one reason: he was a man. He could do all these things and get away with them *because he was a man,** and I had to take it all *because I was a woman . . .* I was intruding in the men's club.(33)

In general sex in the office remains, even in its more innocent forms, a male chauvinist institution, until such time as women gain a working equality in business. As one executive of a major television network said, "What we're fighting against, or what they (women) are fighting against I should say, is *mental* discrimination, the idea that because there's this one special area between men and women which is sexual, the habits and the relationships from that area can be carried over into other areas. Sex is one of those areas in which you can't draw lines or work out what's fair or right or proper—at least I can't. Work *is*. When you mix the two up, and get sexual attitudes in working situations you have waste, bitterness, bad feelings, and probably bad sex."

Good orb ad, one of the first casualties of women's liberation is likely to be sex in the office. As one woman told me, "Sure I got propositioned, and I didn't used to know what to do about it, but these days, I look the man in the eyes and say, 'Sure I'll have dinner with you, I want to know why I'm not making a decent salary for the work I've been doing.' And do you know what? They

* All italics in this passage are the author's.

mostly back off. But if men aren't embarrassed about asking the people who work with them to go to bed, then it's time for women to stop being embarrassed about asking just why we make less money than men and don't get a crack at the good jobs. I just explain to them that I don't sleep with people who don't think I'm equal to them."

FIVE

> *It is only too obvious that a man has no obligation what-*
> *ever to a woman who is considered brilliant. To such a*
> *woman a man can be ungrateful, treacherous, and even*
> *mean, and no-one will think of taking her side.*
> —*Madame de Staël*

THE STIGMA OF SUCCESS

The successful woman contradicts the male chauvinist's ideas about women in general—the greater her success, the greater his discomfort. She cannot be fitted into his view of the world and must therefore be denigrated in other ways, sometimes subtle, sometimes not, to prove that her success is either an aberration or a symptom of some inner fault. Men thus generally believe that success-ful women are neurotics or bitches or both.

A woman who *is* successful is automatically assumed to be deficient in some other, crucial area. Success justifies men's failures in other areas of their lives, compensates for their weaknesses and personal failures, serves at once as an explanation and a goal; success for a woman merely calls into question the integrity and value of her life. We are inclined to make excuses for a successful man: "Sure, he's a lousy father" (or a lousy husband, or a lousy lay) "but not everyone can take a bankrupt business and pyr-amid it into a million dollars a year." With a woman, we are more likely to hear: "She's successful, sure, but I wonder what her *life* is like, anyone who makes it the way she has must be pretty damned tough, I mean, you only have to look at her husband, poor bastard . . ." So pervasive is this attitude that women pay unconscious homage to it, protesting that they really *do* care about hearth and home, that after a hard day at the office, run-ning the U. S. Treasury Department or making movie deals for a million dollars, they want nothing more than to slip back into the Feminine Mystique, as if it were a

peignoir rather than a strait jacket, eager to clean the
bathroom floor, whip up a souffle, darn and perform the
million-and-one boring and distasteful chores that are
the *Schattenseite* of motherhood. Thus, we read of Ms.
Barbara Lynn Herwig, recently appointed to a high post
at the FBI, that bastion of male supremacy, who takes
what would seem an appropriately hard-nosed attitude
toward her new position ("I may take a bit of getting
used to, but I try to act like a professional, and I hope
I'll be accepted as one. I'd better be!"), then qualifies
this, according to *The New York Times'* reporter by
adding that "among her favorite pastimes were sewing
and cooking, at which she is said to be very adept."(34)
God forbid that we should have a successful woman in
the FBI who *couldn't* cook and sew or didn't want to!
But of course it's expected, it's "natural," it comes with
the territory, like Willy Loman's smile and shoeshine,
and nobody durst blame this woman for assuming what
amounts to a protective coloration. It is, of course, perfectly possible that Ms. Herwig does enjoy sewing and
cooking, but I have the feeling that the first woman President of the United States will feel herself obliged to
make the same disclaimer, to throw the same ritual sop
to male attitudes. A traditional picture of the successful,
career-oriented woman is given in the following comment, oddly enough written by a successful woman:

Take the twenty-six-year-old girl I recently interviewed, an editor in a large publishing house, who
after four years, has finally been promoted to an in-
fluential position with her own office, secretary, and
a "stable" of authors. She has not reached this pin-
nacle completely by choice, because if things had
worked out with Bob, or Tom, or Irv, she'd be a
wife and mother. . . . But all these romances failed. . . . She doesn't want her apartment to be too
career-womanish, so it must give off an aura of vulnerability, sexually as well as matrimonially (prefer-
ably the latter). A man looking around her apart-

ment must feel she's happy there, but not so happy
she wouldn't give it all up for him.(35)

Of course, of course, a woman only succeeds because
she's compensating, her success is in some mysterious
way unnatural, it is necessary to make excuses for it. Note
that her apartment must project that air of "vulnerability," as if the more successful she is, the more firmly
"femininity" imposes its demands upon her. Men are always scrutinizing successful women for signs of
conventional femininity. I well remember sitting on the
beach at Easthampton with a group of men who were
staring at Commissioner Bess Meyerson, the head of New
York City's Consumer Affairs Department, and something of a legendary figure. Their attitude was mildly
hostile, as if the sight of an attractive woman in a bikini
who was also a success and a political power were both a
contradiction and an affront. Then Ms. Meyerson drew
from her beach bag a flowered straw hat and took some
time placing it on her head at the right angle. The hostility evaporated: she was only a woman after all; she
had made, quite unconsciously I am sure, a "feminine"
gesture, linking her to all those other—unsuccessful—
women, making her acceptable to the group of men
watching her. Even so, as one man pointed out, consumer affairs represents an extension of women's traditional interest, adding, "I'd like to see a woman run the
Sanitation Department or the Police!" In Jules Feiffer's
words, "Whatever ground woman manages to establish
for herself, man abandons, denying its importance."

There is a certain ambivalence inevitable in the ways
in which successful women project themselves to an audience, never quite certain, it seems, of whether they
should play the role of Bella Abzug or that of *Cosmopolitan* editor Helen Gurley Brown—thunder-and-lightning
or charm. For that matter, even Bella Abzug switches
from one role to another. After one of her famous explo-
sions of temper, couched in language that was until recently thought more suitable for longshoremen than for
women politicians, she will give a small, appealing smile,

and even adjust her hat, signals of femininity that are perhaps unconscious, but in any case represent a kind of apology. Shana Alexander reported that on her first day in the House, Bella Abzug met John Conyers, the head of the Black Caucus, who said, "Bella, I hear you're gonna burn your bra." To which Ms. Abzug replied, "Up yours, black man," reportedly following this shaft with a smile.(36) The *smile* is just the thing men fear most in a powerful, successful woman. They can deal with the temper, the arguments, the rivalry, but the small smile disarms them, reminds them that they are dealing with a woman, deprives them of the possibility of responding in kind. This transition—in Bella Abzug's case, from Amazon to Jewish mother-figure, in Helen Gurley Brown's, from executive to little-girl-lost—represents a powerful weapon in the hands of any successful woman.

Nothing is more difficult for men to accept than that a woman can do what they can, and do it as well or better. Their natural reaction is to probe for those signs of femininity that are, by definition, the badge of weakness and inferiority. Thus Gloria Emerson, the first woman on the foreign staff of *The New York Times*, a gifted reporter who writes with the true voice of informed outrage, was obstructed from going up to the combat zones in Vietnam on the grounds that no suitable toilet facilities existed for women. Thus the Army's first woman drill instructor, Sgt. Diana Oppedal, was allowed to train as a DI on male recruits, but was afterward assigned to a WAC unit. Thus women arguing for a change in church rules to permit their being ordained to the Episcopalian priesthood were told that they should try to imagine a crucifix with a "female form." Thus eight of the country's most successful professional women who were recently honored at a dinner given by Sales Executive Club of New York, were, according to *The New York Times'* report, variously described as "glamorous," "charming" and "distinctively groomed" (Try to imagine male executives being described at a banquet in their honor as "handsome," "magnetic" and "beautifully tailored"!).

"A distingushed woman novelist" is not the same as

"a distinguished novelist" *tout court*: a woman novelist is generally assumed to write about emotions, to have a "lyrical sense of language," to have an insight into people's feelings and emotions; the Great American Novel, that mysterious Moby Dick of American literature, is thought to be in some way masculine, as if only men can unravel the complexities of human society in its larger aspects. "A woman's novel," on the other hand, is often thought to be synonymous with sentimental trash. The addition of a feminine prefix to any profession instantly transforms the nature of it, and never for the better. An editor is an editor, of whatever sex, but a woman editor (they used of course to be called *lady* editors) risks being thought of as a "women's editor," saddled forever with "women's books"—Gothic novels, romances, cookbooks and decorating guides. As one successful woman in publishing said, "It's an uphill battle all the way. Men are always trying to pigeonhole you. You have to fight not to get pushed into needlework books and embroidery, but if you get into politics they say, 'OK, you're a political editor,' and you're expected to do nothing but political books. You could come up with the greatest novel since *Gone With the Wind* and they wouldn't want to hear about it. Men *want* women to be specialists, partly because it's easier to accept their success in one defined area than to accept it in a variety of fields, also because they know the real money for an editor comes when you're free to do anything and make it work. The first time I ever broke through and did a really successful book in an area that was new to me, the editor-in-chief told someone, 'She has a really *masculine* mind'!"

Men can cope with a woman's success so long as it remains within a specialized and defined area, whether it is the promotion of a former Columbia University maid to the post of a campus security guard (reversing the former decision that guarding the university's buildings and grounds was men's work) or the appointment of women to managerial and executive posts in the office. Women are in fact *encouraged* to succeed at those jobs that require specialized knowledge and techniques, for these are precisely the jobs that have a ceiling, beyond which it is impossible to rise. In business, men are well aware of the advantages of mobility, of learning something about every aspect of the process so as to run it, rather than becoming immersed in the details of one department or operation. Again and again, women rise to success, mastering the details of their jobs, only to find that they have been outflanked by men who have mastered nothing but the ability to "manage." In one woman's words, "I started as a secretary and decided I'd know more about this department than anyone else, and after a while I did. I pushed and pushed hard to run this department, and there was a lot of flak, because there had never been a woman in charge before, but since there wasn't any other choice, I got it and I did a good job. And in fact, everyone was very nice about it, except that it didn't take me very long to realize that if I even showed a glimmer of interest in anything else, the iron curtain came down. Anything I wanted in my area, I could have, including a lot of praise, even money and a title, but to get any real financial information about the rest of the company is like going to the White House and asking to see the plans for the ICBM system. If I need a piece of information, I have to go to a senior executive and ask for it, and he tells me. I don't get to look at the paper it's written on, I might see all the other figures on it. They're frightened that I could be a success at something *else* now. When they saw how well I was doing, they pushed the panic button, set up people I had to report to, added new responsibilities to my job, did everything they could to make sure that I'd stay just where I was. It's interesting. I can't complain about money. They'd much rather give me another five or ten thousand dollars a year than let me get involved with management problems or future planning. I even get offered free vacation trips to the islands, as if you had to treat a successful woman like a wife, a fur coat here, a bouquet of flowers there, anything to keep her quiet and in her

place. I took it for years, why not, after all? But I think
the time has come to say, 'I want to play the management game too!' "

Faced with success, men lower the boom, sometimes so
sharply that they injure themselves. A twenty-seven-year-
old woman, recently promoted from secretary to editor
in a publishing house well known for the freedom with
which its editors are allowed to develop books in their
own way, found herself embroiled in a series of controversies about the titles and jacket designs of the books
she was doing. After listening to advice from her fellow
editors (mostly men), the salesmen (all men) and the
management (all male), she weighed the suggestions,
chose the ones that seemed to make the most sense, and
went ahead. In a man this would have been commenda-
ble efficiency. What she had not understood, however,
was that the advice she had received was mandatory in
their effect on a woman. She had failed to appreciate
that while men are always willing to give advice to a
woman (particularly a young woman), they expect it to
be taken, and will use it as a precedent to establish their
authority over her. Thus, she soon found herself del-
uged with complaints from male executives that she had
"ignored" their instructions, when in fact she had
merely solicited their opinions. Each man had seen her
questions as signs of weakness, and had attempted to establish himself in a position of authority over her in the
guise of paternal interest. "Finally," she told me, "the
editor-in-chief called me in and said, 'I don't understand
why you ignored my instructions on these books. I
thought I had made it perfectly clear how they should be
handled.' Well, he hadn't given me any 'instructions,'
and he knew it, and I knew it, and I told him so. 'Look,'
he told me, 'we can't have anarchy here, it's too late to
do anything about these books, but from now on things
like this are going to be cleared through me.'

"I asked him if that would apply to everyone or just to
me. Well, he obviously meant it to apply just to me, but
he couldn't admit to *that*. So he said, 'Everyone, damn
it!' So he had to send a memo to all the editors, some of

whom are successful men, older than he is, setting up a whole *system* for clearing jackets and titles, and the art director went into shock, and all the male editors went in and complained that their freedom was being taken away from them, and the editor-in-chief said that the rules would really only apply to the *junior* editors, which is to say women, which is to say *me*, and the senior editors (men) came to my defense to protect themselves and the art director took me out to lunch to tell me that we all had to stick together, and the system was never put into effect. Instead, the editor-in-chief passed the word down that if he didn't like the titles and jackets on my books, I wouldn't get any 'support' for them, so all the men feel they've saved my ass, and I'm right back where I started from. It's not that they don't *trust* you to make decisions, it's that making decisions is a kind of masculine fetish, and when a woman makes them for herself, she shakes up the whole system. So long as you go to a man and show him a good book jacket and say, 'Which do you like better, blue or red?' he'll let you have the final choice, I mean he mostly doesn't know or care, but you have to give him the chance to put his oar in."

A successful woman advertising executive reports that her boss, who gives her every possible sign of support and encouragement, is in the habit of having lunch with her clients and contacts to check out how she's doing. "I noticed a kind of weird pattern. If I had lunch with someone to discuss anything serious, that same person would be having lunch with my boss a couple of days later. He wasn't trying to take business away from me, nothing like that, he was simply trying to make sure that the client wouldn't think mine was the final word on anything important, and to see how they felt about 'dealing with a woman.' I remember one of my potential clients, a guy I wanted very much to bring in, phoning me to say he'd been invited out to have lunch with my boss, and he wondered why. Well, I wondered why too, so I asked my boss, what the hell gives, why all the

Gestapo stuff? He was really surprised and hurt. He didn't want me to think he doubted my judgment or ability, not at all, but he was just afraid my *enthusiasm* might get me into tricky situations. Because women are *emotional*, right? They get carried away, right? He didn't have to say it, that was what he meant, and I knew it. I hadn't realized that any work a woman does has to be done *twice*, once by her, then a second time, uselessly, by the man who's checking her out. And it's the second time it's done, by the man, that counts. That way they can always sit around and tell themselves, 'Margie got us into a nice situation there, she's got drive, but of course if I hadn't stepped in and talked turkey at the right moment, or gone over her figures or brought in a new media analysis, she'd have screwed the whole thing up.' Woman proposes, man disposes, that's the way it's played, no matter how successful a woman gets, there's always a man looking over her shoulder, saying, 'Very nice, dear, but have you considered this or that, there are considerations you're not aware of . . .' Until a man has put his pawmark on something, it doesn't *exist*. Sometimes I'll give the word on something to a client and he'll call back my boss to check it out—it's not that he doesn't trust me, he just wants to hear it confirmed by a man, it's like it wasn't real until a man has said it. Why does having children, wearing a skirt, disqualify you from being a hundred per cent real person? Men can say of each other, 'His word's as good as his bond,' but has anybody ever said 'Her' word's as good as her bond'? And honest *man* is a guy who won't cheat you, who's on your side. An honest *woman* still means a girl who isn't a prostitute, or a prostitute who delivers value for money. 'He took it like a man,' well, we know that means a guy with guts; 'taking it like a woman' means having hysterics, acting up. 'A man's man' is Clark Gable or Paul Newman, that kind of image, 'a man's woman' is a just a woman who keeps her mouth shut, and pours out admiration and affection without asking too much in return. As an advertising person, I can tell you that our *image* as women is so lousy that it doesn't matter how successful you become in business, you're still stuck with a set of attitudes that are like a brick wall, and that allow men to interfere in what you're doing and control your work and even get the credit for it, while still feeling that they're *protecting* you. The trouble with male chauvinists is that they don't even think they're our enemies. Deep down where it counts, they still think in terms of 'helping the little woman,' and if you act like a battle-ax or a buzz-saw, that just makes them feel more generous and 'understanding.' "

Throughout business, the same attitudes prevail, sometimes institutionalized to the point of caricature. In a major New York talent agency, where most of the agents are women, and very successful women at that, the women sit in a long row of offices, not small, but not large either. At one end of the row, in a huge corner office, sits the comptroller of the agency, a man; at the other end, in an equally large corner office, is the president of the agency. Boxed in by two men, the women work in the architecture of oppression as surely as did the long lines of mill hands or sewing machine operators in the nineteenth century—well paid, able to come and go as they please, liberated, but able to see, each time they step out of their offices, just where the power lies by merely looking down toward the ends of the corridor, where the doors are in sculptured wood and always closed.

In certain offices, a law of natural selection takes place that moves women executives together. One company I know moved to a new and luxurious office, in which the executives were carefully alloted space according to some mysterious master plan in which officers were assigned by seniority and for reasons of prestige. The result was an office in which male and female executives were distributed randomly. When the inevitable reorganization took place, the women found themselves grouped on one side of the building, the men on the other side. No sooner was this done than the women found their functions as

executives being changed in a number of small ways—
more "controls," more emphasis on "committees" (con-
sisting mostly of men), more elaborate "management su-
pervision." By grouping the women together (in
purdah, so to speak) and isolating them, it became possible to treat them as a group, like secretaries, instead of as
individually successful executives.

When I visit any office and see a long row of rooms
with women executives working in them, I say to myself
that here, for the moment, male chauvinism has tri-
umphed. Move them into the same row, and soon we can
stop thinking of them as individuals, and start referring
to that part of the office as "the girls' row," thus giving
everyone there a special and, by implication, *reduced*
status. In most offices, a man who is assigned an office in
such an area is on his way out—to be housed near any
sizable grouping of women executives, unless in a way
that implies control over them, downgrades a male executive and serves as a warning that his pink slip is not far
away. One man I know was hired by a large corporation
and given the only available office, on "women's row,"
where he was surrounded by women making more
money than he did, and who had far more experience in
the business as well. Unable to function in what seemed
to him a harem, he finally invented a pretext for examining the corporations's contract files, which were kept
in an anteroom on the "other" side of the office. He had
his telephone transferred there, and exchanged his spa-
cious, comfortable office for a desk in a small dark cubby-
hole without a window, leaving to his secretary the
glories of his old office. He sat there until he was given
an office among the men. "I knew I was doing the right
thing," he said, "senior executives even apologized for
having put me over there with the women, the president
of the company told me that he guessed it must be pretty
noisy over there, with all those women talking. If I'd
stayed there, they'd have begun thinking of me as the
kind of executive who's on the same level as women, the
kind of guy who is doing a job a woman can do, and I'd
have been out in six months."

In many offices, it is easy to notice that when there are two sides, the entrance and the front desk will usually lead into the side where the men work so that a visitor's first sight is that of men at work in their offices. Few companies want to present a group of women, however successful they may be, as the first impression, unless they're attractive secretaries, which is a different kind of exploitation.

Of course, however successful a woman executive is, and however large her office, it is very important that no meeting should take place there, even if the alternative is to hold it in some place that's inconvenient and crowded. Women executives can exhibit their success with built-in bookshelves, private telephones with push buttons, marble-top table-desks, concealed lighting; it is rare that they can persuade the office manager to give them a conference table. That remains a male prerogative, except at fashion magazines, where it is customary for the woman editor-in-chief to have a conference table for "editorial" discussions, at which most of those present will be women, while the publisher has a conference table in his office for discussion of advertising, budgetary matters and business. In these circumstances, it is desirable for "her" conference table to be as frivolous in appearance as possible, giving the effect of a boudoir or a dining nook in a rather elaborately designed house of vaguely French Provincial decor.

My own experience on women's magazines has led me to the conclusion that women tend to cover up their conference tables with knickknacks—clocks, pencil holders, souvenirs, flowers, photographs, bowls of candy, cigarette boxes—in order to conceal the real purpose of the table, whereas men leave theirs bare and empty in order to emphasize that the conference table is the instrument for making decisions, as meaningless without their presence as a race car without a driver.

It is natural enough for women who run fashion magazines to decorate their offices in the style of the product they are producing, but this has the additional effect of creating a world in which men are made to feel ill-at-ease

and unwelcome. The editor-in-chief of a well-known
fashion magazine for which I once wrote had an office
whose aura was so powerful that even the publisher and
owner of the magazine was unable to cross the threshold
and used to stand in the doorway to talk to his employee,
who added to her feminine armory two secretaries whose
desks were actually in the room itself, so that any male
intruder was faced by three perfectly made-up female
faces smiling blandly at him like Vestal Virgins receiving
an importunate messenger from the Roman Senate. The
carpet was made of imitation leopard skin, the walls
were shell pink, the tables (no desks, of course) were
white marble, a dazzling collection of sea shells was displayed against one wall, the telephones were pink, every
available surface was covered in objects from Hermes,
Gucci, Buccellati and Asprey's of London, and all the
pencils were fitted with small plastic flowers that incon-
veniently covered the erasers. In such an atmosphere any
man brave enough to enter was at a disadvantage, and
most chose to do business by telephone. Even that did
not altogether spare them from embarrassment. I was
once sitting in the publisher's office when he dialed his
editor-in-chief's number to give her his opinion of some
planned promotion scheme. After explaining his doubts,
he paused to wait for her reply. Instead, the line went
dead. "My God," he said, "she hung up on me!" He
dialed her number again, and asked, rather nervously,
"Did you hang up on me?" Her reply was audible to me
from the other side of the desk—a loud click. She had
hung up on him again. "You know," he said with feeling, "women have no *manners*." At which point one of
the editor-in-chief's secretaries appeared in the office,
smiled politely, and said, "Mrs. X wanted to say that
she's awfully sorry, but we seem to have a bad connection," and left. "But they're smart," the publisher said,
and closed his eyes to brood over the misfortunes of a
man who has to deal with successful women, and who by
refusing to treat them as equals in a professional sense
(for none of his editors were members of the board, or
served on the executive committees), had unconsciously

turned them into a separate caste, with special powers and privileges.

As with most magazine empires of this kind, women were allowed to have considerable powers in each magazine, even allowed and encouraged to run their own magazine, but they were rigidly restricted to their own magazines, and kept in a state of fierce competition from magazine to magazine, though they were all members of the same corporation. The functions that involved the company's total product were traditionally reserved for men. Embarrassed as they might be by the arrogance of the women, the men could afford to accept humiliation —they held the high ground, as military tactitians say, and could therefore concede all sorts of limited strategic advantages to the women on the plains below.

By conceding to women just enough ground to keep them busy, they could be forced to adopt a role that effectively precludes them from active competition with men. "We'll give you these areas to succeed in, and stick to them!" Thus: women lawyers who find themselves gradually specializing in "family" cases, women reporters who are relegated to writing stories about the fact that Mrs. Murphy buys her husband's size 8 and one-half shoes, rather than writing stories about the New York Police Commissioner himself, are in effect being bought off, and no matter how high their salaries, they are not really that much better off than traditional "housewives"—for as long as men can select the roles in which women can succeed, as long as male chauvinism sets the ground rules for a woman's success, then a woman's money and status remain meaningless, nothing more than the signs that she is talented enough to make a profit out of her surrender.

I admire any woman who succeeds, any way she can, but there's a world of difference between trying to beat the system and joining it, and men are simply more comfortable with the women who join.

Two offices, two styles:

Barbara Walters' office at NBC, in the small, busy

suite reserved for the *Today* show, is cluttered with the
working impedimenta of a woman who doesn't feel she
needs feminine surroundings—old magazines, books,
stacks of paper, raincoats, memorabilia—of famous
guests on the *Today* show and of Ms. Walters' own trips
—that have collected too fast to be hung or displayed,
several clocks, a huge television set taking up a very large
part of the floor space, cartons of odd objects which in-
ventors, manufacturers or promoters have sent to the
show either to be advertised or to form the subject of
some unlikely discussion. What with the news tickers, the
telephones and the messengers coming and going, there
is a sense of urgency that reminds one of a city news
room, and of course the business of this particular show,
and this particular woman, *is* news of a kind. Amidst all
the busy confusion, Barbara Walters seems remarkably
controlled, a function perhaps of her ability to project
herself on television, a medium which is notoriously
harsh on people who are fidgety or nervous. Despite her
reputation for toughness (Thomas Thompson reported
in *Life* on his relief at the news that Frank McGee
would "do" him, rather than Barbara Walters, commenting on her ability "to bore in on others, as often as
I have admired her asking the questions that Hugh
Downs was too gallant to ask" and adding that he had
"scant desire to be under her gaze myself"), Barbara
Walters doesn't seem at all formidable, and it is difficult
not to conclude that the "gaze" that frightened Thompson and others is quite simply the look of an intelligent
and slightly impatient person who has to listen to a good
deal of bullshit and doesn't accept it easily. *Life*, with its
unfortunate talent for unconscious male chauvinism, described her as "aggressive but feminine," implying with
a remarkable economy of words that aggression in the intellectual sense (which in most men and all ambitious
men is regarded as a valuable asset) is by definition un-
feminine.

Her role on the *Today* show developed into one of
those controversies of which only a small part, like the
tip of an iceberg, has surfaced. It is an interesting situa-

tion because Barbara Walters is by any definition a very successful person, and much admired. Yet her success seems to engender a remarkable amount of explanations, as if it had to be exorcised. Her producer, Stuart Shulberg, a man of broad erudition, ferocious energy and very considerable talent, in an industry where the first and the last of these three virtues are very rare indeed, was quoted in *Life* as saying, "What's happening (in the show) is a shift in roles. Hugh Downs was affable, wise, the great compromiser. He treated every guest as he would someone in his own home. He was not a probing journalist. Barbara would sense a gulf and she'd dive in. Shocked a lot of men—women, too. An aggressive dame! Now we've got Frank (McGee) and Barbara, and she senses she's lost the chance to fill the journalistic gaps. She's very properly developing a different side of her personality . . . warm, feminine, kindly, the peacemaker . . ."

To this Frank McGee added that ever since he took the show over, "friends have been asking me, 'When are you going to gut Barbara Walters?' My answer is, 'Never.' There's room for both of us. There's room for Joe Garagiola, too. Joe's a great big hunk of pulsating humanity. He responds to the warm, the gentle, the furry, the jockstrap side of America . . . Joe's marvelous. He's honest. He says what he believes."

Connoisseurs of male chauvinism can easily detect in these two quotes certain subtle signs of prejudice. One notes the speed with which Frank McGee, having dismissed the rather brutal suggestion that he should "gut" Barbara Walters (and having overlooked the possibility that she might have tried to "gut" him), rushes on to praise Joe Garagiola, another man, as "gentle," "marvelous," "honest." Of Ms. Walters he merely notes that there's room enough for them both. She does not come in, as Mr. Garagiola does, for an extended affirmation of her virtues as a warm and wonderful human being.

Mr. Shulberg, for his part, suggests that Barbara Walters' desire to "fill the journalistic gaps" was in some way slightly unnatural, that having abandoned that role to Mr. McGee, she is now "very properly" finding her own personality in terms of the show, which is, of course, "feminine," "warm," and "kindly" as opposed to being "a probing journalist."

There is nothing *overtly* hostile in the comments of McGee and Schulberg on their female colleague, but a careful reader cannot help but sense a certain reserve, accentuated by what appears to be an effort to smother Garagiola in praise as a way of putting Ms. Walters down. It is also interesting to note that Barbara Walters' opinion of her colleagues was not quoted, as if *she* were the problem, the one who had to adapt, rather than the men.

I began by asking Ms. Walters, who is indeed a very successful woman with a relatively happy working situation, if she felt that her position would be different if she were a man, and she pointed out very sensibly that she had originally been hired as a female. "I used to be the Weather Girl," she said. "I changed. The job changed. Still, there's the feeling that the job is supportive to the man. When Hugh Downs left, people wrote in to ask why isn't Barbara Walters the head of the show? Well, they wouldn't have a woman as the head of the show. For a day, yes. But if it's a week, they bring a man in. I find that demeaning."

I asked about the position of women on network television: "A woman has no authority. Therefore she can't present news. If you try to argue about this, you get told, 'But look, the audience doesn't want to take a woman seriously. Women don't want to watch women . . . When we went to China with President Nixon, John Chancellor got asked all the serious questions. I got asked about shopping! Afterwards men complimented me on the way I'd worked in China, and told me, 'We thought we'd have to carry you.' Why? I've been on this show for ten years . . ."

When Barbara Walters talks about her role as a woman in a business dominated by men, it is easy to see why some of the show's guests are intimidated by her.

She is energetic, outspoken and very clever, all qualities that rarely commend themselves to men when found in the opposite sex (A friend told me, "I watch the *Today* show every morning, and I think Barbara Walters is terrific, but I think she sometimes tears into authors just for the pleasure of doing it, and I'm not sure she's a woman I'd *like*"). On the subject of money, Ms. Walters is succinct: "I make more money than many of the men in the news department, but I don't make as much as the host." Unlike most people, unlike the men around her, she understands very well the ambiguities of a woman's success, the additional pressures that weigh on a woman who has a career. These pressures range from the way some women television reporters instinctively lower their voices while on the air to project a more "masculine" voice to the ways in which women are automatically presumed to be unable to do certain jobs (reporting on serious news, for example) then penalized financially and in status because they don't do the things they aren't permitted to do, however much they would like to. It is, for example, all right for women to read headlines, since this doesn't imply interpretation, it's like reading the weather reports. Reading the news itself, or commenting on it, is still regarded as a man's job.

Here is the paradox: a successful woman, well paid, famous, talented, and yet still conscious that something is missing, that she is not "equal" to men, perhaps never can be, finding at the very top of her profession the same restraints and polite evasions that infuriate women in far more menial jobs, out of the public spotlight. In Ms. Walters' own words, "To say 'She's an intelligent woman' is not male chauvinism. I don't mind, for example, the use of the word 'Congresswoman' . . . Yes, things bother me, but for the most part I'm not angry. I would rather have the advantages of being a woman, but I am aware of the differences every time I open my mouth and do an interview." For of course being a woman, despite the "advantages," is a disadvantage: one has to work harder (for which one is accused of being "aggressive"), prove that one can do a job as well

as a man (for which one is accused of being "unfemi-
nine"), reject the colonialism implicit in male attitudes
toward women (at the risk of making enemies of them).

Or one has to disarm them, by emphasizing the "feminine" image to the point where men are so uneasy
about how to react that they are defeated in advance.

Another office, another person: Again the clutter in-
separable from being busy and successful, endless piles of
magazines, reams of papers with scribbled notes, but the
very definite sense that this is a *woman's* office: glass jars
of hard candy, antique lamps with fabric lampshades,
pastel telephones, cluttered photographs, porcelain ashtrays that look as if they had come from Tiffany's instead of from the mailroom's office supplies, furniture
upholstered in decorator fabrics, china animals . . .

Beyond the door of this inner sanctum, the offices are
small, utilitarian and shabby, places for hard work rather
than for making a public display. Even the entrance hall
is sparse and frayed, furnished with two somewhat bat-
tered sofas and endless supplies of the house product:
Cosmopolitan. For this is the office of Helen Gurley
Brown, successful author, an editorial genius who made
a faltering and dull magazine into the best-known
monthly magazine in the United States after *Playboy*, in-
ventor of a whole philosophy of male/female relationships, whose lessons, reduced to a single memorable
paragraph appear once a month from the mouth of
"The Cosmo Girl" that radiantly beautiful spokeswo-
man for creative hedonism, whose message is that you
still have to get your man, just as in the old days, but
that you can do it by learning new sex techniques, cooking aphrodisiac casseroles, wearing a fall, succeeding at
your job, making yourself a more interesting, more attractive person. And of course you don't have to marry
him once you have him—you can live with him, or even
keep your own apartment. In short, it is the ancient wisdom or the Matriarchy couched in the language of the
sixties. Whatever else can be said of Helen Gurley
Brown, she isn't "The Cosmo Girl." True, she has been
pushing for a Cosmo centerfold pinup of a naked man,

and succeeded in including in one issue a photograph of actor Burt Reynolds lying on a bearskin rug ("We all talked it over and the last thing we wanted it to be was soulful . . . Girls have always been sex objects; it was time for men to have a turn . . . I don't think it's going to turn on readers. Most Cosmo readers will have seen naked men before"), but there is nothing in Helen Gurley Brown to suggest a revolutionary philosopher in the struggle between the sexes, let alone a dedicated supporter of sexual freedom. "The Cosmo Girl" may have a mission, but to meet Helen Gurley Brown is to meet a very busy, slightly nervous, very successful person who has created a startling and effective editorial format and been rather overwhelmed by it. There is a widespread rumor that she is in some ways the invention of her husband, David, the protean associate of Richard Zanuck and a very shrewd man indeed, but five minutes with Helen Gurley Brown is enough to prove that she has a mind of her own, and enough energy and ambition for at least three lesser overreachers. Her style is the opposite of Barbara Walters'. Helen Gurley Brown doesn't make the slightest attempt to beat men at their own game; she behaves just the way a male chauvinist *expects* a woman to behave—flighty, charming, seemingly scatterbrained, given to effusions of enthusiasm and girlish crushes. One needs to be no more than mildly perceptive to see that a good deal of this is a carefully devised mask; the flightiness conceals a restless mind, easily bored, the scatterbrained mannerisms disguise a real shrewdness, the enthusiasm, which comes in bursts, emerges from a real interest in anything that can work for Cosmo. Just as Barbara Walters' intense dark eyes are those of a person who is impatient with any kind of fakery or mental sloppiness, Helen Gurley Brown's, especially when she is tired, are those of an executive with a deadline to meet. Ms. Brown has a certain reputation with men for the frivolous (One man suggested that the perfect 1970s Cosmo article should be called "Multiple Orgasm—A New Way to a Thinner You"), but this attitude toward her ignores the fact that the contents of her magazine,

while sometimes presented in frivolous ways, are of real
concern to women, and that there is nothing at all frivolous about Ms. Brown's success. Just as men find it easy
to laugh about multiple orgasm, ignoring the fact that to
women it is a reality, or would be if men were more sexually aware and competent, so it is easy to overlook the
fact the Helen Gurley Brown's is a success story, in the
Horatio Alger tradition. A man who could take a declining magazine and turn it into a profitable national
phenomenon would be treated with respect and admiration; Helen Gurley Brown, a woman who has, after all,
done just that, is treated as if she were something out of
a joke. The joke is on men, and Helen Gurley Brown
knows it.

When she says that women should be "solvent, sovereign and interesting" she is in fact coming down on the
side of those women's liberationists who look down on
the Cosmo philosophy, seeing in its overt appeal to attracting and holding a man a form of collaboration with
the enemy. The trick is financial and intellectual independence before sexual "surrender."

For underneath the "little girl" pose and the sensa-
tionalism, Helen Gurley Brown believes in making your
own way as best you can, in defeating male chauvinism
by competence and work. She is, in fact, a rather formidable person: "My mother used to tell me, 'Don't just
get married and have children. *Do* something!' I had
nineteen jobs by the time I was twenty-five, when I fell
into advertising. I was willing to try anything and *learn*,
and if it turned out there wasn't a future, that the men
there wouldn't listen to a woman, I didn't fight, I
moved. I learned you had to get *into* a company, even if
it was as a typist, you have to start somewhere . . . Once
you're there, you just have to be better than other people. You just did more work, you used your sex appeal,
your brains, you used everything you could, just like a
man. There isn't a magic formula—sleeping with men is
not the way to become famous, rich and successful . . .

"Maybe it's partly the fault of men, old habits, all
that, but fifty per cent of the women I know aren't

doing the best they can. Maybe it's unfair, but as a woman you have to do more. You need to be charming, tactful, smart, as well as good at your job. You have to forget about thinking there are certain kinds of jobs you won't do. Do them! We'll take the responsibilities of the bad jobs, if we can have an equal whack at the good ones!"

"Famous, rich and successful" Helen Gurley Brown is, but these ambitions, which are admired in a man, are thought vulgar and hard in a woman, for a woman's success is supposed to be quieter, less "obvious" than a man's, if she has to be successful at all. It is all right for them to join in the success game, just so long as they don't succeed *too* well, and don't show that they *enjoy* their success. In the words of one man, "I think it's terrific when women do something and do it well, women *ought* to use their brains, and I find that they often have a greater sense of responsibility than men, they pay more attention to detail, they don't try for center-stage so much." But the real motivation for success is not to be a better colleague, it is precisely to seize center-stage. When men encourage women to be successful it is always on their own terms; these terms do not as a rule include becoming "famous, rich and successful." "I don't like to have limits set for me by other people," said the editor-in-chief of *Cosmopolitan*, effectively and precisely defining just what male chauvinism consists of —the setting of limits for women by men. So long as men are able to say, in effect, "A woman who makes $20,000 in this company is a successful woman," thus setting a goal which defines her success and a limit beyond which she cannot pass, she is systematically held back from emulating the success of a Helen Gurley Brown.

A very successful and highly respected woman told me of the way in which male chauvinism increases with each step upward in a woman's career. Starting as a secretary she had worked her way up to a position of considerable responsibility. "I simply had to push harder than a man," she said. "Then, when I got to a certain point, people came around and told me how pleased they were at my success, and it took me a while to realize that they were telling me, in effect, 'OK, this is it, you're successful, congratulations, now stop. Don't ask for more.' Well, I wanted more, and I asked for a title, and I got it, but it was given to me the way you'd give flowers to your wife, as an indulgence, a pat on the back, it didn't have in their minds the serious connotations that a title would have had for a man, even the same title. I'd put in a lot of years to get where I was, but those years turn a woman into a mother figure, they don't give her the status the same amount of years would give a man. A couple of years ago, it became clear that the job of running the magazine was going to open up, and there were only two people qualified to do it, myself and a man. I did a lot of soul searching about it, and decided I didn't really want to do the administrative work, I wanted to control the *editorial* part of the magazine. So we had a big meeting, and I said, 'I think I can contribute equally in what I do,' and everybody agreed, but it was a mistake, the biggest mistake I've ever made, because I should have fought. The man who took on the 'administrative' job which was supposed to be equal is now making $15,000 a year more than I am, and we've been bought by a big conglomerate that doesn't even know I exist—as far as they're concerned (and 'they' are all men, naturally) he *is* the magazine."

Again and again, women complain that they are given specific areas in which to succeed, then persuaded, cajoled, forced, sometimes even overpaid and overpraised, to stay there. A woman journalist says, "You can write terrific stories for the woman's page of *The New York Times* if you're a woman, but it's hard to break into the rest of the paper. I can imagine a man editing the woman's page, or at least writing for it, but can you imagine a woman editing the *Times*'s 'op-ed' page or the editorials? A newspaper speaks with the voice of men." A woman psychoanalyst says, "There are enormous pressures to push women into dealing with women's problems, or into child psychiatry or school dynamics—women's concerns. I wouldn't go so far as Dr. Phyllis Chester (who believes that women are driven to madness by men, and that male psychoanalysts are the worst offenders, and is suing the American Psychological Association for $1,000,000 in "reparations"), but most male analysts play a double game of male chauvinism. They discount what women therapists have to say about women on the grounds that women are being 'subjective' when they talk about other women and their neurotic problems. At the same time, they discount what women therapists have to say about men, on the grounds that women don't have the same insight into masculine problems as other men do. Heads you lose, tails you lose! I don't count things like the analyst who slept with his women patients as part of the therapy, that isn't male chauvinism, that's fraud, but there's a strong tendency on the part of male therapists to view women as the *problem* in any analytic situation, and to carry this over in their attitude towards women in the profession."

The same kind of restriction to specialized areas can also be noticed in criticism of the arts. Wherever the subject involved is "important"—that is it seems to most men a vital part of our culture—it tends to remain firmly in the hands of men. Movies are usually regarded as ephemeral, rather than as a permanent part of our culture; therefore a good many of the more important film critics are women. The theater is thought to be, on the contrary, a major cultural phenomenon, with the result that most theater critics are men. It's not just a question of cultural importance, however wrongly based: it's a question of power. Women criticize things that can't be damaged very much by their criticism—movies, which tend to succeed despite bad reviews, architecture, which can't after all be torn down because Ada Louise Huxtable doesn't like it. When it's a question of something that can be made or broken by criticism, like a book or a play, the major reviewers are men—*all* the book reviewers of *The New York Times* daily edition are men, as is the theater/ballet reviewer and the music reviewer.

As Grace Glueck has pointed out in *The New York*

Times, art criticism is virtually a male enclave, with results that can be imagined for women artists, who feel, in any case, that "magazines and newspapers give more coverage to men because museums and galleries do"—a far more basic complaint. *Art in America* reviewed in one year (1970-1971) 138 artists, of whom 92 per cent were men. *Art News* devoted 96.1 per cent of its reviews in the same period to the work of male artists. Predictably, *Craft Horizons* gave a generous 44 per cent of its space to women, handcrafts having less status than art, and its editor being a woman, which after all can't hurt. As Tom Hess, the editor of *Art News,* half of whose reviewers are women, said to Ms. Glueck, "The conclusion is that it's harder for women to get shows. That's news?"*

The issue is power, as usual. A leading figure in the gourmet business, a man, told me, "Women are listened to about food in terms of preparing and cooking it, but the people who make and break restaurants are men. Julia Child is a superstar in the kitchen as a *performer,* but people want to know what a *man* thinks of a restaurant. Traditionally, when a man and a woman go to a restaurant, the woman is just going along for a ride. Women go to restaurants to talk or to be seen, not to eat." (There is a long tradition of male chauvinism in the wine and food business, the feeling that cooking in the ordinary sense is a woman's job, while cooking as an art form is somehow masculine. In television commercials, professional chefs are always men, imparting their secrets to housewives.) In a recent article on the woman's page of *The New York Times* Ms. Tina Santi

---

* The fact that art criticism is in the hands of men is perhaps the only sign that our society holds it in any esteem. We may not *care* about art, but we have been taught that it matters—this places it in the realm of men's concerns automatically. A. J. Liebling once argued that the "graphic arts had their origin in the free patterns made in the snow by Ice Age man with warm water which accounts for the fact that there have been few good women painters." (37) I am surprised that no modern abstractionist has tried urinating on canvas creatively, and offering it as an idea to anyone who cares to try it, on the condition that the show is reviewed by a woman.

was quoted as saying that she resented "the chauvinistic attitude of men towards wine," a complaint borne out by one wine expert's opening comments in a coeducational seminar on wine-tasting, when he remarked, "Beaujolais is like a pretty young girl; lovely hair, beautiful features, feminine, with a bright smile—but no sex."

"Feminine." A word as loaded with implications as is the phrase "male chauvinism." Form the point of view of the woman who wants to succeed, who wants to be a person, not an object, "feminine" can be defined quite simply by those qualities that men despise in other men and in themselves. It implies a concern with things that are not "serious," a propensity to emotional response, rather than thought, a failure to grasp the "big picture," self-indulgence, limited ambitions, dependency, weakness. A man who has a "feminine" way of thinking is a man who is devious, bitchy and treacherous. Women who work in business that are "feminine" are beginning to be concerned with the implications of "femininity," as if they now wonder if their success in this field might not perhaps mean that they are merchandising just those prejudices and attitudes that eventually prevent them from becoming really successful themselves, perceiving that there is after all a connection between perfumed vaginal sprays and the restrictions that affect their own careers and lives.

A woman who has become successful in the cosmetics business, and is now trying to puzzle out her position by taking part in a women's consciousness-raising group, remarked, "I'm making a lot of money, sure, but I can't help wondering if fashion, cosmetics, the *women's* businesses, don't represent a kind of Apartheid. It's as if men were saying, 'OK, you take over this because it's frivolous, unimportant, *feminine*.' And doesn't it further denigrate women to succeed in exactly those fields that reinforce a male chauvinist view of women? I worked hard to get where I am, but now I get this funny feeling when men say to me, 'How are we going to sell them this, what makes this eye-liner sexier than any other eye-liner?' I'm beginning to understand who 'them' is—it's *me*."

Even the phrase "a successful woman" has disturbing implications, for it suggests, in men's vocabularies, that a woman is successful *as a woman*. A woman who becomes a successful stockbroker is a lady-stockbroker, but a successful woman is a woman who succeeds in living up to men's expectations of what a woman should do. Indeed, the distinction is often made very precisely: "She is not only a successful agent, but a successful woman," that is to say, she not only makes money, but also manages to look after a house, prevent the children from bothering her husband, deal with problems of sitters, laundry, drycleaning and at any rate pretend to an interest in food sufficient to fool visitors into thinking she enjoys cooking. We all know the criteria for a successful man, and know that domestic failures do not diminish his success in the least. But a successful woman remains by definition a success in the domestic area. If she fails in that, no amount of success in other areas will be credited to her account in men's eyes. Hence the nagging preoccupation of reporters with the domestic details of the lives of women celebrities, as if Gloria Steinem's feelings about cooking, or Jane Fonda's abilities at sewing, or Mai Zetterling's sentiments about her children were somehow a litmus test of feminine success. Perhaps it's a reflexive twitch of make chauvinist thinking: if only we can find one traditionally feminine virtue in a woman it will redeem her. Let Ti-Grace Atkinson confess that she likes to shop for vegetables, let Betty Friedan admit that she sometimes washes dishes, let Germaine Greer acknowledge that she can bake a cake, and all will be forgiven. In large things as in small, all we demand is a small sign that the old order reigneth undisturbed. A man with a secretary who is "into" women's liberation counts himself the victor if he can get her to bring him a cup of coffee, but the game is not as harmless as it sometimes seems, for the small surrender is always exploited, and the more successful the woman, the more ruthless the exploitation.

But how are women to compete against their own image? Our symbols of "successful womanhood" are still Mrs. Onassis (however tarnished) and Ethel Kennedy, mothers, homemakers (on a grand scale, to be sure), acquirers of clothes, judged as super-housewives who carry domesticity to the point of fantasy, but whose activities remain within the comprehension of any woman who keeps a house and looks after her children. When Mrs. Richard M. Nixon visited China and the Soviet Union, she was shown an endless round of kitchens and kindergartens, *creches*, photographed with innumerable moppets. These may possibly be what she wants to see, but one doubts that it was, for example, what Mrs. Lyndon B. Johnson wanted to see—yet her visits abroad consisted of the same round of cuisine and pediatrics. With the television cameras of the world trained on them, our First Ladies perfectly represent the dichotomy between men and women: the weighty, important deliberations of their husbands, elected to high office, the meaningless, smiling inspection of domestic affairs set aside for the wives. Men design, finance, build and command ships. Their wives, if they are lucky, are allowed to break a bottle of champagne against the bows at the launching.

Short of some radical transformation of society, success simple cannot make a woman equal, not so long as she bears the burden of men's fantasies about her, not so long as men have the power to create an image against which she is measured, measures herself, not so long as we arbitrarily assign to half our population a different role, a different set of values, by defining them as "feminine." After all, women are programmed to be what they are, their interests are guided toward the domestic, toward "love," children, home, the fulfillment of private impulses and concerns! If they succeed in a career it must either be at the expense of their own identities, or by using less than the total amount of energy that a man could bring to the same job. Thus an author of my acquaintanceship, a civilized and intelligent man who has a woman as an agent and a woman as an editor, recently asked me to read his manuscript, about which both women had expressed confidence and pleasure. "They love it," he said confidentially, "but what do *they* know?"

Behind men's often petty attitude toward successful women lies the fear of women's acquiring power, both the power to live their own lives independently and the power to influence the lives of men. If women find it hard to get to the top, it is not just because men instinctively band together against the idea of a woman sharing the benefits of great success, but because the idea of a woman ordering their world from above is as unthinkable as a female Godhead.

Perhaps we recognize that power is a kind of freedom, and that what women want is the same freedom to make choices that men have. There has always been, in men, an instinctive fear that the more extreme feminists may be right, that women are in fact a more successful artifact of nature than men. The complexity of their biology, their miraculous ability to give birth to another human being, the early imprint on a mother's power on every man, all conspire to produce in men a slight feeling of awe about the potentials of women once they are unleashed. Men have trained themselves to compete, particularly in terms of power, but nothing has prepared them for competition with women, and behind their dogmatism and small guiles lies the fear that woman may in fact be a formidable competitor, once she has made her choice. As Mai Zetterling said recently, speaking of her career as a movie director (she has been a successful actress, a novelist and seems to enjoy her "domestic" role as a mother as well):

"I've changed more in the last three years than I've ever done before. I was cluttering up my life, I didn't have one particular goal. I wanted to be much stronger, much clearer. Sometimes you want to clear your brain out; crystallize things, clean the cobwebs away, and say to yourself, what the hell do you want to do now? So now I am taking time to find out . . . So what, so it's a woman making a film. So she has to give certain orders. But that doesn't mean to say you have to lose your sensuality. It's so childish, so old-fashioned. I don't think I lose any femininity, it has nothing to do with it."(38)

The sense that women are thinking out their lives, that they want to be "stronger" and "clearer" produces a kind of brooding fear in men, who see in each small step toward freedom and success in the women around them the manifestations of some larger revolution to come. Women are thinking out their roles; men are merely clinging desperately to theirs, hoping that they will survive the coming storm, searching for the means to prevent its happening. So long as they behave like an autocracy, they are, like all autocracies, doomed. One businessman who recently lost his female assistants because he took—automatically and reflexively—a male client's word against theirs, told me, "I can't understand it. Am I a bad boss, a bad *person?* I tried to run the office the way I run my home, I mean I'm in charge, somebody has to be, after all, and I try to be fair, and listen to everybody's point of view, at home and here. Sure I set rules, but I treated these girls as if they were members of my family, and look what happened." But look at the *family,* where in fact, his wife balances the family checkbook, makes all the decisions about money, gives her husband a "walking-out" allowance, and in all things great and small runs the family's affairs, while conceding in public a rather convincing role of "authority" to her husband. The ambivalence and confusion of men's attitudes toward women begins at home and extends to every sphere of a woman's activity and success, making men the prisoners of their own weaknesses.

The male chauvinist, as a rule, does not see the connection. He separates women into those at home, and those at work, fails to associate a failure of communication in one area with a failure in another, acts as if successful women at work were a phenomenon apart from real life, even tries to quarantine them. As a successful woman public relations expert said, "Sure I'm a success, and I'm attractive too, but I get the funniest reactions. One man I was promoting came up to my apartment, and I *liked* him, you know, and I wasn't at all unhappy at the idea we might sleep together, and he put his arm around me and said, 'Listen, you're a terrific PR girl, really sharp and tough and smart, but I bet there's a different person there, a loving, warm *person*. Well, I told him to get out. There isn't a different person there. I'm tough *and* loving, smart *and* warm, or I hope I am. I suddenly realized that he thought that my work was a kind of pose, a put-on, all he had to do is take off his pants and I'd become some fantasy figure out of his imagination. He didn't want to sleep with me, he wanted to sleep with his idea of what a woman he sleeps with ought to be like. And he doesn't even understand that my success is *part* of me, it can't be separated from my character, my personality. Love me, love it: it's part of the package."

SIX

> *Marriage is the hell of false expectations, where both partners, expecting to be loved, defined and supported, abdicate responsibility for themselves and accuse the other of taking away their freedom.*
> —Kathrin Perutz, Marriage Is Hell

> *It is better to marry than to burn.*
> —St. Paul's Epistle to the Corinthians

> *Babbitt was not an analyst of women . . . He was of the opinion that all of them (save the women of his own family) were "different" and "mysterious."*
> —Sinclair Lewis, Babbitt

THE DOMESTIC CHAUVINIST

Marriage is of course the oldest of jokes, the staple of every comic act, its roles as fixed as the stars in their course since the time of Plautus and before: the henpecked husband, the nagging wife, the woman waiting to greet her reveling spouse with a rolling pin, the cuckold, Blondie and Dagwood, Doctor and Mrs. Bovary, Darby and Joan, those famous accomplices in senescence— "We've been together now for forty years, and it don't seem a year too much; there ain't a lady living in the land as I'd trade for me dear old Dutch!" The folklore of marriage is so rich that we hardly even notice how it defines our roles for us, and it is perfectly possible for people to be married for years, sometimes indeed for a lifetime, without having a single feeling or emotion about each other that comes from inside them—the model exists, you simply have to live up to it. Ms. Perutz may be going a bit far in saying that marriage is hell (a strange echo of General William Tecumseh Sherman's famous dictum on war, another permanent human institution that gives us preconceived roles into which we can slip effortlessly), but she is essentially giving the ancient

domestic institution the same cold disapproval that St.
Paul reserved for it two thousands years ago. His pessi-
mistic view of marriage was based upon the view that a
life of chastity and prayer was the proper state for man
(possibly for women too), but that human weakness
being what it was and is, it was necessary to allow an out-
let for man's carnal instincts that was acceptable to God,
however reluctantly He might accept it. The early
Church blessed marriage, but without enthusiasm—an
attitude that survives today in our secular view of marriage, though our point of view has changed
diametrically. In St. Paul's time, sexual relationships
were reason enough for damnation, and marriage a
haven for those weak enough to indulge in them. In our
day we worship sexual relationships, and marriage is
seen as a haven for those too weak to compete successfully in the Darwinian struggle of sexual freedom. To St.
Paul, marriage was not far removed from license. To Ms.
Perutz it is a prison and, as St. Paul preached the King-
dom of God, she demands "the recognition that each
person is himself, married or not; that the journey into
oneself is more important than the ego trip . . ." (One
is inclined to ask whether a journey into oneself isn't in
fact the definition of "an ego trip," but I suspect that
Kathrin Perutz suffers from the modern American delusion that it is more important to spend your time thinking about yourself than trying to learn something about
and from other people, a belief in the efficacy of intro-
spection that seems as little likely to make for human
happiness on this earth as St. Paul's belief in the efficacy
of prayer, which it somewhat resembles.) Hell or
heaven, it is in this institution that men, for the most
parts, make up their minds about what women are, and
it is here that their attitudes become fixed. After all, it is
difficult not to draw certain conclusions from a lifetime's
observation, and even more difficult to accept that these
conclusions may not apply to other situations, other
women. At heart, to the make chauvinist, every woman
is his wife.

It is hardly surprising that men often find it difficult in this revolutionary age to deal with young women who have had no experience of marriage, and don't much like what they have heard of it. Older women know how to deal with a married executive, they can read the signals, guess what approach will work. Young women, especially educated, radical ones, are constantly bewildered by the effects they produce on older men, especially those who hold some position of authority.

It is not necessary to be an expert on marriage to know that domestic considerations influence office life to an extraordinary degree, sometimes in simple ways, sometimes very subtly. It is simple when the wife of the president tours the halls and demands that her husband fire any young woman who is conspicuously pretty, her voice, reminding one of the Red Queen in *Alice in Wonderland*, echoing down the hall with the fatal question, "Who is that girl?" (A young lady reported to me that she was fired from this company for a slightly different reason. "I went to a party at the Waldorf Astoria, and my aunt was going to pick me up in her car. It was a Friday, and we were going away for the weekend. Well, it was pouring rain, and I was standing under the canopy on Park Avenue, and at the other side of the canopy the boss's wife was waiting for a cab. My aunt pulled up in her car, which happened to be a Rolls, and I got in. On Monday I was fired.")

The main thing that men bring from home is the attitude that women are to be bullied, or humored, or charmed, or ignored. Like the hedgehog in the Russian fable, they know one thing, and know it so well that they cannot unlearn it. In marriage men learn that the surest way to protect their freedom is to restrict the freedom of someone else; they attempt, given half a chance, to assert their will and individuality, choosing precisely the institution where it is most necessary to give up a measure of individuality and will, relying upon the fact that it is easier to impose oneself on one person than on the world at large.

"Fay now says she never loved me. . . I can't believe it. When we were first married, we were happier than most couples ever are. We agreed on everything! When I laughed, she laughed. When I was down, so was she. Whatever I wanted, she wanted . . . I'm sort of a sports fanatic. Fay enjoys dancing. I don't. Fay had poor muscular coordination untile I trained her. The first time I put her on a motorcycle, she fell off and cracked a collar bone. On the coldest winter evenings, she would sit with me in an unheated garage while I repaired my motorcycle or worked on my boat. I'm ashamed to say I used to swear at her if she passed me the wrong tool. I wouldn't do that today."(39)

One is not surprised to learn that Fay is now living alone, and has decided that both her husband and her subsequent lovers have merely been "using her sexually." The case of the young wife who has to sit in the unheated garage while her husband (who doesn't dance) works on his boat and motorcycle may seem extreme, but the number of refugees from the institution of marriage who are trying to reconstruct whatever it is they might have been in the foreign land of being alone serves as some indication that is this case the caricature is alarmingly close to the truth. It is not surprising that men find it difficult to deal with the women they work with when their judgment of women in general is based on such simple relationships as that described by one husband, a writer:

"We don't compete, we complement. I write, she cooks. I cut grass, she mops floors. I build bookcases. She dusts them. I pay for the babies. She has them. (Southern wives) will pamper the hell out of you in an old-fashioned way that has no connection with women's liberation. They will wash your socks and iron your shirts and make your bed and cook your meals and have your babies, all out of an unthinking belief that this is as it should be . . ."(40)

It's not just that this attitude is common, but that it remains an ideal, even for men who know well their wives expect a good deal more out of life than this. Most upper-middle-class men have resigned themselves to the fact that their wives may not be altogether happy about ironing shirts, and would hesitate to talk about "my bed," or, God forbid, "my babies," the sexual possessive having come into general disrepute these days, but the notion still remains that this is as things *ought* to be, that in some ways a man is a complete human being, but a man and a woman together "complement" each other and form some other kind of complete human being, in which work, money, ambition, an interest in the exterior world are vested in *him*; housewifery, cooking and child care are vested in *her*. So strong is the male chauvinist's image of what the relationship between men and women *should* be that it doesn't matter to him that the reality may be at variance with the image: his wife may dominate him, he may be afraid of his secretary, he may in fact find himself dusting those bookshelves himself, it matters not at all—he simply cannot accept women as "equal" human beings or deal with them on their own merits.

The problem is that the institution of marriage encourages a false view of the outside world. Marriage, as we have developed it in our culture, is hardly integrated into our society at all. It is in fact an attempt to prove, in a suburban house or a cooperative apartment, that we can somehow exist *outside* the changes, the tensions and the frightening pressures of the American reality. Marriage promises stability, despite the fact that one marriage in every four ends in divorce. Effectively, it ends all questions by providing a structure and a rationale for people's lives, thus providing for our age what religious belief provided for the Middle Ages. In this small world of marriage there exists one overriding assumption: that the husband and wife share certain aims, a common interest in *something*, if only survival. In marriage men think of women as essentially *supportive* creatures, learn to treat their demands as tantrums, their hostility as moodiness, their ambition as unnatural. And why not? We have divorced the ideal of marriage from real life to an extraordinary degree, merchandising it, prepackaging it, idealizing it in every magazine and on every television show as a life apart, every home a protected zoo cage from which one member only is allowed to escape every day. Driving me to his home in the suburbs, a businessman told me, "Right here, where we turn off the main road, I begin to breathe. Look at all those lawns, and those houses! You wouldn't know you were an hour away from Manhattan, would you? This is what it's all about." But is it? Can it be? Only a few miles away from his house lies one of the most riot-devastated cities of the United States, there are drug problems in the local schools, the couple who live in the $75,000 home next door have broken up to everyone's surprise, with the wife suddenly flying off to live in the ghetto with an indicted black criminal ("How did she *meet* him?" one local matron asked, with a hint of envy), there is trouble in paradise. But of course it was always there. Did we ever believe seriously in that world of domesticity represented by a small boy standing on a suburban lawn with his smiling mother behind him, under the caption "His wife will buy him T-shirts that won't shrink—why don't you?" in the hope that copper-toned wall-ovens, home saunas, a separate blender for the bar, would protect us from the pains and decisions of living? Yes indeed we did, we staked everything on the notion that man would *give*, woman *receive*, creating together a domestic fortress that would protect us against the outside world, forgetting that no precedent existed for such an attempt, that for most of human history and in most cultures ordinary women have always been deeply involved in the reality of life. While a large part of our population either cannot find work or is doomed to a succession of pointless and ill-paid jobs, our middle-class-oriented technicians are promising us a shorter working day, more "leisure time," recommending that we quickly learn to enjoy a "hobby" in anticipation of that four-day-week to come. But surely if there is one thing America has too much of it is "leisure." Not *enjoyment*, of course, which implies a purpose, but "leisure," the desperate search for some made-up, commercialized fantasy to fill the yawning hours of nothing; Disneylands, with their mechanized, plastic pleasures, the blank, time-filling boredom of television, the "spectator" sports divorced from any desire or ability to exercise oneself, the sad, upper-middle-class women whom one sees in suburban homes, drinking a little too much, laughing a little too loud, the institutionalized hedonism that hangs like a miasma over life, the sad, weary faces of middle-class men at Playboy Clubs, confronting the make chauvinist ideal of captive woman, and finding it empty and barren, a harem without sex, in which women are reduced to the remorseless vulgarity of their surroundings, plastic abjects of vicarious pleasure in a plastic fantasy whose only purpose is profit. The rich have their active pleasures, so do the poor; the middle class remain consumers of a life-style they have sold to themselves, prisoners of the realization of their own dreams.

It is fashionable to pretend that male chauvinism is in some way *primitive*, an instinctive reaction of men that was acquired at some stage of the evolutionary process, perhaps an attitude derived from the institution of marriage itself—in which case, of course, the institution itself must be scrapped. There *is* a kind of male chauvinism that comes from primitive strength, but it is not the kind of make chauvinism that women's liberationists find themselves dealing with in the average working situation. The fears of the modern make chauvinist have their roots in a sense of guilt, the knowledge that one human being has effectively reduced another to a semi-servile status, paying for the sacrifice of the other person's self-fulfillment with certain material comforts and the promise of security which suddenly seem either meaningless or impossible to ensure. Stay at home, look after the children, enjoy the second car, the freezer, the charge accounts, we said, and life will be good, nothing will change, the future is going to be OK, we promise it. But it isn't.

Marriage was supposed to be a "partnership," but a partnership of equals, not a partnership between a producer and a consumer. In primitive societies men and women share the hardships of life together, splitting up the task of survival in whatever way seems best suited to the circumstances. Among the Pygmies of the Congo, who are gatherers of fruit and seeds (and occasional hunters), women and men are equal, share most of the same tasks and live remarkably free from the idea of make chauvinism. In hunting tribes, where man has traditionally been the killer of food by virtue of physical strength (and the fact that he is not incapacitated by pregnancy and the necessity of nursing a baby), women are relegated to domestic concerns, but they are not thought of as being any less important for that: the functions are separate but equal, each has its own dignity, mythology, importance. In tribal life, marriages are based on mutual dependency; the woman's contribution —whether it lies in performing the same tasks or different ones, as among nomadic hunters—is not considered inferior. The primitive tribesman marries (within the definition of that institution in his culture) because marriage creates a unit that enables him—and ultimately his wife and children—to survive in a harsh and hostile world. One man alone cannot survive, even in a tribal community. He needs a home, another pair of hands, a companion, someone to look after him if he is sick or wounded, children to care for him or his fields when he is too old and feeble to do it himself. The same is true of women, therefore they unite, taking on certain responsibilities and obligations, in order to create a unit of survival. Far from divorcing them form society, it is their only way of confronting it successfully.

Life was not very different in the eighteenth, nineteenth and early twentieth centuries. Women may have been relegated by and large to domestic concerns, but these were visibly related to survival, closely interwoven in the fabric of work that made it possible for a family to endure. Men worked, women worked, in different ways, but with the recognition that both were necessary, and with a certain respect for each other that endures today only on small farms and ranches, where the woman's tasks are as necessary for survival as her husband's. Yes, women cooked, sewed, had babies and couldn't vote; but they also looked after the ranch when their husbands were away, preserved food to keep the family through the winter, learned to use a rifle when it was necessary, shared the rigors of life as partners in their own right. Needless to say, among the poor, nothing has changed, except perhaps that the merchandising of the middle-class image in films, on television and in magazines has led men to accept the work of their wives without giving them the respect they once had. The power of the media to promote meaningless ideas has made the easy assumptions of middle-class make chauvinism available to men who couldn't survive without the pay check that their wives bring home every week, and who, fifty years ago, would have treated their wives with a sense of equality that they need no longer feel, exposed as they are to the artificial national assumption that *I Love Lucy* represents the national position of women, flighty, irresponsible, scatterbrained, dependent creatures who couldn't survive for a minute without the common-sense firmness of their husbands.

By placing women in a separate world, without dignity, cut off from the world of work which man made his own, we attempted to live out a fantasy. You cannot get in·your car and journey out to make a living in the world of real threats, ambitions and problems, leaving behind you a microcosm of peace and contentment to which you can return eight hours later, yet that is precisely the fantasy we have sold ourselves as the "natural" order of society. It is one our ancestors, male and female, would have found absurd and unrecognizable. That it has led women to revolt against the artificiality of their position is scarcely surprising; but it has also formed the bundle of resentments, fears and disappointments that we call male chauvinism, the feeling that women took advantage of us, that they got the better part of the bargain and now aren't even grateful for it, that we can never give enough to make them happy, that the price of our relationship with them is the sacrifice of our manhood.

The truth is that men are not very happy with the world they have created, they sense a certain emptiness there, a feeling that still waters run deep in even the most quiet of wives, that women are perhaps disloyal, ungrateful, resentful, that at any moment things are going to explode. We have committed ourselves to a certain notion of what women should be, and the more apparent it becomes that we were wrong, the more necessary it is to pretend that we were right all along, that we can still impose our own order in at least this one area of the world. If we start taking the women in the office seriously, we may have to take our wives seriously, to listen to *their* ideas, accept *their* desire for change. Worse yet, we may have to accept the possibility that women, in searching for new roles and identities beyond the limits that men have imposed on them, may emerge as far stronger and more resilient people than men. Suddenly it is women, not men, who are taking the great risks, leaving their husbands, like Jennifer Skolnik, "to take on the city alone" with four small children, "intent on the big issues—like whether or not you are allowed to boss your own life." Women are beginning to confront life with determination and courage to succeed as individuals, abandoning husbands, homes, sometimes children, refusing alimony, searching for the big issues while men still pride themselves on their mastery of those small issues that suddenly become irrelevant when the wife no longer cares who earns the family money and who decides where the family will go for the vacation because she may be "departing her husband and many children this winter in favor of hitchhiking around the country with a counterculture hammock saleman."(41). If women reject the artifacts of our culture—the conventional marriage, advertising, the inevitability of the domestic role for females, the underlying assumption that what everyone wants at heart is a quiet and protected life

—then men, however chauvinist, will be left as cautious domestic tyrants who have cut themselves off from the possibility of growth and change, eunuchs in every sense but the sexual one. What every man fears is that women may be *living*, while men continue to exist within the conventions they have invented for themselves. Hence the hostility and mild panic that men feel when they read about the coming out of a woman like Jennifer Skolnik. If she can leave her husband, take her four small children to New York (of all places!), find a job and *enjoy* it all, then why are we taking the seven-fourteen into the city for the two-thousandth time, dreaming of a freedom that we can't even admit to ourselves we want because it involves leaving a wife, children, a mortgaged house? We are the prisoners of our homes, our families, they are our prisoners, and now women are opening the prison doors and leaving, when we always thought it was men who wanted to escape.

"I don't know," one male chauvinist said to me wistfully, as we walked down Fifth Avenue together one warm evening in the early spring, "I look at all these women, and I read about women's liberation, and it seems to me they're having a better time than I am. I mean, I'm looking at *them*, but are they looking at me? Somebody once told me that when he died he wanted to be able to say, 'I've made a lot of money and I've slept with a lot of women,' and that's always made sense to me, but I can't get used to the idea that a woman might say, 'I've done just what I wanted and I've slept with a lot of *men*.' The whole game was always hunting, and the tougher it was to bring in a skin, the more fun you got out of it. Now women are out there hunting too, and it's not the same. Sometimes you used to have to *pretend* they were equals, but now a lot of them are equal, they know who they are. I can laugh at most of women's liberation, but what really throws me is this feeling that women are having more *fun*, that they're beginning to do what they want to do, and getting more pleasure out of it than I get out of what I do."

Behind the male chauvinist's supercilious and patroniz-
ing attitude toward "all the little girls getting together"
lies real fear, the fear that we may no longer be able to
impose upon women our vision of ourselves as men.
Most men do not control their wives, cannot, possibly
don't even want to. Oh yes, they exert as a rule a kind of
spurious financial control, but despite the arguments of
the radical feminists woman's domestic role gives her
far more opportunities for exerting control over domestic decisions than a man, and while it is certainly true
that it is the man who goes out and earns the money in
the average American marriage, it is notorious that
women play the decisive role in determining how that
money will be spent. What men want in marriage is not
power so much as "face," in the Oriental sense. A
woman may dominate a man in any number of ways,
provided she allows him to play the dominant role in
public, and the surest way for a man to lose prestige
among his peers still remains losing an argument with
his wife in public.

The price of male chauvinism is terrible confusion;
the male chauvinist is trying to combine in one person so
many contradictory attitudes toward women that he can
only end by fearing and hating them. A powerful and
successful speculator I know is a good example of these
contradictions. When he appears in public with his wife,
he makes it quite clear that he is the boss, and in private
conversations he emphasizes that his is an "old-
fashioned" marriage. "I make the money, and I don't
put up with any nonsense. Somebody has to make decisions, and it's my job to make them." One visit to his
home is enough to convince any observer that this is a fa-
cade; it is quite obvious that he treads cautiously, stum-
bling around his house as if he didn't really live there,
as if everything in it, furniture, pictures, kitchen appli-
ances, children even, were extensions of his wife's
personality, to be treated with extreme care and delicacy.
Though inclined to make fun of his wife when he's with
other men ("She can't balance a checkbook to save her
life, all she needs to make her happy is a charge account,

she's terrific with children, but you know, women are a lot more *like* children than men are, they understand them better, they have more patience"), he can switch instantly to her defense, and even use her as his reason for doing something ("If I told my wife I'd said yes to a deal like this she'd laugh her head off, she'd say, What kind of a man are you anyway?"). He grimaces and winks at his young secretary while speaking to his wife on the telephone (I'm not taking any of this seriously, he is implying, it's just my wife talking, gab, gab, gab, that's the way wives are), then sends her out into the streets on a hot July afternoon to pick up theater tickets for the very same woman he's just been making fun of. A man I know has a wife who paints; he makes ritual fun of her efforts when he's with his friends and colleagues (for no man is supposed to take woman's occupations seriously), but when she has an exhibition, he dragoons every passing acquaintance into going to the exhibit, and stands by the same paintings he has made fun of, saying, "Aren't they great? Isn't she great?"

What is wrong with us that we are willing to settle for such a mass of contradictory attitudes in the one area of life where we should expect consistency? And how can men be expected to have a consistent attitude toward woman—her needs, her role, her ambitions—when their feelings about women are both inconsistent and self-serving? Most men do not see women as fellow human beings at all; they merely have a set of responses toward the idea of women in various roles, from which they can pick and choose the one that seems most appropriate in any given circumstance: domination, submission, sexual passion, patience, fatherly advice, fear, contempt, sentimental adulation. The same man can, within twenty-four hours, shout at his secretary, make a show of negotiating a contract with a woman lawyer on equal terms, make fun of the same women to his colleagues, appear at a party with his wife on his arm, looking strong and protective, and return home listening to her criticize him for behaving like an idiot at the party. Since all these responses, attitudes and postures are constantly getting crossed—fatherly interest serving as a cover-up for lust, a public attitude of domination concealing a private posture of submission, rage at one's secretary compensating for surrender to one's wife—men are inclined to live in a morass of conflicting umpulses when it comes to women, however clear-minded they may be about politics, business or technology. "Women," wrote Virginia Woolf, "have served all these centuries as looking glasses possessing the power of reflecting the figure of man at twice its natural size." Yes, men use women as mirrors, but the worst of this is not just that it has reduced women to "looking glasses," it has reduced men to creatures who can only define themselves by means of women. And unfortunately for men the mirrory is like the ones in an amusement park that distort and split up the image, showing us to ourselves as a giant with a dwarf's head, or as a pygmy with a gorilla's torso.

Marriage at least serves one purpose: it gives men the chance to come to terms with at least *one* woman. In marriage a man senses the possibility of reducing an infinite problem to finite proportions, of isolating at least one member of this capricious and mysterious species in the hope that this controlled laboratory experiment will either answer his questions or provide a good reason for not asking them. Yet obstinately, women remain as unfathomable as they were for Sigmund Freud ("The great question that has never been answered, and which I have not yet been able to answer despite my thirty years of research into the feminine soul, is: What does a woman want?"). Isolate a woman, reduce her contacts with the outside world, sleep with her on an exclusive basis, share in the business of living, of procreating, and perhaps we will discover what it is that a woman wants, more to the point what she *is*. But no answers are forthcoming so long as we continue to assume that she is radically different and mysterious, so long as we cling to the notion that her biology makes her mind, her "soul" (to use Freud's somewhat ambiguous word) somehow different from our own. If it is different, after all, it must either be inferior or superior, and a large part of what passes for social custom and business convention in our world is in fact a defense set up to convince man that it is he who is superior and she who is limited. The notion that "her" limits are our own is seldom considered. And if we can't find the answer to Sigmund Freud's question, we can always take refuge in the question itself, in the notion that women are after all possessed of some separate sensibility, that there isn't any possibility of "understanding" them in the first place, that by definition they represent a kind of monstrous puzzle that God has created for men to wrestle with hopelessly. We can even be proud of *not* understanding them, for the failure to understand women is the ultimate proof of our masculinity. It is not surprising that Ira Levin, the author of *Rosemary's Baby*, should have chosen as his new horror story the theme of male chauvinism, rightly perceiving that it is a form of modern witchcraft and superstition. In *The Stepford Wives*, Levin shows us a suburban community that seems emptily familiar and unexceptional. A young couple moves there; she is a talented photographer, mildly "liberated," he is a quiet, "reasonable" man. She soon finds that the women around her are remarkably submissive, addicted to housework, unwilling to express an opinion about anything. When Joanna invites her next-door neighbor, Carol, over for a cup of coffee, she refuses, saying, "Thanks, I'd like to, but I have to wax the family room tonight . . . I've put it off too long as it is. It's all over scuff marks . . . There's always something or other that has to be done. You know how it is. I have to finish the kitchen now."

Gradually, Joanna thinks she has discovered that the men of the community have perfected a way of turning their wives into robots, that there is a conspiracy to make each woman into a perfect replica of the male chauvinist husband ideal. As Joanna says, complimenting the owner of the local drugstore, "You have a lovely wife. Pretty, helpful, submissive to her lord and master; you're a lucky man." "I know," he replies.

In the end Joanna comes to realize that her husband is part of the conspiracy, that whatever is being done is going to be done to her too, and though she fights it, she is caught. When a friend asks her, in the supermarket, how her work is coming along, Joanna replies, "I don't do much photography any more . . . I wasn't especially talented, and I was wasting a lot of time I really have better uses for . . . Housework's enough for me. I used to feel I had to have other interests, but I'm more at ease with myself now. I'm much happier too, and so is my family. That's what counts, isn't it?" She has been turned into a robot too.

There is more significance in this than would at first appear, for both Ira Levin's successes represent a kind of horror-myth portrayal of male chauvinism. In *Rosemary's Baby*, a husband sells his wife to the Devil to further his career as an actor, in *The Stepford Wives*, the ultimate fantasy of male chauvinism is enacted, the recognition that the domestic world men created to enclose women is so important to them as a symbol of power that it need no longer be shared or enjoyed—it is sufficient that it continue to exist!

As a psychoanalyst told me, "I have to spend hours breaking through my (male) patients' defenses. They tell me about their jobs, their houses, the money they make, everything they've done for their families. I have to tell them, 'Look, I'm not interested in any of this, I don't care how much your house cost, or about the trip to Europe you took your wife on, you wouldn't be here if you hadn't discovered that your wife doesn't give a damn about any of that, and you have to learn that you don't give a damn either. I don't care how important you are, to me you're a man whose wife thinks he's no good in bed, and it's no good clinging to the $150,000 house as if that were the answer to everything, because if you don't learn to treat her as a person, she will walk out that $150,000 front door, get in her Mercury Cougar convertible, and go off to someone who's alive.' The first step in analysis, for me, is teaching men humility, making them understand that it doesn't matter how well they function as businessmen, they have to function as bodies, as people, as lovers. Success in one area doesn't compensate for deficiency in another. I've seen successful men, with male chauvinist attitudes, sit here and weep because their wives are threatening to leave, and most of them say *How could she do this to me?* Well, she did it to him because he isn't a *person* any more, because he's afraid of feeling, living. All he wants is security. And when women begin to think about themselves, the first thing they realize is what we all know: in an existential world there isn't any security, and there isn't any way a woman can provide security for someone else. As one woman said to me, 'I can't be a liberated woman and his mother and purpose in life at the same time. I refuse to be a living proof that *his* life makes sense. Maybe nobody's does.' "

Men cling to their hope that somebody else will make sense of their lives, trusting in Theodor Reik's dictum that "Women in general want to be loved for what they are and men for what they accomplish." Accomplish enough and we will be loved, hence the propensity of the domestic male chauvinist to accomplish a great deal, to pour into his work a disproportionate amount of psychic energy. Anything is better than admitting that life is a question of feeling, that nobody can guarantee us anything, that we cannot demand of another human being that she cut herself off from life to prove to us that we have the capacity, like small gods, to impose order and security in one small corner of the universe.

Meanwhile, a recent survey revealed that the majority of women don't object to moving to further their husband's careers "even if it causes them some pain," and pointed out that in such corporate moves the responsibility for moving is usually the wife's—she is "the key person in establishing the home and making the move successful."(42) A group of executives' wives—whose attitude might best be described as "loyalist," as opposed to "liberated"—were quoted recently on the benefits of being a housewife. "As an executive wife, you don't pursue your own personal life as much as a career woman would," said Mrs. Graham J. Morgan (wife of the chairman of

the board of the U.S. Gypsum Company). "You gear
yourself to your husband's life." Another wife of a successful corporation executive, who has to be "a ray of
sunshine" at breakfast because her husband "gets a corporate look on his face at dawn" reported that her husband expects her to be "useful, punctual, efficient, pleasant, alert and healthy. He has no patience with the op-
posites of any of these. He wants me to be feminine, to
have a sense of humor without being witty and not to be
emphatic."(43)

There is a slightly hallucinating quality to this litany,
which is not to deny its sincerity. It sounds like something that the husbands of *The Stepford Wives* might
have invented as a credo. "Useful" implies that the husband defines his wife's use, that she's a functional object
at his service. "Alert" is a word that is usually applied
to guard dogs and horses, rather than the woman one
supposedly loves. "Healthy"? Well, of course we want
those we love to be healthy, but the marriage sacrament
itself, outdated as it may be in some respects, is quite ex-
plicit about "sickness and health," and it seems a bit extreme to demand health of one's wife—though presumably this kind of nonhuman freedom from sickness could
be programmed into the female robots of Ira Levin's
imagination. "A sense of humor without being witty"
perfectly expresses the male chauvinist attitude that
women can be amusing, if they're capable of amusing us,
but must never be witty or clever, which might be uncomfortable or ego-destroying to men. ("If I'd wanted
to marry a Dorothy Parker, I'd have married one," a
friend of mine told his wife, a former Bennington girl
with a quick wit and a sharp tongue, who sensibly took
her wit and her child to San Francisco, from whence she
wrote, "Despite my reputation for being the serpent's
tooth of Riverdale, I'm really a perfectly loving person.
It takes a real background of romanticism and masochism to make a good cynic, but men automatically assume
a cynical wife is a disaffected one. When I told him that
a girl can have enough of bed and bored, and he got

angry instead of laughing, I thought to myself, I am *not* a monster, and got out.")

On the other hand, Mrs. Lee Allen Muench, the wife of the technical director of the General Motors Technical Center, commented, during a conference of a hundred thirty wives whose husbands earn more than $25,000 a year (in most cases *much* more): "I just feel appreciated by my husband. That's what enables me to function as a person. Oh, I'm taken for granted like most wives. But once in a while he says and does something that makes me feel important. I get my satisfaction from looking good in his eyes and not anyone else's." Clearly the extreme measures taken by Ira Levin's husbands are not by any means always necessary, particularly since the hundred thirty ladies were given a lecture by the manager of mining at the Ford Motor Company, who told them—a *deux ex machina* in more ways than one—that if an executive wife wanted outside interests "she should take painting, music, go to school but under no circumstances take a job." He added that an executive wife should "watch her figure and don't nag."(44)

One would like to feel that there is some misunderstanding here, that this doesn't really represent a serious view of life, but it does. A woman publishing executive whose success is considerable, remarks that her husband never lets her go out at night. "What do you mean," he asked, "I never let you go anywhere? I let you go to work, don't I?" (Needless to say, male chauvinism at the office does not disturb her unduly—she expects it, hardly even notices it. *His* work is important, meaningful, a part of the universe; *hers* is an aberration, a whim to be humored, like eating pickles during pregnancy.)

The authors of *Open Marriage,* George and Nena O'Neill, point out that "both persons have to put something (into a marriage)." They recommend "undependent living," individual freedom, flexible roles, mutual trust, "the combined, cooperative action of two people working in concert, where, as one person grows, he benefits and also gives the other partner an assist in her growth and vice versa."(45) But this is precisely what the male chauvinist cannot accept. He refuses to grow, refuses to see life as a fluid and changing state, he wants to have one toehold chiseled for him in the rock face of eternity. As one male participant in a discussion of women's liberation said, "Nancy has an idea she thinks is fantastic. She keeps bringing it up every few months: Let's have one month where you do all my jobs and I do all your jobs. Now on the face of it, that sounds like a terrific Women's Lib kind of thing. To me it represents hell because I can tell you what would happen in that month. Nancy, who is an expert cook, would be giving way to me and I would be serving things like Swanson's TV dinners at night, heating up a lot of macaroni, so we'd be eating——. I take, I think, rather splendid care of our bills and bill-paying. Nancy is generally overdrawn at the bank and thinks that I think it is cute. I don't. But she thinks I think so and I certainly can't change her. So if she took over the bills we'd be in bad shape. We'd lose all our credit. But my balking makes me a male chauvinist pig, right?"

Alas, *right!* Why *can't* he learn to cook decently, and if he can't what is wrong with eating macaroni, or alternating the cooking by days so that one good dinner is followed by a TV dinner? And what's so important about food anyway, in comparison to finding a new and more interesting way to live together? As to the bills, surely a little confusion is a small price to pay for an experiment that might, after all, convince Nancy that it isn't "cute" to be overdrawn at the bank? Poor Nancy. When it comes to her sexual fantasies, her loving husband says, "Nancy claims that she has not told anyone the full fantasy—and her only sex fantasy since the age of eleven—and principally the broad outlines are that she is . . . people rip her clothes off . .. I think it's a fairly universal woman's fantasy to be raped, to be used as a sexual object, and so on." (46)

There you have it: they see themselves as "sex objects," their fantasy is rape, and if that's the way they see themselves, what's the point of trying to treat them differently? Men are still desperately looking for the small concessions that will allow them to preserve their greater illusions, unable to face a life that has to be lived, ultimately, among equals, in which the possession of a penis does not serve as a substitute for brains, charm or originality, in which no status attaches to it by divine right, in which money and material objects can no longer be used as weapons to guard a false view of the world, to protect us against the demons. One young woman who has recently gone back to work after marriage told me, "You have to feel what it's like to make your own money and not have to depend on someone, even if it's someone you love. It's the root of women's liberation. I think I'm badly treated at the office, yes, because I'm attractive and young, and I get a lot of fatherly protection that I don't really need and that I have to fight to prevent myself accepting, because it's easier to accept. And at home, we have this system in which we split up all the bills, and each of us writes out a check for one half of whatever it is, and that *works*, but still my husband thinks of things as being *his*, even when I've paid for my half of whatever it is. We bought a camera, and when I wanted to take it to the beach, he said, 'Listen, don't do that, you might lose it.' A year ago I'd have accepted that, but not any more. It's ours, if I lose it, I'm responsible, and why would I be any more likely to lose it than he is? He thinks women's liberation is Ti-Grace Atkinson, or Jill Johnston, a whole big sexual thing, total change right now, but it isn't. It's what we're doing, and we're making it work. I'm not all that 'liberated' myself. I have sexual inhibitions, I'm attracted to other men, and I don't have the courage to do anything about it, and maybe it's just as well, I don't know. And I'm not involved in politics. But I do know that right here, in this life, right now, I'm going to be equal in the relationship I've chosen, I won't accept anything less. And once I've made that work, I'm going to go to work on *this* office, because if my husband can learn that I'm a person and not an extension of what he wants to do, then the men here can learn the same thing

about me and my work, even if they're still treating
their wives like second-class citizens. I took the first step
yesterday, when I told a senior executive, very politely,
'It's my decision. I made it. I'm sticking to it.' He said,
'I never figured you for a women's libber.' And I told
him, 'I'm not one. Try not thinking of me as a woman
at all, try thinking of me as somebody who knows how to
do this job.' And he said, 'To me you'll always be a
woman.' And do you know what? He meant it as a compliment! *That's* male chauvinism!"

SEVEN

"Little did we realize [in creating the research staff] that we were inaugurating a modern female priesthood, the veritable vestal virgins whom levitous writers cajole in vain, and managing editors learn humbly to appease."
— Henry Luce, co-founder of Time magazine, at a
dinner celebrating its twentieth anniversary

. . . A woman with a B.A. degree in English, a Masters degree in journalism, and at least six years of prior journalistic experience in business fields, was hired as a researcher and after six years is still a researcher.
— From a complaint filed by Louis J. Lefkowitz,
Attorney General of New York State,
and certain women employees of Time, Inc.

"OK for researchers, but maybe we should have a separate category for scenery-brighteners . . ."
— Executive discussing a complaint
about job categories on a major magazine

THE REVOLT OF WOMEN

I've just picked up a friend at LaGuardia airport, and we're sitting in the chill of an air-conditioned car while she gives me the late-night story of the Democratic National Convention. Tracy has lost her luggage, been invited to what sounds like a postnomination orgy, sampled Wolfie's chocolate cheesecake, gone without sleep for days and nights, been treated as a celebrity because she writes, and as a power because—yes, of all things— *she's a woman.* "You can't believe what it was like," she says, "I understood for the first time how men *feel* about power. Women used to go to conventions as a backdrop or as nonentities or as hookers, they weren't in on the power games, they didn't know what it's like. Talk about multiple orgasm! Wow! Once you're there and people know who you are, and you're in the game, you find out what it is that men have been keeping to themselves all these centuries, and it's a lot better than having babies."

Already I feel an outsider, as Tracy, exhausted from excitement and lack of sleep, conscious as she had never been before of the power that comes from solidarity, plunges from anecdote to anecdote, high on the euphoria of her own experiences, remembering that Jane O'Reilly of *MS* hired a Harley Davidson motorcycle with a bearded chopper freak as her driver to rush from one headquarters to another in Miami, a kind of journalistic easy rider, retelling the triumphs of Gloria Steinem—the celebrity of the convention—describing how the women forced the pols to talk about such hitherto-forbidden subjects as abortion, filling me in on the obscure details of how they caucused and fought like a bunch of old-time labor leaders, but with a good deal more clout, savvy and muscle than the old-time labor leaders themselves turned out to have in the end . . .

"The greatest thrill of my life was realizing that women could form a bloc, a constituency, that we could make people listen to us as women and not just on subjects that interest women either. Going to the Democratic National Convention in Miami was a mind-opener. All my life I'd read about politicians listening to 'labor' or 'the farm vote,' and suddenly here they were listening to 'women'! We had to learn how to get together for a purpose, how to use the system, when to ignore it, how to use power and pressure. And once you understand power, you understand the whole game, it isn't a mystery any more. For the first time, we weren't outsiders. "We can do *anything*," Tracy says, sweeping her hand toward the sleeping housewives of Queens. "Women can hack it."

Indeed they can, for the male chauvinist is in a weaker position than has generally been assumed. With a few exceptions, such as the International Ladies Garment Workers' Union, most unions have paid comparatively little attention to the problems of women, and most women workers who do in fact hold union membership are still represented by men. There is no way for women to bring their collective force to bear on management, a situation compounded by the fact that a very large percentage of working women are employed in businesses that aren't organized in the first place. The woman office worker, whether a secretary or an executive, is dealing with men who aren't generally accustomed to the pressures of collective bargaining, indeed have no experience of it. "Salaries are an individual thing," one businessman told me, "we don't give out figures, and we don't think you can make rules about it—some people are worth more than others, and that's all there is to it." But this attitude, common to most office management, is out of step with the practice of industry the Civil Service and most large service institutions. Men who make more than $20,000 a year negotiate for themselves; those who make less than $15,000 are generally organized and represented. The vast majority of women still work in a system of paternalism that more or less guarantees them the lowest possible salary for any given job.

Executives who in certain circumstances might sit down to a session of collective bargaining with a union leader representing five thousand truck drivers or lathe operators still react in horror and outrage at the notion that two young secretaries might even be *discussing* their salaries together. Conspiracy! No woman is supposed to know what another woman is making, money is a subject we don't talk about, comparisons are odious, as Nanny used to say. But why? When policemen want a raise, the negotiations are on the front page of *The New York Times*; nobody is embarrassed. When senior executives get a raise, it's published in the annual report; nobody is ashamed. But in most offices, raises are given to women with grim warnings: Don't tell anybody, don't talk about it. No subject is more secret than the list of salaries and the names of those who got raises, each of whom is invariably pledged to secrecy with the result that people must always try to guess what their colleagues are making, a source of constant interoffice *Angst*. One woman may get a raise, but there is no opportunity for a *group* of women to act together, and any attempt on their part to do so would be treated in most places of business as a kind of mutiny. A system which benefits men above a certain salary level, since they are free to bargain for salaries on an individual basis, works invariably to the disadvantage of most working women, who have comparatively little leverage to exert, and who are usually spoken for, rather than given an opportunity to speak for themselves.

To many men of course women's liberation has come as a kind of personal liberation, making it possible to admit at last that women are in fact the enemy, justifying the release of hostilities that were until quite recently politely repressed or denied. The advent of one determined, radical woman's liberationist in an office often unleashes a kind of reign of terror in which all women are forced to pay the price for one woman's convictions. It is an index of men's sensitivity on the subject that a very small number of women, usually young and in subordinate positions, can cause such enormous eruptions of passion and self-justification in the largest of corporations. Like the rumors of revolt in the slave quarters, the first signs of women's liberation provoke instant fear of some larger catastrophe, throwing into doubt the whole structure of a business and of man's place in it. Women have managed, almost by accident, to associate themselves in men's minds with the riots and streets disorders of other civil rights movements, while at the same time making their issue a media concern on a national scale. No man can resist a public issue, even when it is personified in a woman, and the most determined male chauvinist is unable to ignore what he is being told about in every newspaper and magazine. It is odd that radical women have never thought of adopting the methods of other radical groups—a determined group of women could theoretically sabotage the operations of any corporation—but luckily for them, they don't have to. Men already fear them in a deep private sense, and nothing in their lives has prepared them for any real confrontation with women over substantive issues. It is easy to ignore the problems of the blacks, since most businessmen don't after all go home to the ghetto, but most of us do go home to wives, daughters, women we love and live with in one way or another, and the effect is to make men increasingly insecure about their prerogatives—once they allow themselves to *listen*, their curiosity tends to make them vulnerable to liberationist pressure. But, as every woman knows, listening is not enough. When women's lib first hit the office, there was a rash of confrontations, ranging from women's strikes, to locking the editor of *The Ladies Home Journal* up in his own office, to holding endless meetings that paralyzed work and brought the senior executives down to find out what was going on.

But just at the moment when men were beginning to feel that the real problems of job discrimination against women would have to be faced and solved, women offered men a perfect escape. The enormous success of Kate Millett and Germaine Greer can be partly explained by the fact that men were at last being presented with a series of issues and problems that were largely concerned with biology, theory, equality on the existential plane. What a relief to be able to forget about the question of why all the copy editors (salary $150 a week) were women, and all the editors (salaries $15,000 a year and up) were men, and involve oneself in the larger issues of clitoral vs. vaginal orgasm, of woman's identity, of women as sexual objects. Men turned with delight toward the stars of women's liberation, overjoyed to find the movement descending into discussions about lesbianism rather than money. It was suddenly possible to free oneself of guilt by reading *The Female Eunuch* and watching Germaine Greer on television—just as millions of Americans were delighted to admire and applaud Martin Luther King while working hard to prevent a Negro family from moving in next door and reducing property values. The two things were simply not seen as congruent, as being in any way connected. The heat was off.

It's a national failing, we all know, that Americans

prefer personalities to issues, and women's liberation presented us with a few hugely successful and provocative personalities whom it was possible to admire precisely because they weren't working women in any ordinary sense, or wives, or people who had, at least for the moment, a primary interest in the day-to-day problems of work and marriage that is the real area of men's fears and women's concerns. Men could now say, "I'm in favor of women's liberation" and *mean* it—and why not if it was going to lead to a relationship with some Germaine Greer/Gloria Steinem-like figure, a tall, beautiful woman who was equal, strong-minded, independent, exciting to be with and listen to. And if men were in favor of women's liberation, as it suddenly presented itself, in the form of an intellectual *Playboy* foldout of the mind and spirit, with promises of a franker approach toward sex—of, if not endless sex, then endless discussions about sex—then they no longer had to feel guilty about paying their secretaries $125 a week or not promoting them to jobs they deserved. What the hell, they would have promoted Germaine Greer to anything she wanted to be—but my secretary isn't Germaine, for Christ's sake! Women had providentially proved what men always believed: that you succeeded out of some inner reservoir of strength and talent, together with a lot of luck and *chutzpa*, and that a woman could succeed as a woman's liberationist just the way that men succeeded as brokers, publishers, politicians, bankers and generals, yes, even as best-selling novelists, and if they could succeed that way, as equals, then what was all the talk of discrimination about—look at Germaine, for the love of God, show me where there's any discrimination against her! And in the glow of several million television screens, buried by the weight of words from *The Dick Cavett Show, Today, Tonight, The David Frost Show*, driven out of men's consciousness by the heavy exploration of sexual equality, of artifical insemination, of Freudian chauvinism, of Woman's Fate, the practical applications of women's liberation unexpectedly died. Men took a quantum leap forward to grapple with the subject of women in psychological and sexual terms, leaving the question of work and salary behind them, a dull reality which offered no fuel for flights of fantasy, no scope for analytic confessions, no way to make large concessions and admissions of guilt without having to pay for them in terms of hard cash and a surrender of real power and authority.

In this age of liberation the subject of money remains as shrouded in euphemism and polite evasions as sex used to be. It's not just that women usually end up negotiating with men on a one-to-one basis, without the clout to get what they want, or that men disarm them by admitting beforehand that women are badly paid. In some cases women suffer the ultimate humiliation: their salaries are determined by the status of the man they work for. In many companies, secretaries are paid according to the title of their boss, an arrangement that makes them something like a chattel and removes them completely from any kind of merit system. X, a department manager, is authorized to offer $125 a week to his secretary, while Z, a vice-president, is authorized to go to $140, and that's it. X's secretary may be bright, ambitious and hard-working, but nothing she does will earn her more money; while Z's secretary may be shiftless and only holding on to her job because she fills some neurotic or sexual need on the part of the man she works for. No matter. Under this system, the woman is made into an extension of the man. Even in companies where this is not the case, women usually have to go through a complex series of male intermediaries to make known their demands about money, always kept at several removes from the area of decision, knowing their claims will be filtered through men's own needs, feelings and positions in the hierarchy, seldom informed about what is being done to or for other women. So far as possible, management insulates itself from women and discourages any collective spirit.

"You learn quickly," one woman told me. "I went to my boss, a nice man, I thought, and told him that I wasn't being paid enough, and he agreed with me, and promised to take it up at the annual review. And he did, but I found out later, from someone else, that he decided his own raise was more important than mine, and when the management people started to say, 'Well OK, this may be justified, but you have to be a big boy about these things, you can't have everything you want,' he just backed down on my behalf. It makes me furious. All the men around here talk big about money, they run up huge expense accounts, spend fortunes on all kinds of silly projects, and when a woman comes to them and asks for ten or twenty dollars more, suddenly they're full of lectures about the profit picture, and about how bad business is. It's always the same. I overheard a man say the other day, 'Listen, I don't think he's the right man for the job either, but we've got him, and until we fire him we have to pay him a decent salary for a man. So give him another two. It's the decent thing to do.' But whoever things of doing the 'decent' thing for a woman? Men behave as if money were a kind of masculine special concern, as if every man were a potential husband and father of three children, even when he's a bachelor, and every woman were being supported by someone. It's a system, for God's sake. Men try to attach women to a man, and make *him* responsible for her. When he says 'No,' there isn't anywhere she can turn to. It's all on a personal level, as if we were children trying to get an extra fifty cents allowance."

The power of men is in direct proportion to their ability to separate women and keep them in dependent positions at arm's length from the workings of the system. Divided, women are inclined to look upon each other with a certain amount of suspicion. Yet there are signs that women are beginning to recognize just what can be accomplished by forming a bloc, by presenting a united front over issues of pay and position. It's uphill work— business isn't geared to collective demands, if for no other reason than that most men in higher positions have nothing to gain from collective bargaining of any kind. What works well for a senior corporation executive, who perhaps lunches with the president of the company once a week, doesn't work at all for a young woman who has never even met the president. *His* lobbying can be done in a quiet and effective way, aimed directly at the point of decision; *her* lobbying can only be effective if she pushes hard, inevitably creating hostility in the men who make the decisions.

Half of the traditions on which male chauvinism in the office is based are either illegal or maintained only because nobody has ever challenged them, except possibly a single, obstreperous individual. A perfect example of what can be done is the Time-Life *affaire*, where a group of women decided to take their complaints to the State Attorney General, breaking the unwritten law of business that all disputes should be kept "within the family," where they can of course be treated as family affairs, which is to say buried.

In the first place, you have to picture Time, Inc., a world in itself, where small differences in status count for a great deal, and in which, as in so many predominantly WASP institutions, traditions have spawned and taken hold almost overnight, so that the rules, regulations and especially the *habits* of Time, Inc., have acquired in a few decades the sacrosanct quality that social behavior had at Yale during the founders' undergraduate days. Like many large organizations—magazines, brokerage houses, investment bankers—Time, Inc., was, in a sense, an extension of an Ivy League university, which explains the tendency to rely on college men of a certain kind ("generalists," which is to say people who don't know much about anything), the tendency not to take women seriously (serious women don't need to work for a living)—such organizations as these have simply been fixed in the mental climate of Yale or Princeton in about 1925, or at any rate before the Crash and the War, and no amount of modernity, success or new blood ever quite succeeds in changing their basic nature. (I don't wish to get into a racial argument as well as a sexual one, but it is my experience that there exists a considerable difference in feeling between organizations that are primordially WASP and those that are not. From an employee's point of view, NBC has always seemed to an outsider to be a better place to work than CBS, not because General Sarnoff was necessarily a nicer man than Mr. Paley, but rather because there is something about WASP ownership than produces rigidity, fixed hierarchies and a lack of flexibility and sense of humor. One need only remember the famous opening of CBS's new building on Sixth Avenue, and all the complicated rules about where secretaries were to put their pencils, the committees whose permission had to be obtained before the occupant of an office could put a family photograph on his or her desk, the attempt to make the office an *institution*, rather than simply a place where people work for a specific purpose. Similar differences in tone and feeling were reported to have existed between *The New York Times* and the WASP-owned New York *Herald-Tribune*. WASP organizations tend to be run like WASP institutions, in the spirit of the Puritan ethic; non-WASP organizations, however large, tend to be run like families, domineering rather than hierarchical. This is an important distinction for women. In the former kind of office, women do best to use the rules and regulations, that is, to make men live up to them or change them by forming committees; in the latter kind of office, it is more effective to behave like a member of the family—drama, tears, rage and an appeal to personal justice are likely to be more effective, whereas forming a committee would seem like a hostile and treacherous act.)

You also have to understand that Time, Inc., is not exactly a normal business office: it was founded by two young men who took themselves, the world and their magazine seriously, and who believed, at least in Henry Luce's case, in *writers*, by which was meant people who could write a story without being "reporters"—the ideal *Time* story being something like a good, informative term paper from a literate but not too literary Yale undergraduate of Luce's time. Despite the elephantine growth of Time, Inc., and its early commitment to profit and product, the organization is founded on a kind of instinctive feeling that creativity is vital to the company's well-being, which has given rise to a remarkable combination of personal freedom and rigid editorial control epitomized by the necessity of rewriting everything endlessly at the direction of a whole pyramid of editors and management personnel). Time, Inc., was always more than a business; it was a *cause*, propagandizing with evangelical fervor an upper-middle-class, American, male WASP view of the world. Women were interesting only if they were Clare Boothe Luce or Mme. Chiang Kai-shek, or if they had very special talent, like Margaret Bourke-White, the photographer (about whom one staff member says, "Sure she was good, but how many women photographers have there been since then? Damned few! The fact that she was a woman gave her a special status, but it didn't rub off on other women, any more than Clare Boothe Luce's did"). On a practical working level, they were at once protected and exploited. The stress of working to a weekly deadline made Luce's magazines exciting places to be, especially for young women who could pretend that their basically secretarial jobs were somehow more dramatic than they would have seemed in a more mundane office, and the dinners served to the staff on the evenings when *Time* or *Life* went to press, the necessity for working long hours, the opportunities for men to stay late, all gave Time-Life in its lush heyday some notoriety (and status) as a place in which office sex and office drinking were thought to be well above average—though the difficulty a woman faced then in getting promoted to more responsible work could be seen as further proof that sexual liberation in the office merely serves to keep women in their places. At the same time, there was a spirit of protective paternalism that was unique to Time-Life; as one woman said, "We were told that we couldn't do, wouldn't *want* to do, certain jobs because they would expose us to risks, like flying to Chicago in the middle of the night. God forbid, they would say, that one of 'our girls' should get molested or raped . . . We were always *their* girls. That's why we attracted so many college girls from middle-class families. Once you were in, you realized that it was the tradition, if not the policy, to hire only good-looking women, so you had this peculiar sense of equality in most departments, because a good-looking chick *rates*, gets attention. It takes a while to realize that's *all* you're going to get! There was this whole legend about sex, some of it's true, I admit, but at the same time it was 'respectable' work, it seemed like an extension of college. You felt *safe*, and you knew the company wanted you to be safe. Of course all that is gone, and the management never even noticed it was going. The women who work there live in New York City, for God's sake! They aren't safe and they know it, and they don't care. The woman who used to work in the office next to mine was on drugs for a long time, *heavy* drugs, but she used to bicycle in every morning, throw her long blond hair out of her eyes, and get to work. All these management cats used to come by and treat her as if she was Sally Co-Ed, and when they left, she'd turn to me and wink, then go back to work. You need to be a little tough to get by in this city, and if you can make it, you begin to look around you at the place you're working in, and say, 'Hey, I didn't come here to spend six or seven years as if I were still on campus, fending off passes from guys and seeing them get all the credit for my work, and all the money.' The women who worked here before us accepted the limitations of being a woman in a man's hierarchy, took it for granted that the *serious* stuff was decided by men. Time-Life offered them a personal freedom, at the price of whatever ambition they might have had. But we've *got* personal freedom on the outside; it's not such a big deal to us to sit in Hurley's with a couple of drunken executives on the make, having a drink after the book has closed. I came here out of the Peace Movement, and I hassled my way around the city on not too much money at all, and I wasn't hung up about sex, and when I'd done my time and gotten a few pats on the behind for thanks, I said to myself, 'OK, this has got to change!' "

And change things did. In 1970 a small group of women drew up a list of demands to present to the company. These demands differed from one division to another, since certain of the magazines, *Sports Illustrated* and *Fortune,* are not weeklies and have different problems and organizations from those at *Time* or *Life.* Still, the basic preliminary demands the women agreed upon at one such meeting are fairly representative of the sort of things they were all determined to change—

(1) A more open and flexible policy of recruiting and training people . . . without reference to sex.

(2) Referrals from the personnel department shall not be made on the basis of sex. The personnel department shall no longer maintain separate staffs and facilities for interviewing male and female applicants and employees . . .

(3) Job categories shall all have a substantial balance of men and women.

(4) Implementation of this program shall not be grounds for laying off any current employees.

(5) Equal pay, equal job title, and equal recognition shall be given for equal work . . .

(6) A committee shall be established to monitor progress in eliminating sex discrimination at Time, Inc.

(7) In each division of the company, a regular committee shall be created to hear all complaints about sex discrimination. Collectively or individually they shall make a report on such complaints to the staff and the Attorney General's Office.

(8) In each division this committee shall also consider changes in job structure, with a view to dividing up these categories or rearranging them so that job levels and salaries (A) clearly reflect the actual distribution of work being done; (B) create a ladder of training and mobility within the division.

(9) To enable women to pursue professions within the company and not to exclude them from responsible jobs because they are mothers, we ask that

Time extend the present maternity leave in the following manner:

(A) Employees, married or unmarried, working for the company from ten months to two years shall receive six months of maternity leave and all medical benefits;

(B) Employees working for the company two years or more shall receive the year's leave;

(C) Any woman, with the consent of her doctor, can take less than this amount of leave, but with no suggestion from the company that this would be preferable.

(10) A committee be formed to establish within two years a full-time day care center that will be available to all employees, men and women, permanently employed by the company. Fees will be shared between the company and the participating employees . . .*

On each magazine, an effort was made to poll women in various departments to determine just what questions should be asked of management. Replies contained, typically, such suggestions as "Researchers should not have to do secretarial chores" and "Honesty in job descriptions and future should be practiced—people shouldn't be hired as secretaries and told they're going to be made researchers or something, then left sitting behind a typewriter and ordering coffee for the next five years."

A great many of these demands and suggestions are, of course, specifically about status and job descriptions on the magazines, and are of less interest to the outsider than the ten "general demands," though crucial to the women themselves, for in the hierarchy of magazines there is all the difference in the world between a re-

---

* "We threw this in because we figured we'd have to give up some things later," one woman told me. But in fact, it seems to me one of the most interesting proposals, and perhaps the major step that large American corporations could make to end the system by which women are prejudiced in their careers by their sexual and biological roles.

searcher and a writer. The researcher (almost always a woman) looks things up, checks facts, produces the raw material for a story, sometimes even writes the first draft. The writer (usually a man) puts her basic material in shape and submits it to an editor (almost always a man). It goes without saying that the writer gets more money and more prestige, and that the researcher must fight a constant struggle not to be treated as a secretary. Since the researchers are responsible to the head of research, often a woman, while the writers are responsible to the editor (a man), there is a natural tendency for the researchers to form a "gynocracy," and no easy way for a researcher who wants to become a writer to switch to a different chain of command.

These problems and many others formed the basis of a complaint made by the women to the Attorney General of the State of New York, Louis J. Lefkowitz, who issued, on June 10, 1970, a "Determination and order after investigation . . . in behalf of 113 Female Employees of Time, Inc., vs. Time, Inc." It began "On May 1, 1970, Louis J. Lefkowitz, Attorney General of the State of New York, in behalf of 96 female employees of Time, Inc., filed a verified complaint with the State Division of Human Rights charging Time, Inc., with an unlawful discriminatory practice relating to employment, by refusing to hire or employ or barring or discharging from employment individuals or discriminating against individuals in compensation or in terms, conditions or privileges of employment, because of the sex of the 96 females in violation of the Human Rights Law of the State of New York. On May 11, 1970, an additional 19 female employees of Time, Inc., were added to the original 96 on whose behalf the Attorney General filed the complaint; 2 were deleted from the original group . . . After investigation, the Division of Human Rights has determined that it has jurisdiction in this matter and that there is probable cause to believe that the respondent has engaged or is engaging in the unlawful discriminatory practices complained of . . ."

The language of the complaint serves both as a perfect

description of male chauvinism at work and as an example of the means by which women can bring pressure to bear to remedy the conditions they object to:

(5)*Respondent (Time, Inc.) has adopted and implemented a policy of hiring predominantly college-educated women to fill certain categories of lower paying, often menial positions while men are hired and promoted to fill higher paying positions entailing greater responsibility.

(6) Respondent's hiring, promotion and employment practices respecting its women employees bear little or no relation to the qualifications of such women to perform the work they do or the work they aspire to perform.

(7) College-educated women, some of whom have graduate degrees in Journalism, are employed as typists, copy-readers, newsmarkers, letter correspondents, researchers and checkers . . .

(13) . . . A memorandum . . . has stated that . . . few women seem to have the physical and mental energy needed to perform in higher positions at Time Magazine . . .†

(19) Female college graduates are hired and employed by Time, Inc., in non-writing positions, with starting salaries ranging from $110.00 per week for newsmarkers to $148.00 for researchers, whereas male college graduates are hired directly as writers at $232.00 per week.

(20) Respondent's acts and practices at Time Magazine have the purpose and effect of placing college-educated women in lower positions where they can expect little or no upward advancement . . .

(30) Within the "reporter" category (on Life Magazine) the men have all been directly hired into that

* Numbers refer to the paragraphs in the complaint itself, from which these examples have been taken. The document contains seventy-five clauses and is fifteen pages long.
† One wonders what Clare Booth Luce would say to *this!*

position as writers whereas the women have generally worked their way up from lower, often menial, positions.

(31) Graduates of Radcliffe, Vassar, and other prestigious colleges are hired to clip articles from newspapers with scissors and straight edge. No men are employed in the aforesaid positions.

(32) Men hired as reporters are carefully trained by the men in high editorial positions who scrutinize their writing and offer constructive criticism. Women reporters are not offered such training and opportunity for development . . .

(34) In one instance a Senior Editor who had expressed dissatisfaction with a male reporter's writing was told by a female "reporter" that the piece could be written well by several of the women employees currently in non-writing positions. He replied to her suggestion: "If there were any broads around here who could write, I'd know about them."

(48) One female researcher with a degree in Journalism and five years of previous experience on three newspapers as a reporter and writer was hired by respondent at $85.00 per week (on Sports Illustrated) starting salary to work directly on editorial copy—as a typist.

(49) After six years the aforementioned complainant is still a researcher while men with less previous experience before coming to Sports Illustrated, no journalism degrees and less time as researchers, have been promoted to the position of writers . . .

(53) At Sports Illustrated the Managing Editor, Executive Editor, Assistant Managing Editors, Art Director and all 22 Senior Editors are men . . .

(65) Of the 39 Editors and Associate Editors appearing on the masthead of Fortune Magazine, 33 are men.

(66) The 33 male editors were all hired directly as writers, whereas the 6 women, only 4 of whom are

actually working as writers, all worked their way up from research positions, spending 6 to 12 years in such category . . .

(75) By reason of the foregoing, respondent is in violation of Executive Law, Section 296, subd. 1. (a) WHEREFORE, the complainant respectfully requests that the State Division of Human Rights investigate the foregoing complaint and order that:

(a) respondent shall cease and desist from discrimination against female employees on the basis of sex;

(b) respondent shall be prohibited . . . from discriminating on the basis of sex in its recruiting, hiring, promotional and work classification practices and with respect to the terms, conditions, privileges, and rates of pay of its employees;

(c) Respondent shall be required to set up a regular committee within each of its divisions to hear all complaints respecting sex discrimination which committees shall report to respondent's staff, The State Division of Human Rights and the Attorney General's Office the results of its hearings.

Complainant further prays for such other relief as the Division may deem just and proper in order to effectuate the purposes of the Human Rights Law prohibiting discrimination in employment because of sex.

I have quoted at such length from this document not only because of its importance but also because it illustrates that something can be done, that very often the seemingly random and personal course of male chauvinism at work, far from being an entrenched masculine prerogative, is in fact often illegal. Because of the pressure created by the unwelcome news of this complaint, the demands of the women led to a series of mandatory negotiating sessions with the executives of each magazine, attended not only by the women who worked on that particular magazine but also by observers from the other divisions. (It is worth noting that these discussions, some of which I will quote, are not taking place as exchanges of views between management and employees, but as a legal obligation. While there is no time limit, management is at least obliged to *listen* to women, since the complainants can demand a public hearing if they feel that no serious attempt is being made to solve their complaints. One thing should be added for the benefit of those who may want to emulate the female workers at Time, Inc.—under the law, management is specifically prevented from discharging a negotiator during the course of the negotiations.)

It is difficult to summarize the long meetings that took place on various dates at each of the company's magazines, and it would serve no useful purpose to do so. The transcripts run to several hundred closely typed pages, most of which deal with quite specific issues of seniority and job description. One has the impression that the women have dropped the larger societal issues (day-care centers, maternity leave, a general restructuring of the company's approach to women employees), to concentrate on less radical issues. My own conclusion is that the women would have done well to provide themselves with a good, tough labor lawyer to sit in on their negotiating sessions, and one woman acknowledged that this might have been a good idea. "But," she said, "we didn't have the money to keep a lawyer with us over long sessions like the ones we had. The Attorney General's office provided us with a lawyer, since it was a civil rights suit, but he only attended about half the sessions, and of course it was hard to get him in a hurry if the time of the meeting was changed, as it very often was. In fact, the *timing* of these meetings pretty much turned out to be whenever the management decided to have them. They were always changing times and dates, and we couldn't keep a lawyer on tap like that. Then, we'd come so far, we figured, I think, we had them on the defensive . . ."

On June 10, 1970, the first meeting took place, opening with "a general exchange of awkward welcomes and expressions of hope that this would be an opportunity for both sides to educate one another."*

L: (looking at a copy of the complainants' demands): I think this is very interesting . . . In fact, fascinating . . . I'm going to ask a lot of questions and don't want to seem like I'm defending the status quo. I just want to clarify my mind. I'm not trying to entrench myself and my colleagues. This idea of different categories of researcher is fascinating. How can you do this? Would the reporter/researcher also check?

B: *This is open to discussion. Do you think there should be a special category?*

L: I feel two ways. Granted there are some researchers who are better than others. It parallels the junior and senior writer situation. What is not clear is how this distinction could be made. Should we create researcher/reporters and then just checkers? You'd create a group of people who would never see the light of day. Or should we take the position that every researcher should do checking?

B: *I don't know, but right now one category is a grab bag for people performing different duties.*

I have included this exchange not just because it opens the meeting but because it represents a reasonable and constructive exchange which might well be emulated in this kind of office dispute. However, the problems that faced the Time-Life women are already apparent here: neither side has a specific plan or timetable. The women

* For convenience, the comments of the management representative speaking are printed here in ordinary type, those of the woman representative in italics. I have used initials on the grounds that the exact identity of the people involved is not really important, provided the reader knows who is speaking for the status quo and who is speaking against it. The initials have been changed, of course, to protect the identities of all involved.

are putting forward general complaints, the management is expressing interest, but rather obviously preparing to dwell at length on the difficulties. The question of researchers acting as secretaries is disposed of quickly, though rather inconclusively:

C: *The point is that researchers are professionals and should be treated as such. Whether by design or the failure to indoctrinate writers, this does not happen. There is the ordering about of minor tasks that the writer could do himself.*

V: What do you mean? Like calling Pan Am to make a reservation?

C: *Yes.*

V: This should be done by secretaries, and I'll take steps to ensure that this is done . . .

B: *Writers treat researchers as secretaries because they are women and they are there to help them.*

V: Things like this are best worked out by mastering the art of human relations. I'd tell a writer who asked me to do things that weren't part of my job that I'd get a secretary to do this. Gradually he'd get the idea.

I like the appeal to the mastery of "the art of human relations" very much, but it is already clear that management is effectively asking the women for advice, as if it were *their* responsibility to correct the problems they are complaining about, and responding to their advice with avuncular or auntly generalities, as the following exchange illustrates:

B: *We want to emphasize the positive things and find some way to aid writers, but at the same time promote this idea of partnership. Now not enough people feel included. Couldn't you play more of a role in promoting this researcher appreciation?*

L: I'd like to teach a course in this.

B: *You may get the chance.*

V: You don't get appreciated by saying. It's doing it.

Another example of this tendency to offer advice to the complainants occurs a few pages later:

L: Any researcher wanting a crack at writing will get it.
B: *But the steps are not clear. Who do you speak to?*
L: I know this sounds serious but to write you must want to do it very much. To have a real writing ambition is different from just wanting to try. . . .

This amounts to saying that if you want to succeed enough, you will, which hardly seems a positive approach to promoting women. It also paves the way for a somewhat sharper series of comments, based on one woman's suggestion that men should be hired as researchers too, which might put pressure on the management to pay more attention to the researcher's potentials and to pay a higher starting salary, since male college graduates are neither likely to accept nor to be offered the kind of money that young women are still accustomed to receiving:

B: *The idea that men would be researchers too means that mobility would have to be built in.*
V: I'd be happy to hire men, but I need one fall guy to make the rest follow. . . .
C: *The problem in getting men is that the research job is considered a lower, woman's job.*
L: No, it's the same feeling you have when you don't want to eat at Schrafft's. You're surrounded by women and it makes you nervous. . . .

It is some indication of management's view of hiring men to work in what has previously been an all-female category that the first man in is referred to as a "fall guy." The old male chauvinist fear of women is expressed perfectly in L's remark about Schrafft's, which is, in fact, usually full of men these days.

Schrafft's aside, the problem that keeps coming up again and again in these discussions is the question of recognition. From the management point of view, outstanding women will be "noticed," but from the women's point of view this is meaningless—what they want is a *system*. At one meeting of the complainants, a management representative said, "If you want to write, show me what you've done, like over the weekend or at night." But this is hardly job training, or a system. As one woman replied, "I don't think 'keeping an eye open' is a good way to search from within. There is forty years of job discrimination here, and a lot of people who want to try." The answer to this, given later on in the session by a member of management was "We're not geared to a major program." But it was a major program that the women were demanding, a serious attempt to improve the chances for promotion and responsibility for any interested woman—to "equalize the opportunities in a structured way"—rather than a series of palliatives that apply only to a few very talented women, and which would be handed out in a haphazard way, like gifts from the gods. A certain waspishness enters into the discussion from time to time. One management representative commented, "You have some among you that, just from your memos, etc., will never be writers"; and later, in discussing the possibility of considering secretaries for research jobs, said, "These are just *people*, there is no relationship between their jobs and researcher-writers."

"Just people"! Not executives, not "talent," not even men. One would have thought that the negotiators would have leapt to the defense of their sisters, but no such thing! They too suffer from a certain tendency to dismiss the interests of people who hold jobs in lower categories than theirs. There is a certain tone of elitism in the following exchange:

B: *Sitting outside the writer's office makes her available as a secretary, coffee-maker, errands, anything that comes up. . . .*

K: If this is happening, I will put out a memo to put an end to it immediately. . . . Just don't do it.

B: *It's not in the character of many writers to do it, but others just don't view researchers as professional people. If they were respected it wouldn't occur to them to do this. Researchers object to being substitute secretaries. Where there are secretaries it doesn't happen. Maybe we need more secretaries.*

Even more interesting is a memorandum from management that more or less says everything there is to say about the secretarial function in noting that "qualified individuals are not barred from advancement *merely because they are secretaries.*" Secretaries are the Achilles heel of women's liberation in the office, providing as they do a large and visible group of menial laborers, a source of embarrassment to women who have either risen above their ranks or entered business on a higher level; a useful weapon in the hands of men, because they can generalize on women's ambitions and career potentials on the basis of a number of women who may not be ambitious at all.

By the end of the summer of 1970, both the management and the women negotiators were beginning to take stock of the results of their negotiations. On the key question of forming committees to advise and superintend progress in ending sex discrimination, a certain weariness and sense of defeat became apparent on the part of the complainants, one of whom wrote, "If a committee were formed that did not include management at all, it is possible that management might not be very much influenced by its advice, and in fact it's hard to imagine how the committee could function without the participation of management's eye-view. On the other hand, perhaps the committee could be formed without management, but including a cross-section of staff, perhaps on a rotating basis, and its advice could be given solely on the basis of the merit of the work it judges leaving to management the task of fitting the committee's recommendations to the company's needs." It i clear that the value and status of any committee a loosely conceived and powerless as this and which is in

tended "not to usurp the hiring and promotion prerogatives of management, but to advise both parties on such
matters" is very limited indeed. On certain specific job-
oriented problems, the women seem to have made a certain amount of progress, but their attempt to confront
the basic nature of sex discrimination in the organization
is met with an insistence on examining individual cases
with sympathy, rather than on the creation of any organized system. In the words of one management negotiator,
"We would suggest that the goals which we all share—
improving the working relationship of the team, creating
a better working environment for everybody, and reducing the conflicts which may arise—are not best served by
creating a set of rigid, inflexible rules. Those goals are
probably best served by adopting a variety of flexible
measures intended to reassert some continuingly durable
practices, to eliminate or reduce a few practices which
may have grown obsolete, and to adopt some new flexible policies." From day-care centers to the promise that
things will go on pretty much as they were, only somehow a little better, is a long and disappointing descent of
expectations. There seems to have been general agreement that "women should not be asked questions about
their home situations or social status which could not
also be asked of men," a certain guarded agreement on
"job mobility" (i.e., researchers who want to be writers), and a slightly startled and reluctant acceptance of
the notion of hiring men to work in all-female job categories—though as one woman noted of a management
representative, "he found it hard to agree in the case of
secretaries . . . and he seemed incredulous at the idea of
men working in the copyroom." The unfortunate secretaries, in addition to coming in for a good deal of verbal
abuse, were dismissed by one of the complainants in a
memorandum summing up the women's proposals:
"Some people feel (not necessarily the secretaries) that
the position could be abolished in favor of a good receptionist on every floor who answers all phones from a
main switchboard and screens callers." Some of the mis-
cellaneous suggestions seem unlikely, ranging from a

specific one that "researchers should have *doors* on their offices and windows whenever possible," to a very broad proposal that "the content of the magazine should be upgraded to avoid the familiar female stereotypes."

The central problem remained that management has the ultimate right to determine whether a person is in fact qualified for promotion. It is exceedingly difficult to prove that a woman *is* qualified and has been passed over for some job simply because "they" wanted a man to have it. Hence the emphasis the women placed on the creation of a committee. It is one thing for management to "pledge to do everything within reason to give women complete equality of opportunity and treatment" (what is "reasonable," how do you define "complete"?), but the language of one corporate memorandum defines very clearly the nature of the problem: "The determination of whether an individual is qualified . . . must remain in the sole discretion of the management." Finally, the same memorandum notes, "The structure and purpose of the committee seemed to pose a difficult problem. We are agreed in principle that such an entity will be created. We have agreed that it should have as its purpose to continue the kind of dialogue that we have been having, and to attempt to resolve particular complaints of sex discrimination if and when they arise. But we do not believe it should become involved in any fashion in the process of recommending, evaluating, interviewing or promoting individuals, or in record keeping about that process." Next to this, one woman negotiator had written: "Not the purpose as *we* see it!"

The final "Conciliation Agreement," while it hardly grants the rather sweeping reforms demanded by the women at the beginning of the negotiations, at least recognizes both the law and the existence of the problem, which is more than most corporations manage to do.

1. The respondent Publisher shall refrain from the commission of unlawful discriminatory practices in the future. The Publisher does not concede or admit

that it, or any of its employees, has committed unlawful discriminatory acts in the past, and has
agreed to all terms in order to avoid lengthy legal
proceedings and to manifest its good faith . . .

2. All recruitment, hiring, interviewing, referral,
promotion, setting of job classifications, training
programs and compensation of personnel by the
Publisher shall be without regard to sex . . .

3. The Publisher will actively attempt to achieve integration of all job categories by sex . . .

4. Applicants for employment by the Publisher will
not be assigned to interviews on the basis of sex of
either the applicant or the interviewer.

5. Each person hired by the Publisher will be given
a clear, full and accurate explanation of the duties,
responsibilities and career possibilities of the position for which he or she is hired . . .

Other clauses deal with such matters as applying for
better jobs once you're in the company, the setting up of
a company-wide committee to resolve disputes or alleged
sex discrimination, the preparation of a quarterly statisti-
cal analysis regarding jobs and sex, and a whole host of
specific job changes on each of the magazines.

The slightly defensive tone of the first paragraph of
the "Conciliation Agreement" is standard—no company
ever willingly concedes guilt—and does not invalidate
the real gains outlined in it. The way in which these
women tackled the management of a large corporation
and made it listen might well serve as an example to all
those who feel that feminism requires the creation of a
new kind of woman. The old kind will do fine if she can
develop enough clout.

Needless to say, not everyone feels that the end of
these negotiations resulted in a new Millennium for
women, though everyone agrees that Time, Inc., has im-
proved immensely, and one can only applaud the management's willingness to face up to women's demands—
by no means a common response. Once the pressure of
the negotiations was ended, the women had a tendency

to return to their jobs, some having gained something, others not. As one woman said, "It was worth doing, and it was important, but I'm not sure that all that much has come out of it in a direct way. I don't think enough women *cared*. The committees were supposed to be set up, but somehow nothing much came of *them* either. What they can't do any more is to scrape the bottom of the barrel for men when there are plenty of women who could do a job. That's a step forward. And we discovered we could do it, that we didn't have to be nice little girls. I can see now that the negotiations were too loose. They always agreed with us on the principle, but never on the specifics, and there was a lot of strolling down memory lane, you know? Appeals to sentiment and team spirit, and as a negotiator you have to fight against that, even when you feel it. But it made me a much stronger person, to realize I could do something like this, and at the end I wasn't going to be fired, that I'd said what I wanted to say and even helped make some changes!"

The Time, Inc., case is not unique. Similar confrontations have taken place elsewhere, with varying results. At the *Reader's Digest* eighteen women employees filed a complaint* with the New York State Human Rights Commission, charging the magazine with discrimination against women in hiring, recruiting, training, promotion and pay. In the case of the *Reader's Digest*, the complainants described alleged working conditions in terms that make one think of 1984, citing "all-women departments—chiefly clerical—in which employees were watched by closed-circuit television, could not converse and must obtain permission to go to the bathroom."(47) They also alleged that no male employees were subject to such rules. A woman associate editor in the *Reader's Digest* condensed book division said of their complaint, "the women's movement has brought the first group action ever taken at the Digest . . . where seventy-five per-

---

* Which was later dismissed by the court.

cent of the nearly 3,500 employees are women." (A reverse situation is taking place on women's magazines, where two young men have become the first male college guest editors in the history of *Mademoiselle*, in an effort to "put less of a stigma on men who want to work in the fashion field.")

UPPITY WOMEN UNITE! says a button worn by Ms. Bernice Sandler, head of the women's rights program for the Association of American Colleges, who was quoted in, of all places, *Time* magazine, as saying that, "Many men do not act morally unless they are pressured." Ms. Sandler looks forward to "an enormous increase in litigation" on the campus. The colleges have already given way to so many diverse pressures, from athletically minded trustees to student radicals, that it should not be difficult for more women to get hired and promoted on campus. Curiously, a reverse process seems to be taking place in some institutions. Mount Holyoke, which recently voted to remain a women's college, despite the examples of most of the Seven Sisters, now has a male president, David B. Truman, who bore the brunt of the 1968 student riot at Columbia, where he was vice-president. It is easy to imagine that the presidency of a smaller college must come as something of a relief to Dr. Truman after the turbulence of coeducational life in New York, but hard to see why a college that has voted to remain all-female should want a "father figure" as its head. *The New York Times* reported that an increasing number of girls' schools are seeking headmasters. Foxcroft, Miss Porter's, the Abbott Academy, Spence, all have men as the head at the time of writing, a phenomenon which is variously attributed to "the absence of ambition in women" and the need for expert fund-raising and business expertise to keep a private school afloat. One woman educator was quoted as saying, "It's the familiar male takeover. Any kind of upgrading of a profession in which women dominate brings in 'integration' by men. Then the men set up their 'old boy' network to add more men. It isn't that the women aren't competent and competitive. It's the cumulative effect of discouragement that eventually keeps them from trying."

Certainly it is curious to think of Foxcroft and Miss Porter's being run by men, but the answer seems to be that men have taken women's demand for job equality seriously, and moved in on what used to be women's jobs before women have had a chance to move in on men's.

Airline stewardesses have fought successfully to have male stewards on airplanes, but less successfully to have women flight crews. Most of them seem reconciled to the famous "Fly Me" ads, but they are anything but pleased at such signs of male chauvinism as the ad that appeared in *The New York Times* in 1969:

TWA want man who speak with foreign tongue. We're looking for a man with special qualities. Number 1, that he speak at least two foreign languages . . . Number 2, that he have a special way with women. When we find him, we'll put him in charge of our international air hostesses. They'll be his responsibility. He'll coordinate their every move while in flight. Which should give him a chance to make a few moves of his own . . .(48)

Although there are an estimated 1,800 American women who hold commercial pilots' licenses, only seventy-six have air transport ratings, and only one is believed qualified to fly a four-engined jet. The day when women will be airline captains seems a long way off, though it is worth noting that women airline pilots exist in several countries. The Soviet Union has an all-woman international jet flight crew. (It is interesting to note that integrating men and women on the flight deck is as difficult as anywhere else—a Soviet woman pilot gets a crew of women, including the cabin attendants.)

Across the country women are taking to the law. In New York, seven-hundred women faculty members of the City University filed sex discrimination charges with the federal government that "could result in the loss of $34,000,000 in federal funds to the university." More ambitious than the women complainants of Time-Life, the C.U.N.Y. Women's Coalition filed complaints with the U. S. Department of Health, Education and Welfare *and* the Equal Employment Opportunities Commission. They also got the support of New York City Council woman Carol Greitzer and the services of an employment discrimination counsel, provided by the National Organization of Women (NOW). Clearly, the course of the Time-Life negotiations proves the wisdom of getting outside political support, publicity and a good lawyer when dealing with an employer over matters of sex discrimination, though most women are in no position to acquire such aid, and many still believe that it is important to keep outsiders away from these disputes. In most companies women are afraid of "going too far"; they withdraw at the ultimate test of wills.

In some American cities, women are now beginning to patrol the streets as police officers, sometimes even serving as partners to male policemen. In many states, women are seeking to end the sex quotas and separate promotion tests maintained by police departments, not to speak of the attitude typified by Chief Edward Davis of Los Angeles, who was quoted in *The New York Times* as saying, "Are we going to let a five foot two, 115-pound petite blonde girl go in there and wrestle with a couple of bank bandits? I personally don't think that's the role of women . . . In the history of my wife and daughters there were certain times during the month when they did not function as effectively as they did at other times of the month."

Few employers are prepared to tackle the question of menstruation in quite so forthright a way as the chief of the L.A.P.D. Three women who testified against the American Telephone and Telegraph Company merely charged that women were given no opportunity to apply or train for more responsible jobs, and that they "were constantly harassed by supervisors who tapped their personal home phones as well as their switchboards."(49) A-for menstruation, they testified that operators "get no pay for days they are out sick until they have been with the company ten years."(50) Another young woman testified that she had been "laughed off" when she requested a job as a telephone repair-woman or an installer, and that her applications were "spurned, either laughingly or with the remark by her immediate foremen that the telephone company 'wasn't ready for females outside yet.'" A.T.&T. also came in for the wrath of the ubiquitous Councilwoman Greitzer, who gave her support to eight women who filed a suit in federal court in New York charging the company with sex discrimination, in particular of "assigning them to jobs at lower levels of responsibility than those of men with similar qualifications."*

There is even a woman umpire (in the minor leagues) thanks to the law. When Ms. Bernice Gera applied to the National Association of Professional Baseball Leagues she was turned down by its president, on the grounds that she was too old and too small (she is forty-one, weighs a hundred twenty-eight pounds and is five feet two inches high). In a five-to-two decision, the New York State Court of Appeals took Ms. Gera's side, persuaded by Mario Biaggi, the Bronx congressman, who took the case "because nobody else would." As Ms. Gera says, "I'm treated no different than any other umpire. When there's an argument, they storm out, they circle you; all I could see was their jugular veins . . . All through this case, my heart was broken. I've learned to take everything in stride. The majors? What are they

* The telephone company has reacted to this attack with an advertisement showing Ms. Alana MacFarlane, of San Rafael, California, at the top of a telephone pole. She is the first women telephone installer, and presumably the harbinger of changes to come. Women still seem to feel the same about the telephone company, however, perhaps because it has always employed them in a menial capacity. One woman who has worked as a telephone operator commented on the ad, "I don't care what they say, it's still hard to get to the top of the pole if you're a woman."

talking about, the majors? I've always wondered if even this was worth it."

The spirit of militancy among women is growing sharply. The gains sometimes seem small, but they can be observed by anyone who cares to read the newspaper. Two young women recently sued New York City for $50,000 each in State Supreme Court, charging false arrest and detention after they had resisted an order to leave a restaurant that had a sign banning "unescorted ladies." Curiously enough this was not a case of women trying to bust a crusty old male stronghold—like the guerilla warfare that finally integrated McSorley's saloon. The restaurant in question was, of all things, a Child's on East 78th Street, and the women had wandered in to order coffee, with a woman friend from England as their guest. They maintained that their guest was in effect a companion or escort, but were refused service, following which they were arrested and charged with disorderly conduct. Under pressure, the Columbia University Club in New York recently allowed women full membership after a women's squash tournament held there sparked off a controversy, though the Harvard Club voted not to extend its membership to women. In fact, a Harris poll (sponsored by Virginia Slims cigarettes—"You've Come a Long Way, Baby") revealed that most women now support "efforts to strengthen and change women's status in society," though forty-nine per cent of the women polled declared themselves "unsympathetic to the efforts of women's liberation groups," as opposed to thirty-six per cent who favored women's lib. Clearly, women are demanding changes in the practical day-to-day business of their lives, without necessarily accepting the more extreme views of the feminists. And clearly women are willing to stand and fight, when necessary. From time to time, they lose, but one has the feeling that their defeats are temporary—that there is simply no way to restore the status quo ante.

The case of Schattman vs. Texas Employment Commission was particularly depressing to women liberationists, since Ms. Schattman was challenging a state law that required her to quit her job at a certain point in her pregnancy "regardless of her desire to continue working or her doctor's opinion that she could do so without harm." The United States Court of Appeals for the Fifth Circuit ruled against her, upholding the law, finding it "reasonable and rationally related to a permissible state purpose," despite the fact that Ms. Schattman is an office worker, whose job required nothing more physically demanding than "the lifting of file folders." One is inclined to believe that the only "state purpose" in this case is to ensure that women have to leave their jobs for long periods of time when they become pregnant, thus proving that men are more "reliable" workers and better suited for promotion and long-term careers.

But male chauvinists also frequently rely on statutes and regulations for protection. Two young women recently lost their jobs because neither was able to lift a twenty-five-pound barbell over her head with one hand, as required by the New York Civil Service examination for the job. In an editorial on the subject, *The New York Times* commented:

> . . . One of the victims is an audiovisual technician who never had any trouble working and moving her projectors; the other is a graphic artist and audiovisual advisor who, to the best of anybody's knowledge, is not required to lift anything much heavier than a pencil or a file card. The test the two women were obliged to take to gain civil service status and retain their jobs also included running an obstacle course . . . A predominantly male bureaucracy will set predominantly male standards.(51)

A male bureaucracy can nearly always be relied upon to set its own standards in such a way as to exclude as many women as possible, just as men ordinarily assume that a given job can only be done by a man because it always has been. It is difficult to imagine women FBI agents, and yet one of the first steps of L. Patrick Gray, the new director of the FBI was to rescind J. Edgar Hoover's longstanding prohibition against women agents, announcing his decision with what sounds like somewhat less than wild enthusiasm—"I believe it is something we have to do."(52) (For those who are interested, applicants will have to be at least five feet seven—which seems rather tall—and will have to be able to handle firearms.)

Changes *can* be made, are being made, and it is important for women to know about them, and for men to realize that the strength of the women's movement does not lie in the extremists, but in the mass of women who are determined to win an opportunity to compete equally with men. Every attempt to restrict their opportunities merely turns women toward the extremists, and considering their domestic roles, they have awesome weapons at their command. Male chauvinists seem to me to be engaging in a battle with a stronger force, a battle that is, in fact, already lost. Perhaps the most trenchant comment on the subject was made by David J. Mahoney, chairman and president of the Norton Simon Corporation, at a conference on equal opportunity for women in business: "The women's movement has been good for America and will be good for business."(53) Once it is clear that equality *is* good for business, there is no doubt that equality will come very rapidly, whatever the private feelings of men on the subject.

In the short run, of course, equality remains a threat. There are only so many jobs, and increased competition from trained and competent women will inevitably result in fewer men being promoted. In the meantime, men's fear of losing their jobs or seeing women promoted over their heads has been intensified, according to a group of New York psychiatrists, by a sharp increase in impotence, attributed to "the increased sexual freedom of women in recent years, leading them to demand more of their male partners."(54) What with one thing and another, it is not an encouraging prospect for men who cling to the old ways. What with increasing pressures in this country for a fuller and equal participation of women, the entrenched male chauvinist may have to go far afield to confirm his world view. Perhaps they can take comfort in the fact that at a recent rally held in Canton, China, to celebrate Woman's Day, only one of the eighteen senior officials present was a woman! And in Hopei Province, a group of Chinese women workers complained in *Hung Chi*, a periodical published by the Central Committee of the Chinese Communist Party, that "the work is equal, but not the pay."

EIGHT

> Man for the field and woman for the hearth:
> Man for the sword and for the needle she:
> Man with the head and woman with the heart:
> Man to command and woman to obey;
> All else confusion . . .
>
> —Alfred, Lord Tennyson

LIVING BEYOND EDEN

"We're not going to put up with male chauvinism any more," says Z, her face suddenly drained of its usual vivacity. "It's not that I don't *need* men, I do, but I've never met a woman who behaved as badly towards men as men behave towards women every day, without even noticing it or caring much. It's a question of control, of domination. Male chauvinism is just the effort to exert control, and until men have learned to be *open,* to stop trying to control situations as if control were all that mattered, we'll always be divided and have to live like strangers."

I have never thought of Z as a "women's liberationist," but now that I think of it, I suppose she *is*—independent, ambitious, living her own life, making her own way. A friend of mine once described her, in admiration, as "a woman you can treat like a man," but that has never seemed to me true, either as it applies to her or in general, and on reflection is a supreme example of male chauvinist thinking. When men say that a woman can be treated like a man they mean, in effect, that her ambition and independence permit one to dispense with the usual amenities—by the mere fact of her independence, she has excluded herself from our care and protection. Well, Z and I have shared a lot of *Angst* together, but I'm beginning to realize that I've always simply assumed, rather like my friend, that she could be easily categorized, perhaps that *all* women can be easily categorized. In any case, Z and I, who have long ago settled on the quiet attraction of mutual incompatibility, have been pursuing the question of male chauvinism as an abstract question, until, as if by magic, it has emerged tonight as a *personal* one.

"You accept, yes," she says, "but you don't *give*. You see the world from a fixed point of view, and somehow you manage to fit women into it, you twist it a little bit so they can be fitted in, or if they're weak enough, you twist *them*. It's what men do naturally. You look at the world from the point of view of your own preconceptions, then spend a lifetime trying to fit women into the structure, without ever being open to ask us what the hell we want or think, or frank enough to admit that it doesn't work for you either. Male chauvinism reminds me of war. Everybody is against it, but nobody can stop it."

We are sitting in a bar on Lexington Avenue. It is an off night and there are no other customers. We are surrounded by mini-skirted waitresses, one of whom is in tears. Z, who is working on a book about women's liberation, has suddenly dropped her slightly aggressive posture of self-assurance. I have always thought of her as "equal," whatever that means, intelligent, strong in her own way, sexually "liberated," a woman who can deal with men on her own terms, the kind of woman one ("one" being a man) feels comfortable with. Now we are talking about male chauvinism, and it is increasingly clear that my sense of being comfortable around her is a self-willed illusion, a refusal to face the realities of what she thinks, what she wants, what she *is*. How many concessions has she made to me to create that feeling of comfort, now swiftly evaporating to the strident sobs of the waitress, who has apparently been insulted in some unspecified way by a departed customer? "Knock it off," says the bartender, playfully squirting a jet of syphon water in her direction. "You've heard worse than that. And if you haven't you will." Unconsoled, she retires to snuffle by the cigarette machine, while Z moodily pursues her dissatisfaction with my questions. We began

cheerily enough by talking about each other's first sexual experiences, but this jolly camaraderie has begun to
ebb, as she considers just what her relationship is to the
various men in her life, to man in general. She has tried
to make it alone financially, has to some extent succeeded, yet she is still struggling for something else, and
I am beginning to understand what it is: control. "Our
bodies, our selves"—yes, I understand *that*, though it's
hard for a man to imagine what it feels like to live with
the assumption that your body isn't altogether your
own, that your biology is somehow involved with laws,
traditions, customs, taboos that have nothing to do with
you. Understand that, and you understand a good deal,
but not all. For what Z is talking about is control in another sense: the many ways in which men seek to exert
control, the way they assume that it is their *function* to
control things, whether it's deciding where to have
dinner or just how far and on what terms a relationship
should be carried. Perhaps that is the final equation:
male chauvinism equals *control*. As men, we are willing
to take on the burdens of providing for women, on the
condition that we can control them; ideally, we aspire to
give orders; practically speaking, we are willing to settle
for all the subtle and devious ways in which we manage
to make known our wishes and enforce them.

I think of Z as being free, but she does not. Her body
may be her own, but the terms on which she shares it
with someone else lead inevitable and in each "situation" to a new attempt to settle the question of control
between this woman, that man. A married man will fit
her into his life, on his terms, his terms automatically su-
perseding hers; unmarried or divorced men tend to take
over her life, as if in loving any man she were somehow
obliged to give up something of herself, to accept his imprint, pending marriage, should that ever happen, the
ultimate compromise and loss of identity. I argue against
this point of view, but without conviction. For I know
that I too want control, that like most men, I want to
make the decisions. All freedom to women, so long as it's
understood that I get my way in the things that are im-

portant to me, so long as the final decision is mine. Well,
somebody has to decide, as they say. Where will we
spend our vacations, shall we buy a new car or a new
sofa, what will we do this weekend? Life is full of decisions, and we quickly learn to trade the minor ones for
the major ones, conceding to women whole areas in
which they can make the decisions, depending on our nature and our interests, in order to preserve the areas of
decision we care about for ourselves. We have made the
relationship between the sexes a bargaining session, a
kind of cosmic labor negotiation, and because men still
control most of the areas of temporal power, we have
placed ourselves in a winning position, from which it is
possible to offer small concessions and compromises
without abandoning our central concerns.

Z, whom I have always admired for her strength and
ability to deal with life and men, smiles at the morose
waitress, who nods back and grimaces. Sisters!

"It's all so dead," Z says, "this idea that half the
world is a spectacle for the other half. Sexually, the difference between men and women is interesting, it makes
sense. But any other way, it's like talking about Negroes
and whites, Jews and gentiles, it doesn't apply. My life
was a female *Portnoy's Complaint*—I'm not talking
about masturbation, but breaking out, leaving home,
and I *did* it. I picked the man I wanted to take my virginity, made that decision for myself, camped on his
doorstep in my saddle shoes and cheerleader's sweater,
left home when my mother discovered my diaphragm,
made my own way through college because my family
wouldn't pay for it. And all the time, I guess because it
was so exciting, I never accepted the fact that my sense of
independence was illusory, that everything I'd done for
myself wouldn't ever make me equal to men in their
eyes, that the way I'd controlled my own life wouldn't
seem like anything more than an amusing anecdote to
them. You can tell the story of your life to men, and
they're interested or amused, but sooner or later they try
to fit you into their preconceived ideas, they *humor* you.
Well, that's not for me any more. Sometimes I get fright-

ened at the thought that I'm retreating, closing myself
off, trying to live life alone as a woman, and I know I
can't make it that way, but it's a temptation. I have this
fantasy of judging men the way they judge women, of
seeing them all lined up naked and picking the one I
like best, but I don't really want to do that—I just wish
men would stop doing it to us, to *me*. Maybe it's that
women are brought up to expect *feeling*, a kind of reci-
procated warmth, and men aren't. Maybe men are
frightened by the whole notion of women's sexuality.
The whole idea of multiple orgasm is hard for them to
accept but for us it's real, it's something we have, or can
have, and mostly don't, and because we don't get it, I
suppose we try to compensate by asking for affection and
warmth, which are just the things men are nervous
about being asked for . . . I'm radical in a lot of ways,
but when I talk to lesbians, I don't know, I get frightened, I can't cope with a woman being sexually aggressive towards me. And yet, they understand me better
than any man ever has. So I find myself spending more
time with myself, more time with women. It's as if I'm
suddenly very tired, tired of all those endless little
put-downs, of having to give admiration, support, enthusiasm to men who don't give you anything back but a little sexual action, and even then, nothing like what they
think they're giving, tired of being told, 'Well, we really
want a man for this assignment,' tired of playing the
game by their rules and never winning. I always felt
guilty about my work. It was important to me, but the
men I knew never took it seriously, some pretended to,
but really they just felt it was some little thing I did, like
needlework, nothing like *their* work, and not important
enough to get in the way of their having dinner when
they wanted it, or making love when they felt like it.
And my parents felt, 'Well, why doesn't she get married?' Then I went to a woman therapist, and I began to
see that my work was important, it did matter, and when
I had my first success I told her, and she said to me, 'Now
you understand! *That's* an orgasm!' And in a way it is,
I can see why men have it better than women, most of

them are getting all kinds of satisfaction that women never get, mostly don't even know *exist*. I'm too tired to fight it, and anyway I don't know how. I'm learning to talk to other women, that's something I can do, and getting into problems like abortion and rape counseling, where you begin to see what the end result of the whole system is. Maybe we've all been raped all these years, raped of our ideas, raped of our self-respect, raped of our potential. You don't have to bleed to be a rape victim."

I am walking uptown with R, who has just been told that she will have to find a new job because she's "too smart and too ambitious" for the one she has. She is twenty-two, smart, determined to confront life head-on, and bewildered by the consequences of her confrontation. What do "they" want her to be? Her refusal to put up with condescension, to accept the role of being a secretary when she was promised the job of assistant have led her to a dead end. Sometimes she has been treated with amused tolerance, sometimes she has been the target of open hostility. She has now been given two months to find a new job, and half the men in her office are on the phone, explaining that she's talented, clever, really *good*, to men who don't even have to ask why she's been fired if she's really such an asset—they naturally assume that she's had an affair with someone and therefore becomes a liability. She is confused, rather than bitter, at the fact that the very men who have decided to get rid of her are praising her merits to other men in order to find her a job.

"OK," she says, "I can see I made a lot of mistakes, I thought I could be friends with one of the executives, and it never occurred to me that everyone would think we were having an affair, then blame *me* for whatever he didn't do. He wasn't working well for a while, and suddenly everyone was looking at me and saying, 'She's doing it to him, poor bastard.' I can see that was bound to make trouble. I mean, we weren't sleeping together, but how am I going to say that, and if I did, people would just say, Well, that's the trouble, if you were treating him decently, he'd be fine. But it wasn't a question of that at all, we were *friends,* except of course that *he* couldn't say we weren't sleeping together either, because that would have destroyed his male ego. What a mess!"

Yes, a mess, I agree, as the breathless pall of a summer evening in the heat wave locks us into our mutual claustrophobia of sweat and falling soot. What can I say that I haven't already said, and how true is what I've said? She had pushed too hard, I've said that, often, but is she had been a man, those same qualities or defects might have worked for her, won her acceptance. She has been assumed to have been having an affair with someone, but were she a man that would have been to her credit. She has been opinionated and strident, but men are more likely to get fired at her age because they're too timid and quiet. I have warned her to be tactful, to flatter, to maneuver rather than attack, but is it a sign of my male chauvinism that I can tolerate her stridency, her outspoken frankness, that I'm perhaps *amused* by her? Yes, I tolerate, but I don't take her "seriously" either, the sentimentalist in me wants to seek out the vulnerability that's concealed, the male chauvinist in me wants to know what would produce tears in those eyes, sees them there, searches for a way to produce willing submission. There is no advice I can give that isn't cut to my own bias. Is that it? Given ambition and talent, we try as hard as we can—by what complex and devious means!—to narrow things to the personal level, knowing that once we have succeeded we can exert our control over other areas, that we will have diverted a woman's energies away from work, salary, status into the muddy waters of *feeling*—the ultimate weapon, the traditional substitute for recognition and reward. By taking women seriously in one area, we exclude them from the areas of threat in work, a game so elaborate that we are scarcely even aware of the fact that we are playing it, hardly even know the rules because they work to our advantage; we cannot lose.

Refugees from the heat, R and I pause on Amsterdam

Avenue to buy a bottle of iced white wine, revived for a
brief instant by the air-conditioner of the liquor store.
Then we walk north, surrounded by the street life of the
Upper West Side. "Did I really mess it up that badly?"
she asks.

"No," I say, "not all that badly. You thought that
men would welcome brightness and energy and talent,
and you didn't see that they take all that badly from
someone who's young and pretty. You underestimated
the extent to which they're afraid of women, you didn't
imagine that a young woman could be a threat. You
moved too fast. Next time, go slow."

"I don't know if I can."

Across the street, a domestic quarrel is in progress, a
couple screaming at each other, on the edge of violence.
The man looks as if he is about to throw his can of beer
straight at the woman, but at the last minute he turns
away in rage and disgust and flings it aimlessly into the
street, from which it bounces to land at our feet. "It's a
tough neighborhood," I say, kicking the can into the
gutter, "Aren't you afraid sometimes, living in a walk-up
brownstone? If I were a woman and lived up here, I'd
expect to be raped every time I went up those four
flights. I mean, it looks like a set for rape in a movie."

She looks at me coldly. "Rape? What the hell do you
know about it? I've just been raped by a bunch of guys
in two-hundred-dollar suits and Meledandri shirts. Rape
is taking advantage, that's all, and some rapes are just
tougher and nastier than others. I got raped by my father when he made me 'his little girl,' and I got raped
by my college when they gave me an education without
telling me that nobody wanted me to use it, and I got
raped at work when nobody took me seriously except as
a sex object, then punished me because it looked as if I
had really become one. Don't talk to me about rape.
You rape with sympathy, you've spent your whole life
being soulful to rip off more affection than you have any
right to, than you've *earned*. Women get raped every
day, a little bit at a time, and you don't need a knife to

do it, and it doesn't have to happen in a dark hallway. It's happening right now."

"What is the definition of rape?" asks M., a member of "the Feminist Psychology Coalition Therapy Referral Collective," a group of psychologists and analysts who are trying to make feminist therapists available and known to women patients. "I don't know," I reply, "my feeling is that when a woman says she's been raped, she usually knows what she means. Rape is when you feel you've been raped." She agrees, but only partially, and hands me a pamphlet on rape. "Rape is an act which humiliates and degrades woman, establishing her as a sex object available to every man. Rape is an expression of the hatred of women, not of love. It is an act of violence couched in sexual terms. Rape is whenever you feel you've been raped. Rape is the ultimate expression of the existing relationship between men and women . . ." At the Women's Center there is a Rape Group, preparing another pamphlet which includes a section entitled "After We're Raped," another on "Stopping Rape in the Streets" ("We don't think that rape can be isolated from the kind of humiliation and abuse which all women are subject to in the streets every day . . . Get used to defending yourself in these situations"), and recommendations on "Self-Defense for Women" ("We need to get over certain ideas about non-violence . . . we need to get used to feeling a little pain"). The section on "Stopping Rape in the Streets" sounds like a recruit's course for some urban guerrilla movement; the prospective rape victim is urged to "start thinking about how you could use things you usually carry with you as a weapon," to use store or car windows as mirrors, to walk down one-way streets facing the traffic "so you will attract attention and can stop passing cars," to avoid wearing "heeled shoes, clogs, tight skirts or pants, large pocketbooks, capes or ponchos," all of which prevent a woman from moving quickly or from defending herself.

Is this really where we are? Is "the act of rape the ultimate expression of the relationship existing between men and women?" She nods in affirmation. And, on reflection, isn't it perhaps true? Male chauvinism has made us deaf; we do not listen to women, we talk to them, justify ourselves, explain that we don't mean any harm by our feelings, but their words do not reach us unless they're telling us what we want to hear, in our terms. We have simply assumed that the most important thing in life is the connection between men and women, then reserved to ourselves certain areas of our own, without making any similar concession to women. We listen to them with our minds already made up, we have already categorized them before any communication can take place, we do not want to know, need to know, who they are, what they want, we have a programmed series of responses for dealing with women ready-made in our minds; it is only necessary to place this particular woman in the appropriate slot and we know and understand everything: "Divorced, an easy lay," "tough, ambitious broad," "sexually insecure chick who'd probably dig an older man" . . . Click! Make the connection and we can stop listening, we can feed back the appropriate response, confident that we have nothing more to learn. My informant looks at me appraisingly, sitting with her knees folded up under her chin. We are in her kitchen; it's one of those immense apartments that exist only on New York's West Side, vast airy rooms full of abstract paintings, rooms full of huge, bulky, low platforms that might be beds or sofas, it is hard to tell, the noise of the West Side streets—where someone is probably being raped at this very minute—drifting in through the open windows, screened by hanging plants. "Do you think you're so different?" she asks. "Do you really think you're sensitized the way a woman is?"

Am I? I think about it, try to think of some male chauvinist act or phrase I may have let drop, aware that like every man I have this reservoir of male chauvinism within me, hopefully concealed because I've learned to be ashamed of it, but occasionally overflowing, its existence embarrassingly revealed. In the few hours I have known this woman, what I have done that could be construed as male chauvinism? I can think of nothing. But then I already know that my idea of good manners, my studied politeness, the care with which I choose my words—all of these are merely devices, responses plucked from the lessons of my childhood and put together in a new form to ingratiate myself with the women I interview. How much of myself am I concealing? Twice I have risen to empty my ashtray, dispose of my paper napkin, but do these small demonstrations of non-male-chauvinism give me away? Are they merely placatory gestures? Yes, I can't deny it: I will go out of my way to wash dishes, to take women "seriously," to put the coasters under the wet glasses of life. I'm ostentatious in my willingness to perform just those tasks that male chauvinists are supposed to resent, forever willing to agree with women—but is it a disguise, a means of getting my own way, a set of automatic responses? Do I give myself away by making these small gestures, by trying to prove that because I will clean my own plate unasked I really *understand*, I can be *trusted*? Like whites who are always overpolite to blacks, am I trying to screen out my own prejudices? Perhaps the mere fact of talking to women as if they were in some way special creatures is itself a kind of male chauvinism—the recognition that this person sitting opposite me is not just another human being but a *woman*, that she has certain powers over me, that I am supposed to have certain powers over her, the knowledge that our experience of life is far more different than could ever be the case between two men. When she talks of rape she is talking of something that is abstract for me, concrete for her. When we talk about the biological differences between us, and their lack of importance in matters of work and ambition, it is *her* biology we are talking about, not mine. I generously dismiss menstruation as a barrier to a woman's success in whatever work she wants to do, but what can I know of menstruation, or childbirth, or what any woman really feels about a man? But it is in women that we seek our true selves; we want them to pierce through our defenses and hope that

what they find there, beyond manners, charm, sexual
competence, whatever combination of virtues we choose
to project, will find favor in their eyes. "Tell me," we
ask, "what do you *really* think of me?" Which means:
"Tell me who I really *am*."

I nod. I can think of nothing obvious I have done to
betray male chauvinism, find it difficult to explain that
perhaps everything I've said is a form of male chauvinism, concealing itself as curiosity, sympathy, interest.

"You're not sensitized," she says. "You're trying, but
you have a long way to go. Maybe you're too old to
know what it's like to simply *accept* women without giving up what you think of as manhood. Look, we meet in
the park, and start talking, right? And I say I'm a psy-
chologist, and you say you're writing a book about male
chauvinism, and when I tell you what we're doing at the
center, you say you want to *interview* me. Right away
it's a hierarchical situation; you're asking questions, expecting answers. Then, when I tell you what we're
trying to do, you shoot back with what you already
know, you make a *conversation* of it automatically, because that's the way you talk to women, you listen a
little bit, sure, but you still think it's like a dinner party,
that you have to make conversation, join in, get *her* interested and involved. But I *am* interested and involved,
in *my* thing; you're the one who wants to know what's
happening. You still think of women as *social* creatures.
When we agree to get together, you ask me what's a
good time and when I tell you, you say, 'OK, I'll be
there at eleven-thirty,' you automatically pick my apartment, without asking me, and you automatically make
the decision. I don't say that you'd have *objected* if I'd
said I wanted to meet at your apartment or somewhere
else, but you're still used to making the choice, passing
on the orders, it's natural to you. And that's what you
don't understand about women—we're sensitive to all
the nuances of male chauvinism, to the little signals you
don't even notice, to the man who thinks it's enough to
tidy up his ashtray instead of leaving it for the woman to
empty and still makes the choice about a place to meet,

and assumes the woman will agree. Male chauvinism is
no big deal, it isn't going to be fixed by 'giving' women
anything. When we're accepted as human beings—good,
bad and indifferent—when you start thinking that it
isn't a problem, then we can begin to change things. In
the meantime, women need to get away from men, to get
some strength of their own, to learn to make their own
decisions, to find out they're not alone. That's what
we're doing. You'll have to decide for yourself what
you're going to do about male chauvinism. After all it's
your problem."

Our problem? Yes, ours. But where do we begin? Men
will confess to being male chauvinists, sometimes apolo-
getically, sometimes with pride and bluster, but no man
can think of a *reason* for male chauvinism, unless it's
simply that it's convenient and comfortable—a situation
which seems unlikely to remain as common in the future
as it has been in the past. Some men justify their attitude
with spurious biological theories; others appeal to dubious anthropological claims; most take refuge in simple
statements of prejudice, echoing, with varying degrees of
sophistication, the man who told me, "It's hard to make
love if you're up against the wall."

Few of us believe in the religious justifications for
male chauvinism. We can only explain it by saying that
it's a habit, a social custom, that it's gone on for too
long, gotten too deeply ingrained in our souls and our
form of society to be eradicated; that, in the final analysis, it *works*. But it doesn't. We pay the price for our assumptions in unhappiness, divorce, bitterness, the constant sense of being ourselves prisoners of some system
that has separated the species into warring camps. We
need women for our happiness, and hope that we can
somehow snare, entrap, charm, hold one of them, as if by
making our peace (on our terms) with one woman we
can hold her captive in our camp, a prisoner of our side.
We want them to satisfy our needs, but we are not willing to listen to what theirs are, except perhaps in the

narrowest sexual terms, where the benefits to ourselves in terms of sensuality are fairly obvious. In the words of Simone de Beauvoir, "All oppression creates a state of war." The oppression of women is no exception.

Oppression? Like rape, it's one of those words that's much in vogue these days. The male chauvinist "oppresses" women, but how? Does he bind them, force them to his will, chain them? Hardly. The male chauvinist is not usually in a position to exert *direct* control over a woman, let alone women in general. As a sultry day can be described as "oppressive," so the male chauvinist's main weapon is to make women feel *uncomfortable,* on edge, humiliated, powerless, by a series of attitudes and principles as small and irritating as the heat and humidity of a summer's day, when a thunderstorm is endlessly on the horizon, never quite breaking.

As men, we don't see how our behavior is oppressive, can't imagine what it's like to be alternately flattered and abused, to be a successful woman of fifty who can't go into restaurants alone because headwaiters will quite often refuse to give her a table, to be a woman of forty-one of whose daughters has been molested and who herself now carries around in her handbag a container of Mace. The sense of danger, the inexplicable insult, the sudden obscenity, the feeling that one hasn't been understood and isn't going to be—how can men feel what it's like? And if we can't feel what it's like how do we begin to treat women as equals?

I *think* of C as an equal, no question about it in my mind as we dine with a mutual woman friend in London. I try not to make decisions for C, try to ask what she wants to do, try not to impose, but—bullshit!—the old urge to dominate, the simple, crass desire to have my own way still rises, the male chauvinist's power erection, so linked to the sexual one that it is sometimes hard to separate sex from power or to guess which it is that a man really wants.

Across from us, at a banquette, a group of noisy gentle-

men on the verge of drunkenness are staring at us—at C,
to be exact, who is beautiful and tanned and has her
back to them. I, on the other hand, am facing them. Pon-
derously and inaccurately, they toss a few pieces of bread
in C's direction to attract her attention. She ignores
them. A few minutes later the waiter appears with a sil-
ver platter bearing a card, accompanied by the expectant
giggles of our neighbors. Before C can reach it, I pick it
up and turn it over. It is one of those printed trick cards
you can buy at fun fairs or in novelty shops—

I want to sleep with you!
Tick off your favorite love position from the list below,
and return this card with
your telephone number . . .

I tear the card up, then, suddenly transfixed by the
stupid, sniggering stare of the man who sent the card, I
pick up the ashtray from our table and hurl it straight at
his face. Instant scene: the crash of breaking glass, both
of us on our feet, the headwaiter and my two companions pulling me away, the old instincts lurking there as
strong as ever, *"Kill the bastard!"*

Well, it's a scene, we've lived through them before,
but afterward, outside on the street I find C in tears, as
furious as she is miserable. What did I expect? That
she'd be *grateful?* That she'd thank me for defending
her honor? I have made her into an object, *my* object, I
wasn't avenging an insult to C, I was avenging an insult
to *me*—and with what stupidity and low-grade violence!
C, who can after all look after herself, lashes out at me
in the rainy street: "If you ever do that again, I'll leave
you! Do you think I couldn't have handled that, or *ignored* it? Did I ask you to come to my defense against
some poor, stupid drunk? You didn't even *think,* you
just reacted like a male chauvinist. You leapt up to de-
fend *your* woman, *your* honor; you made *me* seem cheap
and foolish and powerless; you didn't even give me a
chance to be a person, to make a decision about *my* situation. Make a remark to *my* woman and I'll kill you! In a

restaurant, sure. I don't notice you defending me from Con Ed workers who make obscene remarks on Second Avenue! But in a restaurant it's a social situation, your sense of honor and propriety is involved, they've insulted you by staring at the woman you're with. In the street, I'm on my own. Can't you understand how it makes me feel? I don't mind being hassled by some drunk, I can take that, but to be treated like a chattel, to be robbed of any right to decide for myself whether I'd been insulted, or how badly, to have you react for me because I'm *your* woman, that's really sickening, it's like being a *slave*."

A slave? No. But yes, there it is, the essential male chauvinist reaction, C is right, *my* woman. It's not that I care about the insult to her—later one can pretend that was the motive—it's that my possession of her was threatened, challenged, mocked, that *my* pride was involved. I do not go down into the street to fight delivery boys who have whistled at her, quite apart from the risk of being knifed to death; they have insulted *a* woman, not *my* woman, they don't even know I exist, so there's no harm done, no honor lost, and therefore no rage. We oppress by laying the dead weight of our masculinity on women, by involving them in the endless struggle of maintaining *our* image, face, *macho*, by assuming that we can determine their relationship to the world at large, that the gift of their body to us gives us paramount rights. A man has only to sleep with a woman once to feel that he has earned the right to her loyalty, understanding and respect, that some part of his being is enshrined in her, that what happens to her affects *him*. If women are oppressed it's because we make them play so many roles in a psychodrama that isn't even theirs in the first place, linking those roles, enlarging them, developing them, until we are no longer capable of seeing the woman as a *person* at all.

C and I cease glaring at one another, get into the car where our friend is waiting, make for home. Are my feelings about her merely an extension of my ego? The possibility hovers between us, separating us momentarily in the night. After all, what stopped me from asking her what, if anything, she wanted me to do, or from letting *her* handle the situation? Was I simply seeing her—her body, her being—as an extension of myself? And don't all men reduce women to Adam's Rib, a part of ourselves once removed, but still somehow belonging?

Thirty-five thousand feet below me I can see the towns, the cities, the vast suburban tracts, neatly spread out like the properties around the edges of a Monopoly board; in some places the ghost streets and subdivisions of a building development that has failed, signs of some bankrupt and tentative effort to settle one more patch of this vast land which perhaps only makes sense and seems at peace from the windows of an airliner. God's country can only be seen from God's position, stretching on forever into the dusk, marked with the determined signs of domesticity, roads, reservoirs, mysterious lights, as elusive as the "green light, the orgiastic future" which betrayed Gatsby, lights that somehow fill one with a haunting loneliness as they pass slowly from our field of vision, sweeping away behind the hard-edged, darkening form of the aircraft's wing. There is no loneliness like that of an air traveler in those moments just before night; it is a time for thinking of one's life, for wondering what warmth, passion, feelings are there below, represented by those flickering and faraway lights, the lights of people we will never know, dramas and tragedies we will never share. Below us is the real world, while we sit encapsulated in the plasticized cocoon of our dream of the future, the marvel of technology that carries us at six hundred m.p.h., prisoners of our own myths, ears plugged in to canned music, provided with a menu that describes in glowing terms an elaborate meal that is merely the futuristic equivalent of leftovers, served in disposable plastic traylets, surrounded by the plastic artifacts of the artificial world of our desires.

We are in a world that presumes all men who wear ties are "executives," in which woman is eternally young, smiling, possibly even willing—for in the airplane, the male chauvinist finds his dream realized:

subservient service with no object in mind but to increase his sense of self-importance. In the airline magazine an advertisement for Hertz: "When you come to the counter all you do is show your license and charge card, sign your name, and go. Or sign your name and stay. Because once our girls are free from filling out forms, they can devote their attention to more important things. Like you."

By what magic has the twentieth century produced in ordinary men the desire to be treated like pashas without power, what insane dream of luxury has allowed us to build a culture in which the flattery of men's egos is the substance of our commerce, as much a part of our popular culture as the endless miles of *schlock* architecture, barbecue stands illuminated by giant revolving cowgirls with teeth that flash off and on incandescently, a giant pair of neon lips to mark the entrance of a tavern now become, by the addition of one go-go dancer, a "discotheque"? For make no mistake about it: male chauvinism in its present form is a reflection of that half-life that is the future as we have imagined it, or as it has been imagined for us. We have become afraid of reality; it's too complex, too messy, there may not even be room for all of us in the real world if our population continues to grow; we have sought safety in artifice, sought comfort in a dream world that is clean, well-lighted, secure, air-conditioned, in which we can somehow buy the pretense of being important, valued, appreciated—"executive-sized" drinks for the minor bureaucrat, "VIP" lounges for the traveling insurance salesman, "our girls" to please the modest functionary while he signs the form for his rented car.

What entitles us to this bizarre vision of ourselves, what possibility is there for strength and feeling when we are content to accept an artificial, commercialized, programmed feedback as the definition of ourselves? We have dreamed of a world in which objects will satisfy, even replace, the Ego, a world in which every man of reasonable solvency can surround himself with the ready-made artifacts of his own importance, a world in which

we are willing to settle for buying someone else's fantasy
as a substitute for any internal reality of our own. But
reality is still there, the sudden flood that strips the
ranch house, the moment when we leave the airplane,
the rented car, and step out onto the streets, the presence
around us of the real women we have to deal with, work
with, live with. How are men to bridge the gap between
that imaginary world which transcends social classes—
the world of *Playboy* magazine, of advertising, of signs,
billboards, of Miss Stock Car Racing 1972 presenting the
trophy to the tune of 50,000 simultaneous wolf whistles,
of stars imprinting their breasts in concrete instead of
the ritual handprints—and the world they really live in,
with real women who do not always smile, are not always twenty-three years old and shapely, have minds,
wishes, ambitions, egos of their own?

Perhaps the most disturbing aspect of our dream of
the future is that it effectively excludes women except in
their role as objects, and in those curiously aseptic modern positions that place women somewhere between a
servant and whore. I remember noticing that the only
women in Stanley Kubrick's 2001 were stewardesses on
the space shuttle that took the Astronauts from earth to
their orbiting launch-off station, fulfilling in this fantasy
of our technological future exactly the role airline stewardesses have now. The men are about to be launched
into deep space, to journey back to the beginning of creation; the women are still standing in the aisles of the pas-
senger craft, smiling, telling people to fasten their safety
belts and picking up trays. At least when H. G. Wells imagined space travel in *The Shape of Things to Come* he
sent a man and a woman off into space together, seated
side by side, with no suggestion as to which one was the
pilot, but then Wells always thought the future was
going to be better than it has so far turned out to be. He
could not have foreseen that we would travel into space
with our capacity for violence, irrationality and false
pride undiminished—if anything, increased. Least of all
could he have foreseen that technology would not liber-
ate us, but would simply serve as a device for reinforcing

an artificial world in which men dream of the stars while women continue to perform menial tasks.

Woman—her shape, her body, her sexuality—has become the keystone of our culture, the central image of our frenzied search to build a new world of machines, plastic, strong sensations, commercialized pleasures on the shifting sands of a reality we have never been able to come to terms with. She is both our means of selling, and the main object of our sales pitch, cheapened and courted at the same time. We talk of education as if it would solve every problem, but what changes could we make in our educational system that would outweigh the ever-present effects of popular culture, with its built-in rejection of women as equals, even as human beings? Change the way we educate our children? But to what purpose, so long as they are exposed to the glittering, multimedia show we have elected to live in, among the billboards, paperback jackets and magazine advertising. It is not the dead weight of the past that oppresses women—the past had its virtues—but the dead weight of the present and the threat of a future in which our national culture will resemble a vast, grounded airplane, in which high technology is used for low purposes and where the intensity of commercialized pleasure and packaged conveniences will hopefully keep our minds off the accumulations of misery, poverty and distress that we are unwilling to face or solve. Fly to the suburbs to avoid having to see the poverty and destruction of our cities! Take the children to a multimedia show on forests at the local Disneyland, because it's too complicated to take them to a real forest, and we might have to explain why there are so few left! Join a Playboy Club so that we can pretend to enjoy sexual experiences that we haven't the time, energy or opportunity to seek out in real life! The world has become so complex, so confusing, so big, that we are, all of us, lost in it, caught between the chaotic past and the organized future, in which we shall all be identified by our Taxpayer Identification/Social Security number, our Diners Club card, abject consumers for whom the sharp sensation of orgasm may be the only means by which we can remind ourselves that we are alive, prisoners of a world in which our prejudices, worst instincts and greed are grossly magnified and transformed by the investment of billions of dollars in advertising and promotion, then sold back to us as our dreams and higher aspirations.

Of course, it's hard for men to stop being male chauvinists. What else have they got left, what other promise does our society hold out for them, what other rewards? Work hard, and you can travel first class and get the undivided attention of "our" stewardesses, drinks and hot towels in hand; succeed and you'll have your own secretary, a human being you can actually control, order about, a woman under your thumb; make money and you'll get your numbered key, your embossed plastic entrance card, your right of entry to the dream land of male chauvinism, whre everything is brushed aluminum or gold-flecked plastic marble, and where the women are forever attentive, cheerful, attractive; proof—by the length of their legs, the shortness of their skirts, their flowing hair, their youth—that you are a very important man.

So long as we live in a world of illusions, there is very little reason to expect that the male chauvinist will give up his. If we have opted for a world of fakery, of vicarious pleasures, if we have decided that we do not want to confront people as they really are, life as it is; if we want everything neatly packaged, a cellophane shield between ourselves and the messy reality of human feelings, then the male chauvinist may as well be allowed to pretend to himself that the assumed limitations of women are the proof of his equally illusory superiority. Except that people are getting hurt in the process.

"I'm a male chauvinist, sure," a man told me, "I'm always catching myself saying things like 'She does pretty well for a woman.' But does it matter, does that make me a bad person? I don't think so." But behind the words and the joking attitudes real pain is being inflicted. The man who thinks that male chauvinism doesn't make him "a bad person" is deluding himself:

he is linked to a set of attitudes that are as unjust, as stupid, as restrictive, as demoralizing and as cruel as ever racial prejudice was. The little jokes about women that pass for a friendly, cozy manifestation of masculine humor are not very different from kike or nigger jokes, not only wounding and contemptuous, but linking us to more overt and harmful acts of prejudice, fear and hatred. Every time we make an anti-Semitic remark we shake hands with the Nazis, however unconsciously: no, of course we don't approve of them, of course we are horrified by Auschwitz, Treblinka, the gas ovens, the whole odious and shameful revelation of our instinctive barbarism, but still they *are* shrewd businessmen aren't they? And if you don't like that, I know a pretty good Polish story . . .

Sexual freedom is all very well, even the male chauvinist is in favor of it, though without facing the fact that you cannot enjoy one kind of freedom while refusing to acknowledge the others. But the greater freedom that now attaches to sexuality does nothing to spare women from the consequences of male chauvinism. Lane, seventeen years old, has just flown from California to New York to have an abortion, but finds that the laws have changed, that it's going to cost her five hundred dollars, which she doesn't have and is going to have to borrow from her sister, who only makes $125 a week as a secretary, because she can't tell her parents who "wouldn't understand," and the man who did it doesn't have any money and anyway doesn't feel responsible—why should he, he doesn't believe in hassles, he's for freedom, do your own thing, live your own trip. Sexual freedom hasn't liberated women as much as it has freed men from responsibilities they were only too happy to relinquish. A woman lawyer who tries to shepherd young women through the bewildering maze of medical and police procedures when they've been raped, comments, "Rape used to be a serious matter, but the idea of sexual freedom has made it very tough for women who get raped. In the first place, nobody really believes in rape any more. To get the cops interested, the victim has to be a twelve-year-old Irish Catholic girl who was wearing her communion dress when it happened and was on her way to mass. Otherwise, forget it. If you're a young woman in a short skirt or jeans, you *asked* for it, right? It's as if you had to be a virgin to get raped. OK, that's the way cops are, that's why we set this whole thing up, but the doctors aren't any better. I brought a rape victim into hospital the other day, and this doctor looked at her and said, 'Young lady, why do you dress that way?' Even the psychiatrists aren't any better. We had to set up a referral center so we could get these girls, who were really shaken up, to women therapists. The male shrinks were just making them feel even more guilty, as if it were *their* fault they got raped. It's as if we were living in two worlds, there's this one world where men display women as sex objects to sell things, to make them feel good, then there's this world where a woman who simply dresses herself comfortably and looks like herself is supposed to have brought whatever happens on herself. You work at this kind of thing long enough and you begin to think that maybe all men really hate women."

But no, they don't as a rule hate them. They just don't want to know anything about them. It is hard enough to compete with one's fellow men without adding the competition of women, difficult enough to face life's uncertainties without adding women's problems and ambitions to the burden. Here, at least, is one large area of life which men can dismiss by simply placing woman into a fixed slot in their minds. But it isn't going to work in the long run. In the words of Paul Tillich, "Boredom is rage spread thin," and what we have assigned to women is boredom, the boredom of repetitive, underpaid jobs, the boredom of looking after children as if that were their exclusive concern, the boredom of knowing that no matter how much they learn, no matter how hard they study, the same old barriers will be raised against them, they will not be taken seriously, treated equally, given the same opportunities. Are women really "educated for failure," as Martina Horner suggests? Yes, to some extent it's true that "if she fails, she is not living up to her own standards of performance; if she succeeds she is not living up to societal expectations about the female role." Our offices are full of women who received at least as good an education as any man there, perhaps better, then were sent out into the world to take a typing test and learn "The rules of Telephone Etiquette" ("Always identify yourself. Be courteous. Remember that your voice on the telephone is the voice of your company"). With a few upper-class exceptions, American education is coeducational; girls and boys sit together in the same classrooms, learn from the same books, take the same examinations. It's not what we teach women that matters, or rather what they learn, it's what happens before and after education that counts; before, when girls are taught that their education is a source of pride, while that of a boy is a matter of grim necessity; after, when they are asked to put their education away and forget about it. As a proud father said, speaking of his daughter's appearance in the Cheshire High School Prom, "It's worth it, it's a night they'll never forget. Put them in high-heel shoes and it's like they're a princess. It makes them feel special, you know?"(55)

A moment of being special, for a lifetime of being ordinary. The message we may convey is that "graduation is not an end but a beginning," but the truth for most women is that graduation is an end. Nico, living in Colorado with her baby and her husband who is going to law school and whose career *matters*, may well have felt at Sarah Lawrence what Norma Rosen describes as "the ecstasy of learning,"(56) that sudden confrontation with knowledge, books, one's own mind, that in the final analysis is what makes college an exciting experience, rather than drugs, sex or campus revolt; but what happens when it becomes irrelevant, a receding moment when all things seemed possible, seldom remembered in a life that inexorably becomes limited and mundane?

What hurts, over the years, is the sense of not having *tried,* of having given in, surrendered to the belief that it couldn't really be done, that one's education was an accident, and aberration, a delusion, coupled with the wistful, corrosive fear that perhaps after all it could have been done, that one's promise and talent were perhaps real. "I wanted," writes Nico, "to be an architect, I really did, I liked making all the sketches and drawings, and I was good at it. Then we had a baby, and it got more complicated, and I realized that I'd signed up for something I hadn't bargained for, that there wasn't room for two grown-ups getting their degrees at the same time, and I began to fade. It wasn't a big deal, we didn't fight about it, there it was, I just slipped into the role of mother, housekeeper, dreamer, failed woman, as if I'd always known that's where I'd end up, as if the work at school and college had been a deliberate exercise in futility. OK, you can say, I ought to have fought back, I didn't need to have a baby. It's true, but what men don't realize is how easy it is to just let it all go, to roll with the punch. It's as if there were this role a woman can simply slip into, and men push her, gently, firmly, into it, tell her it's OK, praise her when she accepts it. If I had been stronger, I'd have fought back, maybe I still will, but what I never realized was how easy it is to give in, and how relieved any man is when you *do.* My husband believed in 'women's liberation,' but when it came right down to living it, he turned out to be like everyone else, which is to say, *he* came first. Maybe I wouldn't have been Mies van der Rohe, but the point is now I'll never know, and nobody but me is even going to think I'm a failure. What for? I'm a wife, my husband has his degree, I have a child, and I love him, I've 'settled down.' But I keep wondering, how serious was everybody when they told me to work hard and get good grades? Did they always know this was the way it was going to be? Was this a gigantic put-on? I really believed it then, I trusted my parents and everyone else who wanted me to succeed, to be bright, and now I'm twenty-seven and I haven't done anything, and nobody except me thinks it matters, or that anything has been wasted, and even I'm not sure any more. When we play the most important moment of your life—you know, you tell the experience that you remember most vividly—mine is going to have to be the night I lost my virginity at the Taft Hotel in New Haven. But I bet the guy who was with me has more important things to remember."

We are living beyond Eden, where God was the guarantor of our happiness and content. Driven out of paradise, we are responsible for each other's safety, happiness, welfare, needs; free beings, we have nothing to offer each other but ourselves, nothing to gain by pretending to powers we do not possess. It is no triumph to prove our "masculinity," whatever that is, by using women as mirrors to reflect our success, our strength, our petty triumphs. Men have taken the easy way out, making half the species their audience, looking out toward it for an applause which is becoming fainter and fainter, putting on a show that is already dusty with age, made up of tired jokes and creaking routines, an ancient hit which deserves to die a merciful death. The time has come to pack up the scenery.

Male chauvinism is dead when we want it to be. All we need to do is to *listen,* to accept the fact that half of us have things to say which haven't been said, or have been dismissed, distorted, ignored because they come from *women.* Perhaps we do not need to fight wars, to spend our best years toiling for an illusory security, driving ourselves to the coronary point in pursuit of wealth to placate the women we have married then confined. We are willing to kill ourselves to show our strength, that has always been the way of men. Is it perhaps time to show our weakness, to admit to our fears, to ask women to join us, instead of trying to exclude them from the struggles we are waging, ostensibly on their behalf? It is only necessary to stop pretending: nothing more.

Accept reality, and you accept woman. The games we play, in the office, at home, in the world at large, are merely devices to protect the fragility of our own egos. Slowly, with infinite difficulty, women are moving, coming to grips with themselves and their problems, accepting, demanding, change. It is time for men to do the same.

PREFACE

1. *The New York Times*, March 4, 1972.
2. Thomas Mann, *The Magic Mountain*. New York, Alfred A. Knopf, 1927, p. 566.
3. Frank Loesser, *Guys and Dolls*.
4. See Robert Graves, *The Greek Myths*. New York, Braziller, 1955, *passim*.

The matriarchal society of ancient Europe, in which women were sovereign ("Men feared, adored, and obeyed the matriarch . . .") persists even today in certain primitive tribes, though without the sacrificial murder of the sacred king-consort. A close study of the ancient myths should convince any reader that a matriarchal society has no natural bias toward humanitarian principles. It is a long time since women have had despotic powers over men, but they do not seem to have used their powers any more sensibly than men have used theirs in the thirty-three centuries that have ensued since the Achaean and Dorian invaders put an end to the custom of killing the king at regular intervals by imposing patriarchy on women. We may guess with what suspicions and hostility men and women regarded each other in politics in the period during which this momentous change took place, and these attitudes have survived in our unconscious even today. More recent history may be of some comfort to women's liberationists, since it proves that women, given the opportunity, can be as irrational, cruel and power hungry as men—think of Messalina, Mary Tudor, Catherine The Great or, for that matter, Ilse Koch ("The Beast of Buchenwald"). Here, at any rate, is one area of equality.

5. Hugh Sidey, *Life* magazine.

ONE

6. Simone de Beauvoir, *The Second Sex*. New York, Bantam Books, 1961, p. 77.
7. In eigtheenth- and nineteenth-century French regiments, the *cantiniere* was a woman who sold spirits

and wine to the troops, usually marching with them,
a one-woman traveling bar. These women gave credit
and often married veteran soldiers.

8. *The New York Times*, March 7, 1972.
9. Lightningwork, as in *Blitzkrieg*, lightningwar.
10. U. S. Department of Labor, *Fact Sheet on the Earnings Gap*. Washington, D.C., U.S. Government Printing Office, 1972, #2916–0004.

TWO
11. *The New York Times*.
12. Norman Mailer, *The Prisoner of Sex*. New York, Bantam Books, 1971, p. 47.
13. Jill Johnston, *The Lesbian Nation*. New York, Simon & Schuster, Inc., 1973.
14. *The New York Times*, March 31, 1972.
15. *The New York Times*, April 1, 1972.
16. Norman Mailer, *op. cit.* p. 111.
17. *Ibid.*, p. 168.
18. *Ibid.*, p. 9.

THREE
19. *The New York Times*.
20. *Ibid.*
21. Felice N. Schwartz, Margaret H. Schifter and Susan Gillotti, *How to Go to Work When Your Husband Is Against It*. New York, Simon & Schuster, Inc., 1972, p. 64.
22. From "What Men Won't Say to Women About Women's Liberation," *Glamour*, October 1972.
23. Joseph Adelson, "Is Women's Lib a Passing Fad?" *The New York Times Magazine*, March 19, 1972.
24. Michael Korda, "A Woman's Success," *Glamour*, April 1972.
25. Philip Slater, *The Pursuit of Loneliness*. New York, Beacon Press, 1970, p. 73.
26. *The New York Times*, April 28, 1972.
27. Jack Olsen, *The Girls in the Office*. New York, Simon & Schuster, Inc., 1972.
28. From—of all things!—"The Single Girl's Search for

Herself in the Big City," by Michael Korda, *Glamour*, May 1972. I am indebted to Stephanie Waldman for pointing out to me this lapse into male chauvinist language on my part.

29. Erik H. Erikson, *Childhood and Society*. New York, W. W. Norton, 1950, pp. 98–106.
30. *The New York Times*, April 29, 1972.

FOUR
31. Pauline Reage, *The Story of O*. New York, Grove Press, 1965, pp. 15–16.
32. *Glamour*, May 1972.
33. Jack Olsen, *The Girls in the Office*. New York, Simon & Schuster, Inc., 1972, pp. 442 and 444.

FIVE
34. *The New York Times*, May 1972.
35. Virginia Frankel, *What Your House Tells About You*. New York, Trident Press, 1972, p. 70.
36. Shana Alexander, "The City Politic," *New York Magazine*.
37. A. J. Liebling, *Between Meals*. New York, Simon & Schuster, Inc., 1962, p. 56.
38. *The New York Times*, April 30, 1972.

SIX
39. *Ladies' Home Journal*.
40. Paul Hemphill, "Thoughts from an Unliberated Woman," Copyright © 1971 by *The New York Times* Co.
41. Jennifer Skolnik, "Notes of a Recycled Housewife," *New York Magazine*, May 22, 1972.
42. *The New York Times*, June 4, 1972.
43. *Ibid.*
44. *Ibid.*
45. George O'Neill, as quoted in *The New York Times*.
46. Robert E. Gould, M.D., *The New York Times*, June 18, 1972.

SEVEN

47. *The New York Times.*
48. *The New York Times,* March 13, 1972.
49. *The New York Times.*
50. *Ibid.*
51. *The New York Times,* June 23, 1972.
52. *The New York Times.*
53. *Ibid.*
54. *The New York Times,* March 15, 1972.

The same article also contains a marvelous description of middle-aged impotence among married men, which I append as a warning to all male chauvinists: "They considered that the excitement had passed and that their wives no longer provided the variety in sexual practices they craved. Impotence was accompanied by minimal anxiety: they usually had conscious fantasies about the secretary at work, the girl next door, etc., and felt confident that novel objects or practices could revive their interest. This conviction prevented the emergence of major anxiety and resulted in relative indifference to their wives' plaints."

Material quoted regarding the Time-Life affair is from the files kept by some of the participants, and from documents submitted to and issued by the New York State Attorney General's Office.

EIGHT

55. Joyce Maynard, "Color My World," *The New York Times Magazine,* June 18, 1972.
56. Norma Rosen, "For Women Only," *The New York Times Magazine,* April 9, 1972.

About the Author

Michael Korda was born in London, England, in 1933, and educated at Le Rosey, in Switzerland, and Magdalen College, Oxford. He served two years in the Royal Air Force and moved to the United States in 1958. Mr. Korda has written for *Glamour* magazine for several years, and is *Glamour*'s monthly motion picture reviewer, as well as a member of The National Society of Film Critics. He lives in Manhattan with his wife and child.